Tele-ology

Tele-ology brings together John Hartley's writings on television. The book assesses TV as a global and local force, a cultural and textual system, a corporate and domestic, political and artistic object of study. It draws on current critical theory in Cultural Studies to develop a wide-ranging and thought-provoking view of television broadcasting in Britain, Australia and the United States.

The collection includes writings on TV truth and propaganda; on populism in the news; on mythologies of the TV audience, which turns out to be as fictional as the shows it watches; on TV drama as a 'photopoetic' genre in the tradition of Shakespeare; on the peculiarities of TV continuity and TV advertising; on the cultural politics of Kylie Minogue and Madonna; on *Edge of Darkness* and on gardening shows as art.

Tele-ology will be invaluable to students, teachers and researchers in media, communication, cultural and literary studies. Its diverse and engaging format makes it a collection that can reach beyond the confines of formal TV study to a readership not only of broadcasters and policy-makers, but, more importantly, of TV viewers who are ambitious enough to want to do their job better.

John Hartley is Senior Lecturer in the School of Humanities at Murdoch University, Western Australia. He has been teaching, broadcasting and writing about TV for over fifteen years in Britain, the United States and Australia. His books include *Reading Television* (with John Fiske) and *Understanding News*, both of which have become standard textbooks in the field. *Tele-ology* aims to stimulate an informed public debate about TV's textual regimes and cultural power, with an entertaining and provocative approach which is designed to be as accessible as it is sensitive to the complexities of the subject-matter.

Tele-ology

Studies in Television

John Hartley

London and New York

First published 1992
by Routledge
11 New Fetter Lane, London EC4P 4EE

Simultaneously published in the USA and Canada
by Routledge
a division of Routledge, Chapman and Hall, Inc.
29 West 35th Street, New York, NY 10001

Set in 10/12pt Times by Florencetype, Kewstoke, Avon

Printed in Great Britain by Butler & Tanner, Frome and London

British Library Cataloguing in Publication Data
Hartley, John
Tele-ology : studies in television.
1. United States. Australia. Great Britain. Television
I. Title
791.4

Library of Congress Cataloging in Publication Data
Hartley, John.
Tele-ology : studies in television / John Hartley.
p. cm.
Includes bibliographical references and index.
1. Television broadcasting. I. Title.
PN1992.5.H28 1992
791.45—dc20 91–17312

ISBN 0–415–06817–7 ISBN 0–415–06818–5 (pbk)

To T.H.
(They know who they are)

Contents

Acknowledgements

It's a long way from Shakespeare to Kylie Minogue. My unfailing guide throughout has been Terence Hawkes of the University of Wales College of Cardiff; without his inspiring example, support and friendship not a word of this would ever have been written. I acknowledge too with pride his role as my first supervisor, first co-author and first general editor, long ago and far away . . . which means I suppose that even if it's not his fault that all this got written, he certainly has to take some responsibility for the fact that it started getting published.

It's a long way too from Cardiff to Fremantle. Along the way there have been colleagues, collaborators and co-writers whose company I have valued: I acknowledge here especially co-authors Martin Montgomery and Tom O'Regan, some of the fruits of whose labours I am glad to scrump herein; and Ien Ang, Mary-Ellen Brown, Roland Denning, David Eason, John Fiske, John Frow, Todd Gitlin, Holly Goulden, Bob Hodge, Niall Lucy, Judith Mauger, David Morley, Horace Newcomb, Beverley Poynton, Clare Richardson, Michael Schudson, Graeme Turner; I thank them all.

More credit than they know is due to students at Murdoch University and previously at the Polytechnic of Wales, as well as to students and staff at places where I have been fortunate enough to give papers, talks or 'brownbags', including the Annenberg School of Communications at the University of Southern California, University College of Cardiff, Curtin University, Farnborough College of Art, Florida Atlantic University, the University of Illinois, the University of London School of Education, the University of Michigan, Michigan State University, the Catholic University of Nijmegen, the University of Queensland, the University of Western Sydney, the University of Wisconsin-Madison, Ulster Polytechnic.

Very few words would have been written without the word-processing skills of Merrylyn Braden; her willingness to use them on my behalf is a substantial contribution to this book and I thank her sincerely.

I am indebted to the following periodicals for first publication of some of the essays appearing herein: *Artlink*, *Australian Journal of Cultural*

Studies, *Australian Left Review*, *Critical Studies in Mass Communication*, *Cultural Studies*, *In the Picture*, *One-Eye*, *Textual Practice*. The original publication of each paper is formally acknowledged at the start of each chapter. The essays are presented here in revised form, with the revisions ranging from minor editorial changes to substantial rewriting, and I thank you for reading them.

I would also like to acknowledge the following for the reproduction of television stills in chapter 11: STW Channel 9 Perth; TVW Channel 7 Perth; and McCann-Erickson Advertising Pty Ltd, Perth.

Part I

Television theory

Chapter 1

Tele-ology

Readers of this book may be familiar with the term 'teleology' as a theological or philosophical concept. It denotes the doctrine of final causes, as in the Day of Judgement, which (it is said) won't happen till the end of human history, but which is nevertheless deemed to explain retrospectively all that has gone before. Teleology is cause *after* the event, a doctrine of knowledge with which neither science nor TV executives are very comfortable. However, whatever scientists might like to think, television executives are right to feel uncomfortable; for them the final cause *is* after the event, the day of judgement does determine every action they take. In deference to the poor benighted television executive, then, and taking last things first, I open *Tele-ology* with a quotation from the *Dies irae* ('day of wrath') of the *Requiem Mass*:

Judex ergo cum sedebit	When therefore the judge takes his seat
Quidquid latet apparebit,	Whatever is hidden will reveal itself,
Nil inultum remanebit.	Nothing will remain unavenged.

The biggest and brassiest rendition of this excerpt must be that of Hector Berlioz, so let it play in the background, TV-style, while I point out that for TV executives there are indeed judges who take their seats every day and night and who reveal to themselves what is hidden inside that TV screen; the audience sits in judgement over all the economic wheeling and dealing, the artistic blood, sweat, tears and compromises that have led up to this one moment. If all's well that ends well, then everyone is blissful, but if not, nothing remains unavenged for long; shows are thrown into the abyss, executives are fired (though not literally these days), whole TV channels lose their livelihood. Teleology is not a doctrine of *foregone* conclusions; some shows are damned and some are saved, but no-one knows which is which until after they're screened.

We, the public, are the final cause whose judgement determines the very survival of the TV executive and the entire world of television. In front of such judges, it is now in fact the case that:

Mors stupebit et natura	Death and nature shall be astonished
Cum resurget creatura	When all creation rises again
Judicanti responsura.	To answer to the judge.

Television, the medium of popular entertainment, does nothing less than re-create the world of nature, and of death too, in both actuality and fiction, for our astonishment, for us to judge.

Tele-ology is a set of essays on television as a cultural, aesthetic, political, textual, industrialized medium. Its aim is not to sit in judgement over television, but to contribute to television studies (*tele-logos*), an academic discipline which does not in fact exist, and which Aristotle, who first pondered such matters, would have been hard put to classify into any of his classical branches of knowledge; in Greek, *telelogos* might mean distant-writing or distant-truth, which is an agreeable metaphor for TV if you're already familiar with it, but not one that would conjure up to an uninitiated Athenian the image of a little black box of Japanese manufacture that lights up the corner of several billion living rooms around the world. So, for the moment, since there's no such thing as television studies, this is a contribution to the un-discipline of tele-ology.

As befits its status it is not a standard academic study; it makes no attempt to present a comprehensive survey of all published studies of television, though a surprising number of these exist; it does not develop a linear argument about one specific topic in the field; and it does not confine itself to traditional academic styles of writing. Instead of comprehensive linearity and plain style, these essays offer polemic, rhetoric and an approach that works *on* rather than *through* contemporary critical theory, in an attempt to provoke new ways of thinking about an all too familiar cultural phenomenon.

The essays have appeared over a period of a decade in a variety of journals, books and magazines, many of which were hard to get hold of at the time, never mind later on. Their publication was dispersed over three continents and over several different types of writing – some were intended as scholarly papers, some as topical criticism, while others were addressed to specific readerships, from independent filmmakers to English teachers. However, partly because they do range across time, space and genre, they represent an approach to television that is appropriate both to the peculiarities of the medium itself and to the need for a flexible and responsive analytical apparatus by means of which some sense can be made of it. At the very least I can take comfort in the fact that the chapters that follow are like television shows that were tried out on a minority channel before getting the chance to be seen by a wider audience; re-runs yes, but new to some readers, and for others, repackaged into what tactful TV announcers call a second chance . . .

It follows that the development of an argument about television in *Tele-ology* is not one of linear progression across a known countryside in pursuit of a predetermined quarry. The relationship between chapters might better be seen as something like that between individual floes in an icefield; they're connected but independent. The explorer will find that it's quite easy to jump from one to the next, but sometimes they may look very similar in appearance. A position arrived at in one paper forms the starting point for another, though sometimes the direction of progress may not be obvious. Matter that is dealt with in one context may need reiterating in another, and the same material may be put to different uses, just as a floe might rotate after one has landed on it, causing a different orientation to the landscape to be established. Needless to say, this approach does leave a fair amount of work to the reader; progress towards landmarks may be swift, or it may necessitate some agile leaps, or it may not be seen as progress at all. Certainly the book as a whole does not lead the reader by the nose towards a teleological final cause; much of what appears here was written in an exploratory, experimental mode, without the least suspicion that the final point of arrival would be somewhere in the vicinity of Kylie Minogue.

INTERVENTION ANALYSIS

While the landscape may change and the route taken might be discontinuous, it is possible to suggest that more than mere leaps of faith link the various essays in this book. As a whole, it is dedicated to what may be termed 'intervention analysis'. That is, integral to it is the contribution its individual parts might make to the field of study that they have helped to constitute. Intervention analysis seeks not only to describe and explain existing dispositions of knowledge, but also to change them. This is an inescapable aspect of these studies because, at the time I embarked upon them in the mid-1970s, an adequate approach to television as a textual-cultural object of study was not fully developed within existing critical discourses, so it had to be constructed out of them. In particular, a textual-formal (semiotic) and socio-political (cultural) approach to television as an instance of cultural production within the context of contemporary, urban, democratic popular culture is constructed out of materials borrowed variously from linguistics, anthropology, literary theory and criticism, sociology, political theory and journalism, as well as certain metadiscourses like structuralism (and its intellectual successors), semiotics and cultural studies. Out of such rich resources what I hope is a useful and accessible theoretical model of television is constructed, in which full account is taken of its textuality, while simultaneously that textuality is seen not merely as a formal apparatus but as grounded in a cultural context which may determine what any given text might mean.

While meaning may easily be determined by cultural contexts, it is far less easily determined by cultural analysts. However, there is one aspect of its determination which informs much of my work and which is at least easily stated: the determination of meaning is a creative act performed by readers, not by texts or contexts as such. The so-called consumers of meanings cannot be thought of as passive or as powerless. On the contrary, everyone performs creative critical work in relation to popular textual forms. This book is therefore dedicated to making the existing practices of *reading* and *understanding* television better informed, less unselfconscious and more systematic. It does not determine meanings on behalf of an incapacitated audience, but it does develop readings which are intended to intervene in the way people might want to watch television. Its perspective is that of the audience; it claims no special knowledge of technical or production processes, and does not explain television's cultural form by reference to the industry's point of view. Nor does it explain audience practices by reference to psychological or behavioural criteria. Since the act of reading cannot be observed directly, the practice of reading television is not susceptible to explanation by scientific means, unless one wishes to propose a modification of Werner Heisenberg's uncertainty principle, which states that an observer can determine the position or the velocity of subatomic particles, but not both at once. Similarly, the cultural 'scientist' can observe people watching television or watch television, but not both at once. Audience practices and textual phenomena can be isolated and described, but what happens when they fuse together cannot be observed without changing the circumstances of fusion. This is a position tele-ology shares with contemporary theoretical physics.

Unlike theoretical physics, however, tele-ology asserts that there is a position beyond the uncertainty principle to which readers can go, equipped with critical discourse, in order to perform their own acts of creation. To understand the act of reading one must do it, and doing it is creative of new meanings. Understanding a cultural practice by doing it is intervention analysis, and understanding the cultural practice of reading television is what the analysis herein seeks to do.

The first intervention that needs to be made is to justify (i.e. construct) television as an object worthy of study as a textual–cultural phenomenon. However, using textual and cultural theory to account for a medium which is all too often ignored or undervalued by the most influential theorists, also means intervening in intellectual culture in defence of popular representations. Thus TV can be used to test textual and cultural theories just as they can be used to understand popular TV.

The defence of the popular is strategically important in certain contexts, but it has to be set within limits, too. For instance, racist and sexist attitudes are undoubtedly 'popular' in one sense of the word, but they are not to be defended for that reason. Similarly, intervention analysis cannot proceed on the Popeian assumption that 'whatever is, is right', simply asserting that anything with a large audience is OK because *ipso facto* it must be popular, and even if its ideology is unspeakable, its mode of address demeaning and its production values woeful, well, that's OK too because the audience is free to negotiate with it or resist it. Such an approach is unable to conclude for itself what is worth defending and what needs to be criticized. Intervention analysis certainly needs to take popular television more or less as it finds it, without high-culture fastidiousness or right-on political squeamishness, but it needs to intervene *in* the media, and in the production of popular knowledges *about* them, to show where aesthetic or political critique is appropriate to popular representations; it needs to *analyse* television in order to be clear about what is worth defending and why. The defence of the popular is not the same thing as populism, for it seeks not to follow and trade on but to shape and invigorate what Trevor Griffiths has called 'the popular imagination', in an enterprise which is perhaps best thought of as a dialogue with the popular.

Intervention analysis is not confined to critical or scholarly writing; it is also conducted on the margins of popular television by creative producers working with (and against) the medium itself. Hence avant-garde art and independent production are by definition outside the domain of the popular, but still they have something to offer it, both aesthetically and in the way they organize the relations between textmaker and audience (i.e. politically). However, neither radical production nor critical theory can achieve their full explanatory leverage without taking account of what is going on within the domain of popular representations. It still amazes me that many people who embark on the formal study of the media, or who make video, or who comment on television in society, are not only relatively ignorant of mainstream television, but seem to regard the whole of popular culture as something to avoid like the plague. Instead of such fear of contamination, I'd argue for an understanding that includes a thorough knowledge of popular television in its own terms, if only to be better equipped to challenge or change it.

Intervention analysis can thus be seen as a strategy for interrogating various centres, whether intellectual, aesthetic or political, from their margins, seeking to interconnect the domains on whose margins the analysis stands, but not, be it said, to propose a new centre in opposition to those observed and criticized. In other words, the resources from which a critical discourse about popular television can be created, including radical politics, critical theory, avant-garde art and independent production, are marginal to the mainstream practices of popular culture, but their value consists in their marginality – and so it is with this book.

One of the margins upon which it stands is the theoretical one between discourse and reality. The position adopted is precarious – an uneasy balancing act with one foot on a floe called reality and one on a floe called discourse, with nothing more to connect them than the muscular energy of the analyst, whose intervention is always jeopardized by the fact that the two floes are always drifting apart as well as touching. Preoccupied with keeping one's feet together in conditions where any observer can see that sooner or later there's going to be a nasty accident is the occupational hazard of the intervention analyst. But such an undignified stance may be instructive. Choosing to avoid the customary scholarly practice of grounding one's theory firmly, and choosing instead to go out on a limb, is a risky enterprise. Even now I can feel my legs beginning to drift apart on the shaky grounds of this slippery metaphor. But it is worth the risk, if only for the amusement and edification of the onlooker, who will be able to tell where the ice is thin simply by watching what happens when I skate on it.

In common with all those who had the ground taken from under their feet by the structuralist enterprise, I was unsettled but thrilled by the discovery of the constructed nature of the real. However, it soon became clear that it is equally important to hang on to the material reality of the resulting constructions. Just as in contemporary physics subatomic particles (matter) are also waves (non-material), so in the discursive realm it is necessary to imagine reality as material (beyond discourse) and as textual (produced by discourse) at one and the same time. For instance, news is a discursive construction of the real, but its texts are themselves real and can be used to reconstruct extra-discursive reality, most obviously on spectacular or charismatic occasions, like the bombing of Tripoli to coincide with US prime-time, or the staging of media events, from elections to the America's Cup.

Given this stance in relation to discourse and reality, the methodological implications are that in this book evidence takes the form of texts which can be recovered and scrutinized; discourse in real, material form. For instance, 'the audience' is accepted as evidence not in the form of individual behaviour (except where such form is itself textual, as in behaviour which is statistically reduced to the textual form of ratings), but in the form of real discursive constructions which are produced and circulated for various purposes by various agencies. The 'text' that constitutes the object of study for tele-ology is thus not confined to what is on the screen, but includes the discourse of television wherever it is deployed. And, as I hope will become clear from some of the essays in this book, one of the more weird and wonderful fictional creations associated with popular television is not to be found on the TV screen at all; the image of the TV audience that suffuses both the industry and the domain of public discussion about TV is a fiction which is just as susceptible to textual analysis – and just as real – as Pam Ewing.

TEXTUAL INTERVENTIONS

To read texts is also to write them. The point of departure for the essays herein is the work represented in two earlier books: *Reading Television*, which I co-wrote with John Fiske (1978), and my *Understanding News* (1982). Both books have twin aims: first, to provide an adequate (and where necessary original) theoretical and analytical framework for the studies of TV texts that they undertake; and second, to provide a teaching text for the use of readers setting out on the formal study of television for the first time. These aims inform the present volume too; television studies, in so far as such an enterprise can be given a proper name, comprises both studies of television and, simultaneously, the provision of principles, protocols and provocations for studying television in a more or less formal institutional setting.

Before *Reading Television* was published, the study of the medium had concentrated on three main problems:

1 television's behavioural effect on individual viewers, as discerned by psychologistic observation and experimentation;
2 television's cultural effect on the quality of life, as seen by critics trained in certain kinds of evaluative literary discrimination;
3 television's socio-political effect as one of the mass media – owned, controlled and institutionalized along the lines of capitalist commodity production.

Each of these 'inventions' of television as an object of study concentrated on its effects, which were generally understood to be negative. Critical attention to television really had very little to say that was positive. Television was said to cause individuals to behave badly (never well), to have a depressing (but not uplifting) effect on the quality of cultural life, and TV's social effect was said to enhance the power of the already powerful (but not that of its viewers), both by its economic location in their investment portfolios and its political propensity to trumpet their values in fact and fiction alike. Individually, culturally, socially, economically, politically, TV was not held in very high critical esteem.

The gap left by this history was in the region of television's textuality. Criticism was often so thoroughgoingly negative that it made one wonder why the critics in question bothered (and what on earth they themselves had been watching, if anything); if TV was so irredeemably awful, surely it didn't need such obsessive denunciation. Part of the problem, clearly, was that television represented something else for such critics. The trouble with TV was not that it was so bad, but that it was so *popular*. What made me personally interested in television as an object of study in the first place was the shocked discovery that 'anti-TV' opinions, which were at that time and still are quite respectable, simply couldn't be shifted by informed argument, because they weren't based on any such grounds. The passion and fury surrounding television's reputation in the public domain and in everyday conversations seemed to me to be a symptom of something much more disquieting than anything on TV itself: fear of popular culture.

Studies of television always did stand on the margin between popular culture and popular democracy, because the history of television is also, in part, the history of a continuing struggle for popular representation at both the symbolic and the political level. A rather shameful component of the intellectual history of TV criticism is that it has often been used to mount attacks on democracy in the guise of critique of popular culture. While it is not often seen as politically permissible to rubbish democracy, popular culture is another matter; open season on television has allowed those who weren't game to make clear their distaste for democracy to shoot at easier targets. As a result, a fair amount of critical distaste has found its way via schools and periodicals into the common-sense wisdom of the very people for whom popular culture is popular, permeating popular culture with guilt about its own practices, and with nostalgia for the outmoded forms so beloved of the critics.

In this context one strategy for taking account of television's popular-democratic potential is to begin from what may be understood as the viewer's point of view, namely the 'message' on the screen. However, it is also necessary to position across this very point of view an analytical lens; a systematic mode of looking which seeks to focus on problems beyond the immediate plane of personal preference or evaluation.

That strategy was certainly one that appealed to me, as I surveyed the then field of TV studies for the first time in the mid-1970s, wanting to contribute to the development of textual theory in relation to popular media, and, at the same time, to teach or popularize the approaches on which the theory is based. In other words, to put an analytical lens over the viewer's point of view is also to imagine a viewing position that one wouldn't mind occupying oneself. This is a practical method for dealing with what is in fact a difficult issue: the relationship between the observer and the object of study in the human 'sciences'. Theoretically informed observation of the cultural phenomenon of television is not the same as watching telly, and watching television for the purposes of study, teaching and publication does not tell you how other people – 'the' people – watch it for themselves; this is the inescapable uncertainty principle of tele-ology. However, to begin from an imagined viewer's point of view is to presume, *a priori*, that what's sauce for the goose is sauce for the gander. That is, the connection between me as watcher–theorist and the popular audience, via the programming that we both watch, is just that, a connection, and one that makes theorists out of the popular audience just as it makes a 'vidiot' out of the theorist.

This perspective does bring a certain landscape into view; not one in which the observer can pronounce on the individual, aesthetic or politico-economic 'effects' of television, but one in which the general cultural terrain which surrounds both analyst and audience can be viewed from within (just as, say, scholars of the English language can study it from within, but without reference to its 'effects'). Such a perspective encourages a general view of TV as playing a positive cultural role for modern societies, one that Fiske and I dubbed 'bardic' in *Reading Television*. Television performs a 'bardic function', rendering into symbolic form the conflicts and preoccupations of contemporary culture.

From this vantage point, which seeks to survey the terrain upon which meaning is created and circulated, in circumstances where individuals (the traditional source of meaning) are not the sole authors of the sense they make, the exploration of television can begin. As an instance of the industrialization of sense-making, television can then be used to explore larger issues, which reconnect its cultural aspects to questions of power. For example, categories such as class, nation and gender are not only socio-political but also meaningful, and TV is one of the mechanisms for producing the categories themselves, and the relationships within and between them, as meaningful (and therefore as true – 'existing in fact') for those of us who live among such categorizations. Similarly, the erection of discursive hierarchies such as the difference in prestige between oral and literate culture, or between television and literature, is not just a cultural matter of critical opinion placing literature 'higher' on a discursive scale than TV, but a matter of power too, where what is at stake is more than merely the taste of individuals, but the conditions of possibility for entire media like TV.

The proposal of a theoretical, critical apparatus capable of explaining the social and textual power of television is not a one-off enterprise that is achieved at the first or any attempt. Hence the textual interventions initiated in *Reading Television* and *Understanding News* have continued in an endeavour which is represented by the following chapters. *Tele-ology* develops analyses in response to new ideas, and to debates within the field. In addition, television studies is now much more responsive than it used to be to television's own institutional imperatives; technical, generic, economic or aesthetic developments within the industry, and the social relations with the various publics that TV channels create and sustain for themselves, are now capable of being folded into the mix of textual and cultural analysis that characterizes my approach to TV.

GOING WITH THE FLOE

As well as justifying and establishing television as an object of study, television studies has to establish a mode of address which is not only sensitive to its subject matter but also to the reader. Thus the essays that follow are responsive to different intellectual constituencies and to different kinds of readership, who must be addressed in order to establish the textual–cultural study of television with a critical discourse of its own. Hence an essay written for readers trained in literary studies would differ from one written for sociologists. Likewise independent producers cannot be addressed in quite the same terms as those who read scholarly journals. Having said that, however, I believe that each such constituency is or should be aware of what is being said and thought in neighbouring areas; once again my position is not squarely within any disciplinary or practical discourse but on the margins of several, seeking to illuminate each from the perspective of the others. The relations between different essays and their intended readers may differ, but what is represented does cross from essay to essay. Where TV itself is often described by the well-known concept of flow, my television criticism is connected by means of the less well-known concept of *floe*.

'Flow' is used by both Raymond Williams and network TV schedulers to conceptualize time, especially the flow of time within the medium. Floe, on the other hand, is a mixed metaphor of space, including the geopolitics of TV as an international industry, the relations between critical positions and the spaces between viewers. Part of its appeal to me is based on my own experience of TV in different geographical locations, from the British, Australian and American systems with which I am most familiar, to others I have only glimpsed in passing, from Malaysia and Singapore to Luxembourg and Castellon, wherein local peculiarities can be both recognized in their specificity and compared with each other in more general terms. When you leave home to see world television, however, you might find *Neighbours* dubbed into Catalan, or discover that the first programme ever broadcast on Singapore television was *Hancock's Half Hour*, or that the most popular show on Indonesian TV was the Australian mini-series *Return to Eden*, or that news footage is the same, vernacular voice-overs notwithstanding, wherever you go. Television systems the world over are apt to bump into their neighbours, and share each other's jokes and journalism. But you don't have to go far to find world television. Here at home in Fremantle, I can see the news from the USSR, *Vremya* ('Time'), every weekday, live and unsubtitled, beamed in by satellite and broadcast nationwide on the multicultural channel SBS, while on the three commercial TV channels I can catch the American NBC *Today Show* (Channel 7), the UK's *ITN World News* (Channel 9) or the American Cable News

Network (Channel 10) overnight. Ditto for drama series, sports coverage, chat shows and sitcoms. Meanwhile, my children are watching the Australian version of the BBC's *Play School* on the ABC, whose guest presenter today, singing about apples falling from trees, bump, bump, bump, is Annette Shun Wah, better known as producer–presenter of late-night international avant-garde TV and music on the SBS's *Eat Carpet* show.

The internationalization and cross-fertilization of broadcast programming is routine and unremarkable – it merely follows the pattern of publishing, fashion, recorded music and cinema. So it is with *Tele-ology*; readers will find references to unfamiliar shows, localities and personalities, but I think such references do more than give a local habitation and a name to more general matters. They demonstrate that in television, as in other public arts, 'the local' is a contradictory term; it is both vital and defunct. The same shows, formats and structures are found around the world, but what they mean can depend quite crucially on how they are scheduled into the public semiosis of a given locality. But simultaneously, although the resources available to any one household in that locality may be similar to those available in others, what is selected from the repertoire may differ crucially from one house to its next-door neighbour, or even from one member of the same household to another. Television is utilized not only according to the location of the antenna, but also according to the semiotic allegiances of the viewer, which are both local and global, just as a music fan will follow local bands and international stars, or a reader will buy local newspapers and international bestsellers, without confusion or a sense of contradiction.

What this 'multi-consciousness' in respect of symbolic space means for *Tele-ology* is that I have tried to retain the twin realities of planetary circulation and privatized sense-making in the essays that follow. Some of them are much more local in their references than others, and it's tempting to hope that any resulting opacity for readers from elsewhere will be seen as the richness of local colour rather than the murk of confusion. But I'd probably be on safer ground, or a steadier floe, to claim that television requires a situated analysis to enable its peculiarities and its generalities to be teased out. It might also be worth adding that in the international circulation of ideas, to which *Tele-ology* is a contribution, readers will be much more familiar with 'local' references to, say, the UK or USA, presented not as local at all but as typical and binding on readers from Seoul to Santiago. One of the many advantages of living in Australia is that its 'local' is irreducibly unique while at the same time it is unusually open to the international flow of television and other cultural tides. So what is local for Australia is not claimed as typical for the world; its unfamiliarity is a reminder of the way things look differently depending on where you stand, its marginality is a floe from which to survey the ceaseless currents of both television and television theory.

TELE-OLOGY

The essays herein are gathered into five sections:

Television theory

Part I colonizes some terrain for television theory, setting up a number of concepts, analytical procedures and theoretical preoccupations by means of which a textual–cultural approach to television can be undertaken. It argues that television ought to be understood not as a technology, nor even as an aesthetic system, but much more broadly as one of the fundamental human mechanisms for sense-making, comparable with speech itself. In order to make this claim, it is necessary to adopt two basic theoretical tenets: first, that communication is social not individual, and second, that it is textual not behavioural.

That is, first, the 'power of speech' is not individual but social, therefore subject to technological development and historical change in what should be understood not as an innate personal capacity for speaking but a global economy of sense-making. The so-called power of speech is socialized, and therefore subject to economic exploitation, technological expansion and, most importantly, to power relations. Certain people and classes of people have historically taken the power of speech much further than others, gaining power over the means of its production and social circulation.

The second tenet is that communication depends on the production of texts and the practice of reading in any medium whatever; it is neither based on the self-presence of the speaking consciousness nor on face-to-face communication. Writing and other media like TV are neither extensions of speech nor are they, as is sometimes held, corruptions of it. On the contrary, 'media' are preconditions for sense-making.

It is no longer necessary to fret about television's supposed effects on individual behaviour, for these are marginal to its main business of developing the social power of speech into a hi-tech industry. Individual effects are small beer compared with the social effects of widespread belief in them; effects which include forms of censorship, licensing, restrictive regulation and moral policing that are reminiscent of the edicts of Star Chamber against the new medium of printing in the sixteenth century. From this perspective, fretting about TV's 'influence' is based on the presumption that there is something tainted or contaminating about a socio-technological medium of communication *per se*, a duplicity made all the more scandalous for being tainted with the seductiveness of pictures, images, icons, as opposed to the worthy, even godly, medium of print. In this respect TV shares a history of being disciplined *as a medium* with its visual predecessors such as Hollywood, advertising, comics, right back to music hall and the illustrated 'penny-dreadfuls' of the Victorian age, all of which attracted the same discourses of abuse until they ceased to be popular, and were then recognized as art. Contemporary preoccupations with television's individual, behavioural, psychological effects are, historically, a *symptom* of the post-medieval world's suspicion of visual images, not an explanatory framework; even more fundamentally, they are a symptom of that mystical faith in direct, self-present, face-to-face communication as the only real, authentic kind which television and all the other media, including print and writing, challenge.

It follows from a socio-textual approach to television that the object of study is the text in its social setting – institutional, historical, political, economic and personal. The most fundamental concern that the analyst has to confront when constructing such an object of study is the question of textual power. 'Television and the power of dirt' puts the view that television's textual power derives from its marginal status at various different levels: its 'dirty' boundaries, the potency of rites of passage, the power of ambiguity, the excess of scandalous categories. Television's institutional status is also marginal, ambiguous and scandalized, which suggests that the semiotic and the social, the textual and cultural, are capable of being explored in relation to one another, even if they cannot be read off from or reduced to each other. This analytical preoccupation with TV's textual power remains a concern throughout the book, though in different manifestations. Once communication is understood as social not individual, and as textual not behavioural, it may even be possible to argue, as I do towards the end of 'Television and the power of dirt', that speech itself should be understood in the same way.

Truth wars

Part II shows how the production and representation of truth on popular television and in the press is not a matter of philosophical definitions of truth, but a practical requirement in an industry which is attending to other things, like survival, profitability, audience maximization, entertainment, deadlines and competition. Meanwhile, this industry is turning out truth by the ton, wholesale warehouses of words, images, imaginings and sound effects whose effect is to establish in a pragmatic way what counts as true for whole communities. Without having to distinguish in the abstract between truth and falsehood, truth and propaganda, truth and fiction, the news media construct the concrete world into stories, which are narratives whose *form* is already written by the genre-expectations of the medium and by the professional practices of journalists and producers.

Forgetting their scolding grandmothers, for whom 'telling stories' is synonymous with 'telling lies', the manufacturers of the nightly narrative render the immediacy of unpredictable incidents into circadian semio-rhythms, whose familiar components of sight, sound, story and sentiment, cemented by endless talk, continuously invent 'us', our community, nation, alliance, species, as intelligible and as different from 'them'. Thus truth on television is textual, a coherence reached by quotation and memory, but it's also adversarial, being what's inside 'our' boundary *as opposed to* what's outside. Telling news stories becomes a matter of fitting unknown facts to known narratives, making the truth of the news result (like the *quod erat demonstrandum* of a theorem) from the strategies of inclusion and exclusion by which home is distinguished from foreign.

Unfortunately this strategy makes 'foreigners' – beyond the pale not only of 'home' but of truth itself – of all those within a given community who don't fit the 'we' pronoun in the narrative. So if the story happens to be told from a white, professional, male, conservative, first-world point of view, which does sometimes happen, then those whose point of view is organized around different subjectivities are automatically exiled from the community whose news story this is. For such instant outsiders, the news is not true but racist, sexist, biased and propagandist. But for those who occupy or endorse the speaking position of the news narrative, the story is familiar (it creates our family). It is not only *common* sense, or sense-making understood as common-to-all, it is *true*; it has power to command *others*. The occupants of different speaking positions are thus, inevitably, outside of truth (un*trust*worthy), and if they're not liars, then they are at least seen as incapable of self-representation. The 'we' speaking position of news narrative thence reckons itself empowered to speak on behalf of (to colonize) those others in the name of truth, providing interpretation and explanation, usually in the form of 'helpful' voice-overs which literally silence other voices.

These are truth wars, and they have both winners and losers. Current champion is an image of democracy that simultaneously represents freedom of speech ('both' sides of a story) and leadership, participation and government, as well as covering the variety and plurality of public affairs and human interest. This fictionalization of pluralist democracy takes the form of multiple voices and faces speaking for about fifteen seconds each in a dialogue which illustrates the truth of the reporters' narratives, set into a choreographed sequence of familar genres (domestic politics–economy, foreign affairs, disasters, sport and weather) which are linked into audio-visual if not logical coherence by the measured rhythm of alternation between studio anchor, talking heads, graphics and actuality. These are the weapons of truth wars, which certainly make losers of all who cannot wield them.

Paedocracy

Part III concentrates on viewing practices, though once again it is hard to avoid the conclusion that the only real audience for popular television is the fictionalized image of it that can be found in various texts and discourses. The practice of watching television is real enough, but what anyone actually does in this context hardly counts; how we watch television does not determine how television works either textually or institutionally. In any case, although watching TV is easy to do, it is very difficult (in my view impossible) to observe or describe in objective or neutral terms, so no-one really knows what happens. It is only in texts and discourses that you will find identified, unified or explained the myriad unseen goings-on that are collectively lumped together as 'the audience'. The TV industry, for instance, works towards and addresses an image of the audience which I've called 'paedocratic', that is, governed by childlike qualities. However, the TV industry is not alone in this; critical and regulatory discourses, including much of what passes as objective academic or scientific research, also paedocratize the audience, setting it up as an 'other' which is in need of protection from its own innocence, vulnerability and unbridled urges.

Since the publication of the papers in which I first introduced the concept of the paedocratic audience ('Out of bounds' and 'Invisible fictions'), I've begun to realize that the term covers up a struggle, a battle of wills, as it were. Television networks, government regulators and critical institutions all construct TV as a paedocratic regime, but as often as not they only do this as a prelude to some form of *coup* in which they try to snatch power away from the wild, undomesticated and irresponsible audience they've imagined, in order to govern it (for its own good, of course). In other words, there's a struggle between what are presumed to be *paedocratic* audience practices on the one hand (governed *by* childlike qualities), and *pedagogic* discourses on the other (government *over* childish tendencies). Pedagogic interventions range from attempts to guide, channel and inform viewers (usually found inside TV and the press in the guise of promos, reviews and features) to those which seek to control, scold and chastise them (often encountered in schools, so there are few viewers who escape this battle for their imagination).

This struggle seems endemic to a system in which TV has a life of its own, whatever the audience is or wants, and that life is conducted inside a textual realm, surrounded by neighbouring discursive domains, some of which are friendly, some less so. In such a world, the community under discussion – the TV audience – is not and cannot be present to or speak for itself, but nevertheless, perversely, it remains *sovereign*, in the sense that individually and collectively the audience can exercise 'capital' power over what it watches – the power of life and death (i.e. on and off), if not power over the way that the life of TV-land is conducted. TV-land operates from day to day as an institution, relatively autonomous from the audience, but inexplicable without its absent presence; similarly, the audience that is called into being by the world-historical forces of television remains relatively autonomous from that institution at the level of sense-making practices.

The will to control audiences is historically no match for the audience's will to watch. But I do think regulatory, pedagogic, censorious discourses of criticism and control have had a depressing effect, not only on TV texts but on the *ambitions* of audiences, who endlessly settle for less than they want because the only freely available frameworks for making sense of what they're doing make it seem trivial, scandalous, habit-forming, narcotizing, boring, ideologically unsound, hegemonic and, well, bad. It's the critical chorus that needs to be restrained for a while, rather than the audience. The audience doesn't have much to go on if it ever does decide to look around for guidance on how to do its job better. An important job for those who take a scholarly or critical interest in television and its audiences is thus to take a hard look at their own practices and presumptions, some of which I criticize in 'The real world of audiences' and in 'Out of bounds'. It is also salutory, and it may be suggestive, to share with others one's own personal formation as a practising TV viewer, which I do in 'Regimes of pleasure'.

The creation of the audiencc as a paedocratic 'other' often says more about the critic than it does about the audience. However, I would argue just as strongly that audiences, precisely because they are a creation of the institutions that address them, should not be left as they are found. In my view, telling the public that TV is an idiot-box or boob-tube is not calculated to inspire a rich variety of viewing practices, of different kinds and quality from the careful to the carefree. However, to show how TV texts and discourses construct not only the world but also places in it that from time to time everyone might want to call 'me' is also to alert viewers to what they can achieve in the act of watching television. Viewers cannot be made to behave themselves; that's not what TV is for. But they can understand how TV behaves, including their own part in it. That's what tele-ology, finally, is for.

Photopoetics

Part IV takes up this rallying cry by arguing in favour of certain traditions of creative imagination in popular culture both historically and in specific cultural contexts. 'The politics of photopoetry' crosses the frontier between popular and high culture, showing how certain visual artists, from Humphrey Jennings to Troy Kennedy Martin, are doing no less than

Shakespeare did, while conversely Shakespeare has been reduced to an ideological blunt instrument with which the popular media themselves belabour their unsuspecting readers, to the detriment of all concerned.

Meanwhile, over on commercial television in neglected backwaters of the cultural landscape, things are afoot which definitely require explanation. 'Continuous pleasures in marginal places' looks at TV continuity – the TV genre that isn't there – in the context of some communities which are, historically, not sure if they're there either. One such is Western Australia, and another is the community of tele-ologists. Luckily for Western Australia, there is some evidence (in 'A state of excitement') that indeed something is there, even if it isn't the America's Cup. The euphoricization of democracy is one of television's contemporary photopoetic creations, and you saw it first, or rather felt it, on Channel 9. As for the worldwide community of tele-ologists, there's still some doubt about their existence. Watch this space.

The art of television

The final part of the book is devoted to a series of essays which narrow the critical focus, hopefully to increase the intensity of illumination, to television in Australia; what it's for ('Local television'), how it got there ('Quoting not science but sideboards') and what's going on ('Two cheers for paedocracy'). This last chapter shows how traditional ways of understanding both cultural politics ('The 18th Brumaire of Kylie Minogue') and art ('Getting the picture?') simply don't apply to what is going on in the electronic media. Kylie Minogue, Elle Macpherson, Joan Sutherland, Madonna, Mel Gibson and Jane Rutter (all but one of whom are Australian, though all are global figures) are, through their bodily images, caught up in various ways in the politics of electronic aesthetics, storming the Bastille of popular consciousness while falling victim to the *ancien régime* of cultural prejudice. The way that these performers, simulacra of contemporary art, are handled by journalists and commentators, is explored in 'Two cheers for paedocracy', showing (I think conclusively) that cultural journalism is in much greater need of critique and improvement than the culture it purports to explain.

* * *

Since personal computers became cheap enough even for academics, the potential for creativity of small screens in the home has begun to be recognized. It's no longer so easy to presume a division of labour between critical movers and shakers on one side, and awed, passive audiences on the other; creative criticism and watching TV turn out to be one and the same thing. Where culture, meaning and power are concerned, structures (e.g. discourses) and artefacts (e.g. texts) are simpler than their individual end-products, whether semiotic or social, just as a skeleton is simpler than the body that depends on it. And just as a living, breathing body and its actions depend on but are not caused by the underlying skeleton, so TV texts and audiences cannot be accounted for as effects of the structures that determine them. However, when people decide it's time to exercise their bodies, or to use them creatively, they strive to understand the general framework, the skeleton and all the attached bits and pieces, so as to make the best use of what they've got within the limits of the structure. Just as bodies can be made to do remarkable things by such means, increasing personal pleasure as well as functional performance, so it is with the study of textual–cultural structures like television. To understand TV better is to anatomize it, but to do that can help to improve its performance and the pleasure of its audiences.

Chapter 2

Television and the power of dirt*

> Men make their own history, but they do not make it just as they please; they do not make it under circumstances chosen by themselves, but under circumstances directly encountered, given and transmitted from the past. The tradition of all the dead generations weighs like a nightmare on the brain of the living. And just when they seem engaged in revolutionizing themselves and things, in creating something that has never existed, precisely in such periods of revolutionary crisis they anxiously conjure up the spirits of the past to their service and borrow from them names, battle-cries and costumes in order to present the new scene of world history in this time honoured disguise and this borrowed language.
>
> (Karl Marx, *18th Brumaire of Louis Bonaparte*)[1]

This chapter takes up the theme of borrowed languages; both those of television itself and those that have become established within analytical discourses in the study of television. I want to argue that some of the most familiar analytical categories we use to study television are in need of rethinking, and that television itself will emerge from this process shorn of its time-honoured disguise. Instead, television will be seen for what it is – a new scene of world history that supplants what has traditionally been understood as the power of speech. Despite our habit of anxiously conjuring up the spirits of the past to exorcize its power, I shall argue that for modern, industrialized societies, *television is the power of speech*. To begin with, then, I want to make a problem out of some of the received notions of textual analysis, especially where texts and readers have been conceptualized as an abstract binary opposition with meaning somehow batted back and forth between the two.

* Originally published as John Hartley (1983) 'Encouraging signs: television and the power of dirt; speech and scandalous categories', *Australian Journal of Cultural Studies*, 1(2), 62–82. Published in the USA in Willard D. Rowland and Bruce Watkins (eds) (1984) *Interpreting Television: Current Research Perspectives*, Beverly Hills: Sage.

TEXTS

The practice of reading television texts has demonstrated fairly clearly that individual segments, programmes, series and so forth are far from unitary in their meaning. In fact television provides a convincing instance of the structuralist axiom of 'no intrinsic meaning'. Television texts are polysemic, and they resist attempts even to identify their smallest signifying units, since there are so many different kinds on the screen at once: visual, verbal, aural, discursive, narrative and so on. But even though television texts are saturated with meaningfulness, there is no textual warrant for any particular meaning to be privileged as true. The best that the analyst can do is to show, without ascribing agency to them, how texts try to limit and close their own meaningfulness with ideological 'preferred readings' and so forth.

But the problem of the text goes further than this. Television is recalcitrant when it comes to identifying where the text should stop. Quite apart from the problem of rationalizing what must in the end be an arbitrary act, namely the choice of this rather than that as the 'text' to analyse, television cannot be reduced, even for the sake of analysis, to 'what's on telly'. The forms of television representation are not specific to television; its discourses are produced, regulated and reproduced just as much off-screen as they are on it; its institutionalization of *these* rather than *those* signifying practices cannot be explained by looking at the practices by themselves; and even its own programmes are made meaningful 'outside' television itself, in newspapers, magazines, conversations, learned papers and the like. In short, television texts do not supply the analyst with a warrant for considering them either as unitary or as structurally bounded into an inside and outside. If television has a distinctive feature, it is that it is a 'dirty' category.[2]

READERS

The notion of the reader is similarly a problem. Traditionally conceptualized (for the sake of analysis) as either one individual reader or a mass of individual readers, the category 'reader' has become established as both unitary and abstract. But, as anyone who studies television must know, there are differences in the way the same bit of television can be watched by the same individual reader. Such differences may depend on mood, company or place, but there is also the question of which discursive resource, or combination of resources, the person brings to bear on the programme. Today I may be 'reading television' as critic, but tonight I'll be 'watching television' as audience. And sometimes (always) these two ways of watching will slide into or even contradict each other.

Following from this, it is hard to sustain the notion of a unitary individual who is in possession of a unitary subjectivity in view of television.

Without (necessarily) claiming that everyone is schizophrenic, it is possible to use television as a way of showing how no individuals have unitary subjectivity in their possession. Rather there are clusters of significant identifications that may combine, split, contradict or confirm each other in provisional orientations that will for the time being serve the purposes of a social 'I'.

These identifications form an extensive, changing and informal paradigm that is carried in various discourses. What sense 'I' might make of television depends, therefore, on the discursive resources available. But although 'I' might identify with them, not all of them fit each other – some will necessarily marginalize or deny others, and some are more obvious, well-worn and time-honoured than others. Both paradigmatically (the discursive identifications) and syntagmatically (their combinations or contradictions), 'I' is a 'dirty' category too.

DIRT

It seems to me that the dirtiness both of television texts and of individual readers is a matter worth looking into further. The notion that both of these categories are by definition dirty is not a new one. In respect of television, Hans Magnus Enzensberger has put it forcefully:

> The electronic media do away with cleanliness; they are by their nature 'dirty'. That is part of their productive power. . . . The desire for a cleanly defined 'line' and for the suppression of 'deviations' is anachronistic and now serves only one's own need for security.[3]

As for individuals, this is how Edmund Leach puts it:

> Individuals do not live in society as isolated individuals with clear-cut boundaries; they exist as individuals interconnected in a network by relations of power and domination. Power, in this sense, resides in the interfaces between individuals, in ambiguous boundaries. The logical paradox is that (i) I can only be completely sure of what I am if I cleanse myself of all boundary dirt, but (ii) a completely clean 'I' with no boundary dirt would have no interface relations with the outside world or with other individuals. Such an 'I' would be free from the domination of others but would in turn be wholly impotent. The interface is the opposition:
>
> clean/dirty = impotence/potency
>
> and hence that *power is located in dirt*.[4]

The idea that power is located in dirt, which itself can be defined as ambiguous boundaries, strikes me as useful in respect of television. It suggests that the interface between texts and readers is capable of producing both meanings and 'relations of power and domination' precisely because it is not a clean opposition but always and necessarily ambiguous. What I shall be looking for, then, is not texts and readers as opposed entities, but the way boundaries between them are erected, transgressed and policed.

THE POWER OF TELEVISION

But first I would like to introduce just one more dirty category into the discussion, and that is the so-called power of speech. The power of speech, as commonly understood, is a natural attribute of the human species, and is therefore distributed evenly (barring physical damage) between all members of the species. Not only is this power (or competence) reckoned to be equally distributed, but speech itself is understood as natural, direct communication, as natural language. Small wonder that speech is taken as the model for linguistic and other kinds of analysis, such as semiotics, that are interested in meaning. However, the work of Jacques Derrida has shown that this is by no means an innocent act – on the contrary, as Jonathan Culler has explained:

> Privileging speech in this way by treating writing as a parasitic and imperfect representation of it is a way of repressing or setting aside certain features of language, or certain aspects of its functioning. If distance, absence, misunderstanding, insincerity are features of writing, then by distinguishing writing from speech one can construct a model of communication which takes as the norm an ideal associated with speech – where the listener is thought to be able in principle to grasp precisely what the speaker has in mind. . . . Writing, supposedly an external accessory in the service of speech, threatens to taint the purity of the system it serves.[5]

If writing – the medium of literature, philosophy and science – can be reckoned 'parasitic', 'imperfect' and a 'taint' because of its supplementarity, its distance, absence, misunderstanding and insincerity, then what are we to say of television? The medium of trivia and sensationalism, of sex, violence and bad language, of corruption and moral decline, is commonly seen as the ultimate supplement. It threatens the purity of both speech and writing. It does not even have the artistic pretensions of cinema to redeem it.

None the less, Hollywood had already provided a model of impurity and rehearsed a discourse of contagion for later use against television. Here is the report of the Spens Committee of 1938:

> Certainly it would be an advantage if all our children could learn the same English speech, though we agree . . . in recommending the preservation of true dialect, as distinct from affected or debased forms which have no roots in history. Teachers are everywhere tackling this problem,

> though they are not to be envied in their struggle against the natural conservatism of childhood allied to the popularization of the infectious accents of Hollywood. The pervasive influence of the hoarding, the cinema, and a large section of the public press are, in this respect as in others, subtly corrupting the taste and habits of the rising generation.[6]

Television has been policed by this discourse continuously since its earliest prehistory. It is still beyond the pale. Here is one commonplace example, immediately to hand as I write, of the common-sense barricade between literacy (hooray!) and television (boo!). It is from the London *Sunday Times* (10 April 1983):

> The great TV and literacy debate which has been rumbling on for 30 years or so shows no sign of reaching a conclusion yet. The impression – always strong among adults – that a race of square-eyed and weirdly dressed non-readers, non-writers and non-counters is in the making isn't the sort of thing that statistical proof or disproof does much to shake or confirm. It isn't exactly a sign of literary attainment or public spirit when half the adult population is counted as 'readers' of the tabloids; and it's not necessarily a sign that television encourages children to read when publishers produce so many spin-offs from children's programmes.

In the teeth of its own concern with the ambiguity of television's boundaries with its media neighbours (the piece is a review of spin-off books), the article seems to need the security of a cleanly defined line between itself and television. Television isn't much good for anything from this point of view, except to encourage children to stop using it in favour of 'literary attainment', and naturally it's not even very good at that. But the main thing is to reduce contact with the contagion to the shortest possible time. The review as a whole is headlined 'Ways to Wean Children Off TV'. Clearly the power of speech is a dirty category, but here the source of the dirt is identified equally clearly as belonging not to speech itself but to television, the other electronic media, and popular tabloids. The power that is located in this dirt is of course of the negative kind – it infects and corrupts the rising generation, turning them into a race of weird monsters with square eyes and dubious habits. What is it that makes television into such a potent (dangerous) extension of language? Can you imagine a headline that read 'Ways to Wean Children Off Reading' or even 'Ways to Wean Children Off Speech'?

Another way of asking these questions, without having to weigh the merits of the concept of TV-as-motherhood that is implied in the weaning metaphor, is to return to the notion of the power of speech and to concentrate for a moment not so much on the speech as on the power. For Saussurians, the power of speech is not only separated from the taint of writing, it is also protected from the grubby world of speaking: the power of speech is *langue*, an abstract system that lies beyond individual and social will. Only *parole*, the abstract binary opposite of *langue*, is allowed contact with the social relations that, as Saussure concedes, are the sole precondition for the creation of *langue* in the first place.[7] It seems that the protection of *langue* from the social/individual will has more to do with the power of binaries than with the logic of the case.

For Chomskians, the power of speech is an attribute of the species – innate competence. Here too it is regarded as almost unthinkable to suggest that such a power can be interfered with socially. But when it comes to the networks of power and domination that characterize social relations, individual natural capacities are neither here nor there. The notion of linguistic competence does not raise the question of who has power over it, just as the notion of a natural capacity to eat or to make tools does not explain who goes hungry or who owns the means of production. It appears, then, that both the concept of *langue* and that of competence have the effect of defining power out of the terms of study. But, as Stuart Hall has very briskly put it:

> Of course, a language is not equally distributed amongst all native speakers, regardless of class, socio-economic position, gender, education and culture: nor is competence to perform in language randomly distributed. Linguistic performance *and competence* is socially distributed, not only by class but also by gender. Key institutions – in this respect, the family–education couple – play a highly significant role in the social distribution of cultural 'capital' in which language plays a pivotal role.[8]

Perhaps here we have a clue as to why television is commonly regarded as a dirty, dangerous medium that 'our' children must be weaned off. In the first place, it has none of the abstract purity of *langue*, nor the natural pure individualism of competence – it is all too evidently a social relation of sense-making from which power cannot be excluded. And second, maybe even consequently, television is threatening:

> The electronic media are entirely different from the older media like the book or the easel-painting, the exclusive class character of which is obvious. . . . Potentially the new media do away with all educational privileges and thereby with the cultural monopoly of the bourgeois intelligentsia. This is one of the reasons for the intelligentsia's resentment against the new industry. As for the 'spirit' which they are endeavouring to defend against 'depersonalization' and 'mass culture', the sooner they abandon it the better. The new media are oriented towards action, not contemplation; towards the present, not tradition. Their attitude to time is completely opposed to that of bourgeois culture which aspires to possession, that is to extension in time, best of all, to eternity. The media produce no objects that can be hoarded and auctioned. They do away completely with 'intellectual property' and liquidate the 'heri-

> tage', that is to say, the class-specific handing on of non-material capital.[9]

It is perhaps just as well that Enzensberger prefaces these refreshingly optimistic remarks with the word 'potentially', since television as presently instituted does not always conform to its potential. But it is important to consider what that potential or 'productive capacity' might be, in order to demonstrate the extent to which its development is not determined by innate capacities as such, but on the way these are organized socially and institutionalized. In fact, television supplies us with a model for understanding how the social power of communication – the power of speech – is neither abstract nor innate, but a power relation. Further, television demonstrates that the production of senses, knowledges and meanings is thoroughly socialized, marking a decisive break with the kinds of cultures associated with the 'older media'.

BORROWED LANGUAGES

The implications of this argument for the analysis of television itself will, I hope, become clearer later on. For the moment, I want to take up Enzensberger's point about the analyst. He points to the cultural (class) monopoly of the intelligentsia, and their/our 'resentment against the new industry'. Such resentment may be expressed openly and with vigour – ('Ways to Wean Children Off TV') – but it may also have something to do with apparently neutral, respectable intellectual activities like reading texts. For texts, as commonly understood, are nothing short of institutionalized meaning; they are fixed, owned, and have clearly identifiable boundaries (usually in the form of covers). They can be 'possessed' in different ways by clearly identifiable authors and readers – they are a very good way of ensuring 'extension in time, best of all . . . eternity'; they can even be hoarded and auctioned. As Roland Barthes has argued, this concept of text produces characteristically authoritarian social relations:

> The notion of the text is historically linked to a world of institutions: the law, the Church, literature, education. The text is moral object: it is the written in so far as the written participates in the social contract. It subjects us, and demands that we observe and respect it, but in return it marks language with an inestimable attribute which it does not possess in its essence: security.[10]

Television analysts, especially those of us who are institutionalized within education, are notoriously susceptible to the appeal of security, whether of text or tenure. But television is, equally, resistant to classification into texts, and its ambiguity extends even to the dirty boundary that surrounds its institutionalized study (there is no 'pure' academic discipline called 'Television'). Small wonder that we are driven to borrowing the costume of the text in order to dress this scandalous subject in respectability. However, the consequence is that we tend to analyse the costume, to use television to demonstrate an inestimable attribute that it does not possess in its essence: security of texture.

In short, we need to find 'Ways to Wean Critics Off Texts'. But of course the notion of the text is a thoroughly naturalized term in analysis. And as Stuart Hall has put it:

> Changing the terms of an argument is exceedingly difficult, since the dominant definition of the problem acquires, by repetition, and by the weight and credibility of those who propose or subscribe it, the warrant of 'common sense'.[11]

Hall invokes Volosinov's concept of 'sign as the arena of class struggle'[12] to suggest that 'the same term could be disarticulated from its place within one discourse and articulated in a different position'.[13]

Hence, it is not necessary to abandon the notion of the text in respect of television or its analysis. But the ideological inflections of the term need to be recognized, and where necessary changed (though that may prove 'exceedingly difficult'). What is needed is not to reduce television to texts, but to disarticulate the notion of the text from the discourse of possession, and rearticulate it in the position(s) of television.

ACCESSING

Before I attempt that, however, I would like to bring the other side of the text : reader binary opposition back into play. First, rearticulating the notion of the text calls into question the separability of text and reader. Recent work on subject positioning, by *Screen* theorists for example, suggests that subjectivity itself is an effect or product of textual relations. Readers, in this model, are written on by texts. Of course television is not written, it is produced (which is itself a suggestive metaphor for its relationship with its audiences), but I would like to propose that the relations between television and its viewers might be thought of in terms of accessing. Viewers 'access' television discourses and representations both in and beyond the act of watching television ('accessing' goes on after the television set is switched off). And vice versa: television accesses its viewers' (culture's) discourses and identifications in the act of production.

I have argued elsewhere that accessing on television has some peculiar features.[14] It is not a case of information retrieval. When you are quoted or interviewed or appear on television (when you're accessed), you may have your say but you do not speak for yourself. Your contribution is semiotically stolen, that is, appropriated by the overall television discourse. It is made to mean something different from whatever you may have intended, by its status as a 'quote'. You are rearticulated into an actor in the drama, and what you say is like fictional dialogue – it is subservient to what else is being said, to who is saying it and to what the drama is about. Further, accessing lends the credibility and legitimacy (realism) of your authenticity and authority (truth) to television.

If television can be thought of as a means of accessing a multiplicity of discourses and representations, so can the viewer. Everything I have just said about the way television accesses applies equally to the individual viewer. We are all a means of accessing a multiplicity of discourses and identifications. Not only is what we say and the way we make sense of the world largely quoted, but also the resources from which we take these discourses and identifications cannot control the way we use them in combination. However, although I take the relation between television texts and readers to be similar in that it is a process of mutual accessing, I am not arguing that it is uniform or evenhanded. It is still a hegemonic power-relation in the way it is currently organized socially. In brief, some viewers have more discursive resources than others, and television has more than all.

SEVEN TYPES OF SUBJECTIVITY

I shall return to the power inequalities later. At this point I would like to take up the idea of individuality (subjectivity); not as a self-contained and clearly identifiable entity, but as a dirty structure of accessed identifications. In order to be more definite about what I am referring to, I will suggest seven of what I take to be the more important identifications that are available or encouraged. They are what I am tempted to call seven types of ambiguity: namely *self*, *gender*, *age-group*, *family*, *class*, *nation*, *ethnicity*. The list is both abstract and analytical (I do not have a textual warrant for it), and in the concrete instance of television it is not even a list, since the seven categories get very mixed up, and some are encouraged more than others (family more than class), while others do not co-exist very peacefully (some notions of nation with some types of ethnicity). These identifications are neither self-evident nor essential, in either television or individuals. What I hope to do is to show how they are textually produced. In the context of this chapter that means I shall pay attention to the way ambiguous boundaries are erected and transgressed within and between the identifications.

I am looking, then, for textual processes and representations that may encourage reader identifications. It is implicit in my argument that none of the seven types is represented in isolation. Further, the way each one is taken up ideologically (the way it's produced) is similar in structure to the way each of the others is treated. They can be seen, structurally, as homologous transformations of each other. Thus, each type of identification (together with others I've not included in my list) serves to define and limit the others. And there are what I will call condensations of them, where, for instance, particular senses of all seven are collapsed into one star-sign, the signifier for which may be a person, like Prince Charles or the Princess of Wales, or it may be an emblematic object or practice, like a car, a landscape, or a sports event. Television produces its own star-signs, from news-presenters to more obviously fictional characters, and these too are available as condensers for our seven types of subjectivity.

EX-NOMINATION

In this chapter I am going to have to concentrate on just one identification to serve as an emblem for the others. The one I have chosen is that of age-group. In the spirit of the chapter, however, what I am looking for are the marginal, ambiguous edges of the category, and the way these offer what looks like a settled, positive, natural inside for us to access as our own selves. In this respect I have found Barthes's notion of *ex-nomination* very useful. Barthes suggests that 'capitalism' is quite easily *named* in economic discourses. It is uncontroversial to say that ours is a capitalist economy. In political discourses, however, capitalism is less easily named – there is no Capitalist Party as such. In cultural discourses, capitalism 'disappears' – it is completely ex-nominated. As Barthes puts it, the bourgeoisie is the social class that does not want to be named.[15]

This notion can be applied to all of our seven types of social identification, to show how within each one there arc ex-nominations going on. The way to spot such absences, of course, is to look for those nominations or namings that are in play. In the case of gender, women are frequently named or nominated as women. They are represented in terms of gender – defined by their looks, procreative ability, femininity and so on. Men, on the other hand, are often shown as beyond gender – they just get on with whatever they are doing and are defined in terms of their job, character, actions and so forth; men are ex-nominated as men. Similarly, in the instance of class, there are plenty of representations of working-classness, which is nominated as such, whereas middle-classness is rarely presented as a significant signifier on its own; more often it is taken for granted, while the focus of the story lies elsewhere (see *Dallas*, or interestingly in view of its title, the film *Ordinary People*). Middle-classness is an ex-nominated category. In the case of ethnicity and nation, blacks and foreigners are often signified as belonging to their respective race or nation. For white locals these attributes are apparently devoid of significance – they are ex-nominated. Finally, the family is a thoroughly ex-nominated category (despite evidence that the classic family is now statistically rare) unless you belong to a broken one, a single-parent one, etc.

YOUTH: A SCANDALOUS CATEGORY

As for the identifications within the category age-group, these too have a naturalized, ex-nominated centre – the category of *adult* – with other more ambiguous, marginalized identifications on its boundaries. Like television, I am going to concentrate on one of the nominated ambiguous boundaries, namely youth.

Youth is a very dirty category indeed. First of all I will explain in general terms why this is so, and then have a look at some examples to see how it is represented. Youth is a scandalous category because it offends against binary logic. Binary systems are two-term universes, and binary logic requires the two terms to be not just equivalent-but-opposite, but also mutually exclusive. For instance, there are plenty of such binaries in play in analytical discourses – signifier : signified; subject : object; text : reader; producer : consumer; speech : writing; domination : subordination. Binaries are also capable of being applied to both the physical and social world. The surface of the earth can be understood in terms of the binary land : sea, and the people on it in terms of the binary child : adult. All very neat and clean. But if we look closer at, for instance, the binary land : sea, we find things are not quite so simple. There is a margin between the two that is ambiguous. Sometimes it is land, sometimes sea. It is neither one thing nor the other, and both one and the other. I refer, of course, to the beach – the very same ambiguous category that people flock to in order to escape all sorts of otherwise strict social boundaries. The ambiguous beach is the place where you can do all sorts of scandalous things, from taking your clothes off in public to being more or less continuously preoccupied with pleasure, sex and self, without getting arrested. And of course you flock there in the ambiguous nontime of Sundays and other holidays, especially (in Britain) on Bank Holidays.

Youth is just this kind of scandalous category. It is neither child nor adult. To see why youth is so very dirty, then, all that is necessary is to list some of the most general, naturalized, and common-sense attributes that separate child (as a category) from adult, and to notice how completely youth transgresses them all. For instance,

child : adult
family of origin : family of destination
not working : working
single : married
asexual : gendered sexuality
irresponsible : responsible
and so on : and so on

With youth, all such oppositions are transgressed; youth has the attributes of neither child nor adult, and both child and adult. Just to show that the scandalousness comes from the categorical ambiguity of youth and not from what it does, I have located several examples of media stories in which age group is significant. I have taken these from popular newspapers; I hope these fixed texts will illustrate at least part of what goes on in the more complex moving text of television, especially in view of television's own ambiguous boundaries with its media neighbours.

What would you think of someone who brutalized a goldfish, terrorized a cat (three times), assaulted his father, set fire to his aunt, vandalized a car, disrupted a social club, and pinched people's bottoms with a pair of pliers? Normally, this is just the kind of behaviour we are encouraged to think of as scandalous and to associate with the excesses of youth. But not in this case, for as the London *Sun* (5 November 1979) tells us, 'little imp Colin' is a child of 3; leaving a 'trail of havoc' is cute, not culpable. Leafing through the same newspaper, we come across someone who at 21 is closer in age than Colin to the category of youth. This person is shown sitting at a school desk, wearing virtually no clothes. Again, however, the action is not represented as scandalous; quite the reverse, for of course this is a pin-up, and thus firmly within the realm of gendered sexuality. Susie the 'Oh!-level girl' may be (must be) youthful, but the representation is addressed to adult men. Despite the reputation of youth, then, it is not violence or overt sexuality as such that scandalizes. The problem is that youth transgresses the naturalized limits of both childhood and adulthood. In anthropological terms it is a rite of passage, a crossing of boundaries, so it becomes the subject of taboo and is subjected to ritual and repression.

The next example is from the London *Sunday Mirror* (17 May 1981). It describes, in detail, the youth 'cults' known as skinheads. The whole story is a ritual condensation of boundary transgressions and scandalous categories. It is set in that special place and time – the seaside on a Bank Holiday. The story is presented irrationally, as 'disturbing', 'frightening', and as about 'victims', 'fear' and 'thugs'. The transgressors themselves are called 'Britain's young tribes', 'sworn enemies' and 'like animals'. In the accompanying pictures, they're shown as Nazi-sympathizers whose appearance is precisely tribal, even their faces are made to look like masks, and their clothes and haircuts are all paraded to confirm our worst fears. The story itself comprises a succession of transgressions: of speech (they swear); of the peace (they fight); of patriotism (they parody the national flag); of politics (they are racists and admire Hitler); of sexuality (they stir up your murky psychological depths); of gender (the women swear and fight); of marriage (they insult a happy young couple); of the home (they live alone with a naked light bulb, greasy plates and a crinkled picture of Hitler); and of sobriety (at least one of them gets drunk while being plied with pints of lager by the reporter).

Mixed up in the unfolding of all these transgressions are almost all of the seven types of subjectivity I have mentioned. Of course, the story is not encouraging its readers to identify with the skinheads. But it is not just a

THE FUN PICTURES ARE ALWAYS IN THE SUN

TINY TERROR!

CAPPING the lot . . . little imp Colin   Picture by PETER LEA

Colin, 3, leaves a trail of havoc at home

By ANDREW PARKER

TODDLER Colin Shinton is a tiny terror . . . because he thinks he's Dennis the Menace!

The three-year-old's passion for copying his comic-strip hero has led him into a series of scrapes that Dennis would be proud of.

This is the trail of havoc left by cheeky Colin at his home in Wednesbury, West Midlands:

OUCH! He didn't like the black spots on his goldfish so he scrubbed them off with soap powder.

PHEW! His pet cat Tiger felt hot, so he popped him in the fridge to cool off.

SQUELCH! Poor Tiger he's on the receiving end again. Colin put him in the bath and sat on him.

Sprint

WHEE! Tiger in the tank . . . Colin gave him a spin in his mum Sharon's washing machine.

BANG! Sharon asked him to awaken his dad Colin who was snoozing in an armchair.

And dad came round with a bang as Colin Jnr. hit him on the head with a bottle of pop.

WHOOSH! Colin has surprises up his sleeve for all the family.

One of his aunties was peeling potatoes at the kitchen sink when he set her dress on fire with a cigarette lighter.

Colin is even more of a menace outside the house.

Spin

He let off the handbrake on his dad's car in a busy shopping centre, leaving roofer Mr Shinton with a 50-yard sprint to catch it.

But the most embarrassing moment came when Sharon and son were banned from the local bingo hall.

"Colin would sneak into a corner, wait until the game had really got going and then shout, 'House'," said Sharon.

"He stopped so many games that the management eventually kicked us out for good."

Colin is also the youngest bottom-pincher in Britain — and he uses a pair of pliers!

Sharon, who also has a six-year-old daughter, Sarah, said: "Colin is convinced he's a cartoon character like Denis the Menace.

"He never means to hurt anybody — and he loves his pet Tiger. He just thinks he's helping them out.

"He's a little angel really, but it was quite a shock when I went to the fridge to get some cheese and Tiger stepped out looking rather uncomfortable."

The Menace also has days when he likes to play the Incredible Hulk.

Fling

Sharon said: "He will unbutton his shirt, pick up things like bikes and chairs and fling them across the room with a roar.

"But you have to forgive him because he's always got a lovely big smile on his face."

THE SUN'S PAGE THREE OH-LEVEL GIRLS

Susie is sum girl

★ Susie Bessant, 21, has four O-levels, including maths, which makes her as good as any computer, in our opinion—and a lot better to look at.

Susie, who topped the class to become Miss Brighton, is a history, geography and English brain, too. More Oh!-level girls this week.   Picture by STEVE LEWIS

A disturbing Sunday Mirror

OF ALL Britain's young tribes, the skinheads are the most feared for the atmosphere of violence they bring to modern life. Our special report reveals that for many skinhead kids the reputation is undeserved—their haircuts and clothes are just part of fashion. But a hard core of thugs have reached new lows of race hate and violence.

by COLIN WILLS

The

NEXT weekend, Spring Bank Holiday, Britain will head for the seaside. And among the crowds, ever ready for trouble, will be members of the country's most violent group of youngsters.

CHELSEA soccer supporters give Nazi salutes at Watford Junction station..

Of all the factions the young have formed themselves into, the skinheads, or "skins," with their close-cropped hair, are the most disturbing.

For many the main attraction is "aggro" directed against rival groups and, particularly, blacks.

I have spent the past month with them attempting to understand the reasons for their fearsome reputation.

Skinheads have the capacity to strike terror wherever they go. You could see the fear in the eyes of the onlookers on Southend sea front on May Day Bank Holiday Monday two weeks ago.

Nazi salutes

Two hundred skinheads had been cornered by the police into a small section of the promenade. Ringed by blue they stood shoulder to shoulder like caged animals, oozing hostility, occasionally breaking into chants of "Sieg Heil" or giving Nazi salutes.

What were they doing like this, surrounded by police?

"They've only f—ing rounded us up, aren't they?" said a boy with an 88 symbol tattooed on his neck. "They're going to escort us to the station and put us on trains back to London."

What about the risk of vandalism?

"They put us in old clapped-out trains that are wrecked anyway," said a girl called Karen from Barking, Essex.

Sworn enemies

"Yeah, I think it's a dead liberty," said the boy. "We paid for our f—ing tickets. Why shouldn't we get proper trains to wreck?" Everyone laughed.

Suddenly the merriment stopped. Down the hill from the town centre to the seafront marched a group of about thirty mods, the skinheads' sworn enemies, with their neatly combed hair and their parkas.

"We are the mods," they sang at the tops of their voices. "We are, we are, we are the mods."

It was too much for the skinheads to take. In one surge they drove a human wedge through the police cordon and set upon the mods.

Before the police regained control, fists and boots flew in a spasm of brutality. Total strangers kicked and punched each other, snarling, swearing, tearing at each other's faces. "Die you bastard." "F—ing mod pig."

Of all the disturbing aspects of the skinhead phenomenon, it's the casualness of the violence that affects you most. Offhand violence that means about as much to the perpetrator as swatting a fly.

All of us may lose our tempers, lash out when provoked, or fight in self-defence. But skinhead violence is different. It has the horrific quality of being impersonal.

When they're in the mood—and almost always in superior numbers—anyone from an opposition group will do: mod, Ted, punk, black.

Some incidents have given a whole new meaning to the word sadistic. A lone Teddy boy was thrown into the sea and pelted with pebbles. He was being swept away to almost certain death until

RICHARD LEWINGTON
"White kids suffer, too."

he managed to clutch hold of a rowing boat and was saved.

Once three Skinheads tried to hang a nine-year-old child from a tree because he said he liked mods.

Allied to the violence, feeding it and feeding off it, is the sickening cancer of racism.

Nazi emblems are everywhere. Most skinheads need no second bidding to show off swastika badges and armbands.

The Nazi salute was even given in court by a 17-year-old skinhead sentenced to be detained indefinitely (he was too young for a life sentence) for the brutal murder of a Pakistani.

In a sick parody of all I understand our national flag to stand for, painted across a Union Jack sewn on to the back of one skinhead's jacket were the words "Skins Kill."

Some skinheads have tramlines of bare skin running across the sides of their cropped hair just above their ears.

This is a sign that they are supporters of one of the two main right-wing extremist parties, the British Movement or the National Front.

Both actively solicit support among skinheads, especially young football fans.

In a pub near the Stamford Bridge ground, before Chelsea's last

'Any victim will do for

eport on Britain's most frightening youth cult

SUNDAY MIRROR, [illegible]

SKINHEADS

gangs who feed on fear

ome game of the season, talked to a 16-year-old kin, Richard Lewington, om Carshalton, Surrey.

He showed me a copy of ulldog, the paper of the oung National Front, ought outside the atch.

In Leeds another young kinhead, Peter Stobart, ld me of an experience 'd had on his way to a otball match.

"A bloke I'd never seen efore came up to me and id: 'Are you interested joining the National ront? We could do with rong lads like you.'

"I said: 'No, I'm not terested in politics. I'm st here for the football.' d went to walk by him. e grabbed me by the oulder and said: 'What e f— 's the matter with ou? Are you a nigger ver or something?'"

Admires Hitler

I remember having a olitical discussion — if at's the word for it — th a 20-year-old skin in irmingham, Billy owarth.

He invited me to the edsit where he lived one. The room was lit a single, naked light- lb. The sink was clut- red with greasy plates d on the wall was a inkled picture of Hitler a staff car.

Why did he admire tler so much?

"Cos he was right, asn't he? He wouldn't stand no nonsense from no Jews."

What would he do if he were Prime Minister now?

"Send all the blacks home on the first boat. Put the Commies up against the wall."

Half an hour of that sort of stuff and you've had enough.

Some skinheads do express a genuine sense of grievance far more intelligently than Billy.

Richard Lewington, who leaves school at the end of this month to face an uncertain future, felt that much of the skin- head appeal was to white youngsters who believed themselves to be ignored and forgotten.

"It's always the blacks who are doing all the suffering. They're always the ones who need help and sympathy," he said.

"Let me tell you, white kids suffer just as much as they do." He doesn't attempt to play down the violence. "I admit skin- heads cause trouble. But anyone would think we were the only villains.

"Black kids cause trou- ble, too, but [illegible] nobody says anything about that."

In the world in which our rejected kids find themselves some despair and give up. Some get lost in music, drugs or booze.

And the unpalatable fact is that some find in violence the great orgas- mic excitement, the only glamour, the way of hit- ting back at an adult world that doesn't care.

There are skinhead girls, too. They tend to dress in the same way as the boys: tight jeans, but- ton-down shirts, braces, black boots with white laces.

Their hair, too, is shorn to within a quarter-inch of the skull. Sometimes it is tinted in vivid colours.

SUE NEWMAN

"They're real men"

Like animals

Mandy Stapleton, 17, from Basildon, Essex, and her friend Sue Newman, also 17, told me they'd never consider going out with a boy who wasn't a skinhead. Neither of them has ever personally taken part in violence.

What's the attraction? "Well, they're real men, aren't they?" said Sue. "Nothing poofy about them.

"They're not always going round looking for trouble. But, when it starts, they change in a second. They become like animals really."

Many skinhead girls, with their close-cropped hair, sparse make-up and skin tight around the cheekbones, can look tot- ally breathtaking—mak- ing you wonder what murky psychological depths in you they are stirring up.

But other girls with their loud-mouthed effing and blinding and their constant egging on of the blokes to fresh violence, seemed to me totally unwomanly.

One bragged to me that she had stabbed a black boy with a pair of scissors in a street fight.

It must be stressed that by no means all skin- heads are thugs or active racists. It is a "look", a fashion, and playing with the body image is one of the great pre-occupations of the young.

They can be bright, chirpy, quick-witted. Uninhibited, too, bounc- ing up and down to their beloved "Oi" music with its groups like the Cock- ney Rejects.

But throughout my time with them, violence never seemed very far away, and in the end it is the violence that you remember.

Like listening to one saying that early one morning he'd helped paint, in letters a foot high on a wall near Tottenham Hale Under- ground station in North London, slogans like "Wog On Fire," and "Burn The Niggers," and "Black Shit."

I overheard four skin- heads insulting a happy young couple in a West End hamburger bar, cal- ling the girl a slag and a tart, inviting her to a gangbang.

Telling the boy they'd all had her, driving him to the verge of tears.

Ask about the violence and you find no remorse.

"Makes you feel good, bashing some coon in. I like it," said one.

How can you feel pity for such as these? Yet pity should be the first emotion to spring to mind for their lives are very, very empty.

They have substituted violence for kindness, hard looks for loving glances.

No girls

After Billy Howarth and I had had our "political discussion" in Birming- ham, we went to the local pub for a drink.

As pint of lager followed pint of lager, the disap- pointment flooded out. He had not made much of his life. His mates had gradually deserted him.

"If you really want to know, I'm pissed off gen- erally.

"The blacks, the Pakis, the Commies, well, if it wasn't for them things would be better, wouldn't they?

"I have to get by on my own," he said. "Why the f— should they be mol- lycoddled?

"I hate them ... hate them."

He clenched his fists so hard that his knuckles turned white. Suddenly he gave out a huge sob and dropped his chin on to his chest.

When he raised his face to me again, I saw to my astonishment that it was running with tears. Tears of frustration and emptiness.

AGGRO as skinheads clash with mods at Southend. Pictures: MICHAEL DAINES.

some skins: Mod, Ted, Punk or Black'

matter of excluding them as foreign, or as unlike us, since that would not implicate the reader in the various identifications. I think there is an (ex-nominated) we : they binary in play in the story's mode of address, but once again the object of attention, youth, is significant precisely because it transgresses it. The skinheads certainly are not us, but they are not foreigners either (which is why they are 'frightening'). The reporter can talk and even joke with them, and he gets invited to bedsit and pub. He purports to understand and even like them: 'playing with the body is one of the great preoccupations of the young. They can be bright, chirpy, quick-witted.' He pities them and advises us to do the same: 'for their lives are very empty.' He fancies the girls too: 'Many skinhead girls, with their close-cropped hair, sparse make-up and skin tight around the cheekbones, can look totally breathtaking – making you wonder what murky psychological depths in you they are stirring up.' None of these concessions would be possible if the skinheads really were alien 'tribes' or 'animals'.

In fact one of the appealing aspects of this story is the uneasiness of its movements between skinheads and 'all of us': 'All of us may lose our tempers, lash out when provoked, or fight in self-defence. But skinhead violence is different.' As the story thinks through this Derridean observation on the transgressions of the skinheads, it establishes boundaries between we and they identifications. It establishes a narrative point of view that takes for granted – ex-nominates – the we identifications it requires its readers to access in order to make sense of the story in its own terms. Thus, the skinhead girls mark the limit of sexuality for women, and it is not without significance that the story is written from a male point of view while speaking for all of us. This point of view carefully differentiates those girls who look 'totally breathtaking' from those who, 'with their loud-mouthed effing and blinding and their constant egging on of the blokes to fresh violence, seemed to me totally unwomanly'. In another instance, what the skinheads do with the Union Jack is differentiated from 'all I understand our national flag to stand for'. And so on.

EXCESSES OF MEANINGFULNESS

It seems to me that this is a highly risky strategy if the story's scandalized tone is taken at face value. Carefully separating the transgressors from us is of course one good way to encourage fantasy identifications, but quite apart from that there is another risk too. The strategy generates far more meaningfulness than it can control. Ambiguous categories are by definition more meaningful than the two (or more) categories they transgress, since they partake of the attributes of both. On television, the more complex modes of representation generate an even greater excess of meaningfulness, since television signifies by colour, motion, sound and time as well as by pictures, words and composition. All these are variously affected by their internal juxtapositions and their external relations with discourses and social relations off-screen. Thus, beyond a *social* risk (of encouraging love rather than hate, attraction rather than repulsion), there is a *semiotic* risk that is even more fundamental. For excess of meanings and overlapping opposites are among the defining characteristics of madness, or at least of nonsense.

It is hardly surprising, then, to find television itself characterized by a will to limit its own excess, to settle its significations into established, taken-for-granted, common senses, which viewers can be disciplined to identify and to identify *with*. Disciplining is done partly by television's conventional codes of composition, lighting, movement, narrative, genre and the like, and partly by external limits such as those professional, legal and other exclusion devices that limit who and what gets on the air. However, I would argue that television can never succeed in its will to limit its own excesses of meaningfulness. For in order to think through abstract problems associated with various kinds of categorical ambiguity, television must necessarily scandalize the overlapping boundaries. In order to limit meanings, then, it must first produce excess. It does this in both fictional and factual programmes (so much so that the separation of fact from fiction is another abstract binary that has a dirtier boundary than is commonly admitted).

In fictional programmes, characters rarely act as mere persons. Usually they signify some mighty opposite, like man : woman, individual : institution, good : evil, active : passive, efficient : inefficient, normal : deviant, nature : culture, rural : urban, heart : head, and the like (a good example of a text that unfolds its narrative by means of an unusually obvious series of such binaries is the film *ET: The Extra-Terrestrial*). So the barroom or bedroom brawl is a ritual condensation of the opposites being distinguished and thought through. Action sequences are calculating machines and their outcome is as pure as a mathematical QED. But meanwhile, of course, the action itself may be as dirty or excessive as the budget allows. In factual programmes – especially news – the *raison d'être* is scandal, conflict and the disruption of normally settled categories. Internally, such programmes make sense by producing abstract binaries (we : they, etc.), which serve as the ex-nominated point of view from which the particular event or person can be recognized as ambiguous, marginal, scandalous and hence newsworthy. In short, television's signifying practices are necessarily contradictory – they must produce more than they can police. Concomitantly, for the viewer, the discipline of the preferred reading must be disrupted continuously by the presence of the very ambiguities it is produced out of.

It seems that the signifying practice of mainstream, broadcast network television is not so much to exploit as to control television's semiotic potential. The ideological strategies it uses continuously to draw the line between categories are, I suggest, the 'text' that should constitute the object of analysis. Both in general and in detail, television's efforts to make signification into sense, representations into reality, and to interpellate this rather than that reader–subject, raise important theoretical and political issues. These include its strategies of inclusion and exclusion; the exnomination of dominant identifications and the marginalization of what might be recognized in Raymond Williams's terms as 'emergent' ones; the attempt to clarify ambiguous categories while scandalizing their overlaps; using the power of ambiguity to collapse or condense different social identities into each other in order to represent them as naturally fused; and the transformation of different identifications, and different scandalous categories, into each other.

Such analysis would, of course, be impossible if these ideological strategies actually *worked* – the analysis is founded on the active contradictions within television discourse.

VIDEOLOGY

Television's active contradictions can in fact be quite revealing, and the kind of analysis I am suggesting – which, I confess, I would like to call *videological* analysis – offers principles by which we can select from television's dirty texts and social relations those that reveal what television is up to, as opposed to those that merely reflect back to us our inherited or established presumptions about what a text should look like. Here are one or two brief examples. The national commercial television news (ITN *News at Ten*) for 25 October 1982, in Britain, carried as its lead story an item about two kidnap/murders in Northern Ireland. Despite the obvious political implications of this, the news story was not made sense of in terms of nation, nor of ethnicity, nor of class, but almost exclusively in terms of family.

Verbally, the story foregrounded the numbers of children each of the two victims had and described details of their family situation, including how one of the bodies was identified by a watch his family had given him for his birthday, and how many 'orphans' the killings had produced. Visually, one victim's daughter was filmed against a domestic background, a bishop was filmed inside the victim's home, and the reporter did his closing piece to camera in the setting of a residential street. ITN's textual strategy, then, was to disarticulate the Troubles from any national political discourse and to rearticulate them in the discourse of domesticity. In this context, the events are literally senseless, and this is how they are described in the story.

Interestingly the source of this description – 'a cycle of senseless depravity', and 'vicious primitivism in its most depraved form' – was that of Authority in the shape of chief constable. The local bishop was also quoted as expressing his 'horror' at the 'acts of violence'. These accessed voices of (balanced) Authority allowed ITN to accomplish the double move of ex-nomination and marginalization without appearing to editorialize. The acts of violence themselves, together with their history, politics, agents and so forth, are marginalized with the strongest possible rhetoric – depravity and primitivism, senseless and horrible. Meanwhile, the category of the family is ex-nominated – it is taken as self-evidently the natural point of view from which to observe the events. Without having to deny that such events are horrific, it can be said that these discursive strategies belong to ITN and to television rather than to the events, and that we are being informed more about the ideology of the family than about Northern Ireland's troubles (see also chapter 8).

Similarly, political and industrial news offers a point of view that is television's rather than ours (the viewers) or theirs (the participants in the event). Again, families are foregrounded, usually as victims or consumers. The parties to industrial disputes are sorted out by both camera and narrative point of view into we and they positions. But just as youth is ambiguous in this respect – it is both us and them – so too are the initiators of negative action, strikers. They partake of the attributes of foreigners (the paradigm examples of which, of course, until the late 1980s, were the Russians), which is what makes them scandalous (see chapter 5).

HEGEMONY

It may by now be apparent that this chapter too is ambiguous as to its boundaries. I am aware that the material I have introduced has been excessive and is not entirely under my control – certainly there is more to say about the examples I have used than I have said. Perhaps I should try to clean up some of the remaining dirt. The point about dirt, crudely, is that it encompasses notions of ambiguity, contradiction, power and social relations all in one. This strikes me as a helpful condensation, since part of my purpose here has been to show that analytical discourses tend sometimes to operate with categories that are too unitary, pure, abstract and clear-cut, especially in a field of study that holds as axiomatic that nothing is intrinsically anything, but that entities are defined negatively by what they are not.

Working back through my argument, then, I have tried to show that TV is a prolific producer of meaningfulness which it seeks to discipline by prodigious feats of ideological labour into familiar categories that it proffers to us as appropriate identifications for our subjectivity to access. But I have also tried to suggest that television's meaningfulness is, literally, out of control. For instance, despite rearticulating the Northern Ireland story into the discourse of domesticity, the news could neither ignore nor silence all of the event, some contradictory aspects of which were even able to irrupt into and disrupt the videological text. Even as the 'daughter-scene' established a powerful chain of family-significations, the drone of an unseen military helicopter above provided an appropriate metaphor for all the absences the videological text itself sought to repress. It is at this point that my argument can be referred to the concept of hegemony. It is by now well established that television plays its part in the diffusion of consent for a power monopoly – not least in its own social relations of production and consumption (never have so many been readers of the texts of so few). However, the concept of hegemony should not be collapsed into the old pure text : reader binary, where there is a clear-cut division between the hegemonic text and the subject reader. Hegemony is a good deal dirtier than that – it is not just a matter of 'them' telling 'us' what, how and when to think. Television is not just videology – it is also a resource. There are contradictions even in its most confident assertions of the supremacy of natural categories, and there are marginal places and times on television where 'common' sense slides into 'good' sense (Gramsci's distinction). Even as it is presently constituted, television's productive capacity cannot be policed at every point. And what it says depends on how you look at it (see chapter 9).

Even so, how you look at it depends on what it says, which brings me back to the beginning of this chapter, where I suggested that what any one viewer can bring to bear on a television programme is a combination of discursive resources. Such resources are determined by the same social relations as are represented on television, and by institutions such as education. They will, of course, include aspects of the hegemonic (hegemony is a social relation, and hence an attribute of the individual bearers of that relation), which is what makes hegemony dirty – it is an attribute of 'us' not 'them'. But television plays a part in distributing and popularizing hegemonic discursive resources too, simply because it is itself a discursive and representational resource.

THE POWER OF SPEECH

One way of demonstrating just how potent it can be is to take each of my seven types of subjectivity in turn, and try to access one of its marginal, nominated, scandalous identifications while watching mainstream television. How can you watch the national news and, at the same time, be interpellated as, for instance, a non-unitary self, and/or not-male, and/or not-adult, and/or not-family, and/or not-middle class, and/or not-national, and/or not-white? You will soon, I think, discover that television is not addressing you at all, and that it does encourage certain social relations and discourage, deny or marginalize others.

One regular response to this discovery is to develop an understandable but, I think, mistaken, hostility to television. Such a response takes television not for what it is but for what it sometimes aspires to be – a private conversation between two friends, excluding outsiders from their private world. But television is not like that. It is social, public, open. It is for this reason that I want to open up the apparently closed frontier between television and the power of speech itself.

I think it is possible to argue that the power of speech should no longer be seen as the primary model for all signification and communication, but as a primitive technology that occupies in the economy of sense-making the sort of position that wood-burning does in the economy of energy. Speech may, historically, be one of the original forces of production, but it has been transformed in line with other forces. Like them, it is barely recognizable in its modern form: the power of speech is now industrialized, a product of technology and corporate imperatives. In short, the power of speech is located not in the body of the abstract individual human subject, but in the electronic media in general and television in particular; it has developed historically into the social power to create and circulate discourse, to popularize particular *paroles*, to suffuse the natural, social and personal worlds with meaning and to use the resources of visual language to promote certain ways of acting in those worlds. The source of the power of speech is no longer (if it ever was) the individual, but society. Speech is nowadays characterized by socialized production and family/individual consumption; by a division of labour between and within producers and consumers; and by the exchange of a subsistence wage that is just sufficient for the sense-making economy to sustain and reproduce itself and its social relations – the wages of common sense. Speech is, of course, supposed to be exempt from all these impure influences, because of its general availability and individualized production, but I do not think it is (or ever has been). The example of television, in fact, leads to questions about speech – about who has appropriated, historically, the power to produce discourse (to make speeches), and how speech as a force of production has been organized socially in relation to the prevailing mode and phases of production. It also suggests that in speech, as in television, there are marginalized, muted and scandalized identities for subjects whose powerlessness entails that the only means they have to represent themselves to themselves represents them as marginal, muted and scandalous.

The reason why I want to pursue this line of thought is not to discredit speech. On the contrary, the notion that speech is more like television than is commonly realized allows for some highly embarrassing questions to be asked. It would be truly scandalous to discover that whole sections of the population were systematically being denied access to speech by a power bloc of professionals and their allies in commerce and government. But this is just the situation that obtains in television. Conversely, the model of television suggests that discourse is socially produced and disciplined in ways that our sentimental attachment to the individualism of speaking only masks. Speech too is a power relation, but we need to be reminded of that fact by the poor relation whose productive power is greater than that of speech but whose reputation has been scandalized by segments of the very power bloc that operates it (the intelligentsia). Could it be that this behaviour itself signifies that television is beyond the control of its controllers, that its potential for socialized sense-making is being resisted because it is not a boob-tube, goggle-box, or any other dangerous, silly or contemptible thing, but a valuable weapon that is currently in the hands of those who despise but must use it in the struggle to maintain cultural supremacy?

Part II

Truth wars

Chapter 3

Regimes of truth and the politics of reading: a *blivit**

These days – the days of *Whoops! Apocalypse,* nukespeak, deconstruction, Rajneeshis, *homo ludens*, Memphis design, Popemobiles, Foucault, Lindy Chamberlain, Wapping, semiotics, remote-control TV – these days it is necessary to start with incommensurables; with things that don't fit.

Perhaps it is appropriate in these days that high academic theories, like Popemobiles, scour the terrain of popular culture, searching for truths in the domain of the profane, the commonplace, the demotic. Kurt Vonnegut has coined the term *blivit* for his own incommensurable combination of fact and fiction: an 'all-frequencies assault on the sensibilities' made of 'fiction, drama, history, biography and journalism'. A *blivit*, writes Vonnegut, can be defined as 'two pounds of shit in a one pound bag'.[1] Somewhere in the bag, Vonnegut records his own great-grandfather's belief that truth 'must always be recognized as the paramount requisite of human society'. Vonnegut comments: 'As I myself said in another place, I began to have my doubts about truth after it was dropped on Hiroshima.'[2]

* * *

In the mass media too, truth matters: it has power to command; it is an instrument of power to be dropped on the unsuspecting. Unlike theoretical discourses on truth, which can (at least in principle) keep their boundaries pure and uncontaminated by quotidian incident, existential hum or ontological murmur, the media are structurally *blivitous* – the only boundaries that cannot be crashed here are deadlines. Songs, sights, stories and speech are continuously produced and deployed, after the manner of Vonnegut, to combine and intertwine 'the tidal power of a major novel with the bone-rattling immediacy of front-line journalism . . . the flashy enthusiasms of musical theatre, the lethal jab of the short story, the sachet of personal letters, the oompah of American history, and oratory in the bow-wow style.'[3] Such a mixture of genres, rhetorics, referential domains and bodily

* Originally published as John Hartley (1987) 'Regimes of truth and the politics of reading: a *blivit*', *Cultural Studies*, 1(1), 39–58.

experiences clearly needs something pretty powerful to keep it all sorted out.

Regimes are conditions under which processes occur, the prevailing methods or systems of things, the governing assumptions. Among the regimes of representation, performance and classification which are used to keep order in the media *blivit*, there exist regimes of truth. But a characteristic of all the modern media – the press, radio, cinema, publishing, television – is that, in each case, incommensurate regimes of truth co-exist. The two principal regimes of truth are fact and fiction. Strenuous efforts are made, within each medium where both are found, to keep them apart. Factual and fictional truths are produced and circulated on the same channel, but by different professions, different companies or units, by different practices, in different genres with different semiotic systems and rhetorical conventions, invoking different codes of recognition and different modes of reading, for different audiences, at different times of day.

Not only do different kinds of truth result from this process, but they are maintained in an uneasy hierarchy too. A rank order is imposed in which fact is more important (has greater power to command) than fiction; the 'real' is more true than the 'imagined'. News and the domain of public affairs – the world of what E.M. Forster (in *Howards End*) called 'anger and telegrams' – has priority over drama and fiction.

* * *

For those who produce news, truth has the status of a professional ideology: it is what they profess. Rule 49(a) of the Constitution and Rules of the Australian Journalists' Association, for instance, sets out the AJA *Code of Ethics*: 'Respect for the truth and the public's right to information are overriding principles for all journalists. In pursuance of these principles journalists commit themselves to ethical and professional standards', of which the first (of ten) is: 'They shall report and interpret the news with scrupulous honesty by striving to disclose all essential facts and by not suppressing relevant, available facts or distorting by wrong or improper emphasis.' The gesture of glossing 'truth' as 'facts' is, of course, characteristic of journalistic discourse, so much so that the *Style Book* of West Australian Newspapers, for instance, does not contain an entry on 'truth'. But this is what it does have to say about 'facts': 'Do not say the true, real, or actual facts. There are no untrue facts.'[4]

* * *

The domain of facts is large and varied: from the craggy heights of hard news to the lush plains of human interest, comment, current affairs, features, documentary – right up to the dangerous boundaries of 'docudrama', 'infotainment' and 'faction'. Or, as the BBC has put it in a guide book to the terrain, written for its own documentary producers, 'at one extreme, documentaries border on current affairs programmes; at the other, on drama'. This booklet tries to map difficult country, where, for instance, the 'material' might be documentary but the 'techniques and intentions' are dramatic; such programmes 'aim more immediately at dramatic truth than at documentary truth'. Thus it asks the question: 'In its broadest form, what sort of truth ought documentaries to be concerned with?' The answers are, of course, practical, not philosophical: producers must have clear intentions; they must execute professional, responsible programmes; they must 'label' them properly both internally and in publicity; they must bear in mind differing audience interpretations and levels of engagement. These are 'the four elements which convey truth to the audience'. Philosophy is not forgotten, however; producers are 'constantly faced with questions of ethics', which boil down to what can be *simulated* and what can be *selected*. Simulation is variously glossed as 'preparation', 'fabrication', 'reconstruction', 'slightly different situations', 'go[ing] through the motions', 're-creations' and 're-enactments'. All these are 'permissible', but 'construction', 'prompting', 'invention', 'a wrong impression' and 'a fake' are not. As for selection (and editing), these are 'essential for the preservation of truth'. For instance, producers must decide whether a person featured in a programme is 'typical' or 'part of a lunatic fringe'. In the latter case, the producer must either 'present him [*sic*] clearly as such' or 'refrain from the temptation to include him at all, despite his obvious programme value'.[5]

Apart from labelling loonies or leaving them out, producers face another 'matter of great delicacy', namely how to deal with the unpredictability of 'real life' and the impossibility of conveying an 'accurate impression' of an event simply by filming it as it occurs. The two criteria for avoiding 'misunderstanding' in this area are, first, to 'give the audience a true and accurate impression of the facts' by simulating 'a true picture of a real type' of the given situation; and, second, to ensure that 'people outside television', who 'have to be present' during filming, 'understand the need for the "fabrication". Otherwise dangerous seeds of doubt may be sown which could lead to a disbelief in the BBC's documentary methods'.[6]

Truth, then, turns out to be a *blivit* after all; the end product (hopefully) of a mixture of fact, fiction, fabrication and faking whose chief characteristic is that the audience – with much encouragement – continues to believe in it despite the odds. Indeed, the principal requirement for the preservation and communication of truth is that no-one 'outside television' realizes that it is founded, literally, on an 'as if' premise; despite the need for 'a mass of equipment and a whole team of people', a 'great deal of [the documentary producer's] skill is devoted to presenting his [*sic*] subject matter as if the equipment and the technical processes were not there'.[7]

Or, as Kurt Vonnegut himself said in another place: 'This is the secret of good storytelling: to lie, but to keep the arithmetic sound.'[8]

* * *

One way to keep the arithmetic sound is to make sure that the pictures tell the same story as the script. Even in news programmes there are unadmitted constructions which are designed to jolly along the audience by making it think that the so-called real world is like a feature film. Sound is added to recalcitrant pictures to make them tell a particular kind of truth. These matters are rarely discussed 'outside television', but in a letter to the London *Guardian* (1 March 1985) a professional picture editor called Andrew Lewis let the cat out of the bag. He had spotted the use of sound effects in several stories put out by the commercial news organization ITN. Having a professional eye for shoddy work, he cited examples where the arithmetic had failed to add up – for instance, the use of 'hospital effects' over still photographs showing the Pope recovering in hospital, 'making the frozen Pope look like a corpse', or the addition of sound effects to a 'silent video of Mount Everest, complete with car-horns going in the background'. Wondering why ITN keeps a sound-effects library at all, Lewis commented: 'It is bad enough that there is bias in what our newsreaders say, but there is no excuse for deliberately faking the relationship of sound and vision to reinforce their scripts.'

* * *

Truth is a product of struggle: struggle between technology and subject matter, certainly, but more than this. Truth is a product of war, and is itself adversarial. There is not, and never has been, an original truth, or, if there has been, the origin is that of the word 'truth' itself, where interestingly, it is a social, discursive, adversarial sense that predominates, not an abstract, transcendental, absolute one. In Old and early Middle English, 'truth' could be glossed as steadfast allegiance, fidelity to a cause or person, faithfulness, loyalty. It was the same word as 'troth' (one's faith pledged or plighted) and as 'truce' (a singularized form of the plural of true – 'trues' – that is, an exchange of faith to allow cessation of hostilities). In such usage, truth is not conceivable as an abstract object or as a quality of an objective world that can't answer back; it is a relational or orientational term, expressing the social relations of often warring parties.

The process of abstracting and objectifying truth has, however, been going on for quite a while, though contradictorily it remains an adversarial notion. Indeed, the modern notions of truth are literally a product of war; the wars between different kinds of Christian truths that took the form of the Reformation and Counter-Reformation. One aspect of that struggle was semiotic, as it were; a war of representation, fought to decide whose discursive strategies would convey the most accurate impression of objective – divine – truth. The outcomes of that war have lasted right up until today.

The medieval Catholic church was an effective mass medium. Like more recent and more obvious mass media the medieval church was a complex of institutions dedicated to mass communication. It had centralized policy-making bureaucracies of great power ('controllers' and 'managers' from the curia to the episcopacy), it included 'producers' and 'presenters' (people in holy orders), 'contributors' (professional specialists, from masons to vestment-makers), and also 'consumers' (the laity itself), whose vast numbers dwarfed any other social community of the day, including nations, empires and language groups, just as television audiences do these days. Like television, the medieval church was riddled with internal contradictions and fierce competitive struggles, but, like television, it nevertheless spanned the known world and was designed to cut across established political, demographic and cultural boundaries. It was a force for both social cohesion and social control.

For its consumers at least, the medieval church was a peculiarly non-literate medium, conveying its truths to its audiences in audio-visual and performative form: songs, sights, stories, speech. It employed the highest, leading-edge technologies and massive capital investment to produce its hardware (cathedrals, carvings, Latin, manuscripts) and its software (liturgies, laws, rites, rituals). Its output was organized into genres, schedules and seasons, and it was dedicated to audience maximization – seeking, at least in theory, a world rating of 100 per cent. It was, like television, free at the point of consumption, but, like television, it was paid for indirectly by consumers. Unlike television, whose truth has often been doubted, it discouraged doubts about its truth with weapons that were the then equivalent of what was dropped on Hiroshima.

The Protestants, opening a competing channel, were determined to put a stop to all this. Their truth was a product of war with this mighty opponent. Among other things, the audio-visual medium of the medieval church was to be supplanted by a new medium, a new technology of truth, which was taken at the time (and still is) to be intrinsically more truthful: the medium of print. The art of printing was held to be responsible for 'the manifestation of truth, propagation of the Gospel, restoration of learning, diffusion of knowledge, and consequently the discovery and destruction of Popery.'[9] Printing 'shed light' on the 'tedious and deep dungeons of loathsome ignorance', and the dawn of 'purer doctrine' enabled the 'liberal sciences' to disperse 'the soggy and darkened clouds of this old motheaten barbarousness'.[10]

But, like the BBC's television documentary producers, Reformation truth producers devoted a great deal of their skill to presenting the subject matter as if the equipment and the technical processes were not there. Truth was understood as a property of an objective, natural world. Its discovery was held to have been impeded by the elaborate verbal and visual arts so beloved of the opposition, but to have been revealed by print. Thus the Protestants were against drama, poetry, dialogue, visual images; they were for monologic prose ('plain style'), logic, method, diagrammatic spatializations of knowledge, books. Their theory of representation held that art imitates nature: truth is attained by observation and study of nature, so that the 'truth of art' corresponds to the 'truth of nature' as a portrait should correspond to its sitter.[11] And that correspondence was understood as literal, not metaphorical: thus 'it is unknown of what form and countenance' God, Christ and the saints of antiquity were; 'wherefore, seeing that religion ought to be grounded upon truth, images, which cannot be without lies, ought not to be made'. Truth, then, was deemed to be dependent upon a one-to-one relationship between a sign and its referent, and if there was no empirical, ocular proof of the form and countenance of that referent, then any sign of it would be 'false and lying . . . the teacher of all error'.[12]

* * *

The traditional emblem of the teacher in this period was a figure of the schoolmaster holding, in either hand, the book and the rod. One of the features of those times was the escape of that figure from the confines of the classroom, from whence it tramped, militantly, across the whole social domain. A regime of truth, using the technologies of print, pedagogy and preaching, was imposed throughout the popular media of the day, promoting truth for teenagers, understanding for the 'simple people'. This popular, pedagogical truth was still adversarial, produced out of the war of words with the opposition. Naturally, the opposition was stirred up by Satan (*Satan* = Hebrew 'opposite'), and comprised 'cruel tyrants, sharp persecutors, and extreme enemies unto God and his infallible truth' who are 'pretending, most untruly', that reading 'God's word is an occasion of heresy and carnal liberty, and the overthrow of all good order in all well ordered commonweals'.[13]

The stakes, then, were high: threats to the soul (heresy), the private body (carnal liberty) and the public body (well-ordered commonweals), taken together, spell the end of the world. To prevent that, the Protestants were determined that their transparent, referential, natural truth should prevail. In this fight, technology and teaching were counted better allies than theology or theory. The trouble with the visual culture of the Papists was that it was a bad teacher – a teacher not only of lies but of sexy ones at that: visual images are 'trimly decked in gold, silver and stone, as well the images of men as of women, like wanton wenches . . . that love paramours'; therefore, 'although it is now commonly said they be the layman's books, yet we see they teach no good lessons'. Indeed, what they teach is 'other manner of lessons, of esteeming of riches, of pride and vanity in apparel, of niceness and wantonness, and peradventure of whoredom'. So says the official *Book of Homilies*, whose message was to be 'declared and read by all parsons, vicars and curates, every Sunday and Holiday in their churches'.[14] As in those days, so in these; truth is – must be – for teenagers. Its limpidity must be measured against their literacy, at least for Kurt Vonnegut: 'The Bible opens with a sentence well within the writing skills of a lively fourteen-year-old', and so, it seems to follow, 'any person who can't explain his work to a fourteen-year-old is a charlatan'.[15]

* * *

King James is, as is well known, the name both of a king and of the Authorized Version of the Bible (1611). What is less well known, perhaps, is that it was in his reign too that the first ever English licence to print news was issued.[16] As usual, the granting of such a licence in 1622 indicates a will to control and fix the dissemination of news as much as a willingness to encourage it. The licence covered only foreign news; the authorities permitted only Authorized Versions of domestic events. One newsworthy foreign event in that same year of 1622 was the story from Rome that Pope Gregory XV had instituted a new body of cardinals to oversee the Catholic church's missionary work. This body was called the Congregatio de Propaganda Fide.

So entered a new word into the English language – a foreign, adversarial, oppositional word. While Protestant discourses prated constantly about 'propagation', 'diffusion', 'teaching' and 'manifestation' of the truth, and while the Reformation was noted for its missionary zeal on that truth's behalf, none of this was understood as 'propaganda'. On the contrary, propagation is a property of nature: the word applied originally to the propagation of vines, and became applied metaphorically to 'the best end of marriage' (*OED*), namely propagation of the human species. Such a term signified increase, abundance and profit too, so it was clearly not just natural but also good. Propagation of the truth, therefore, was the very opposite of what the nasty, scheming, Latin-speaking Catholics were up to. Ever since, propaganda has been understood as 'a term of reproach applied to secret associations for the spread of opinions and principles which are viewed by most governments with horror and aversion' (*OED*). Even so, it wasn't too long before there were Protestant associations just like the Congregatio de Propaganda, but of course they didn't say so. What could be reproachful about 'one Body Politick and Corporate, in Deed, and in Name, by the Name of the Society for the Propagation of the Gospel in Foreign Parts', set up by Royal Charter in 1701? And what could be secret about the famous SPCK, the Society for the Propagation of Christian Knowledge?

* * *

Propaganda still has a bad name, but these days it is understood not so much as an organization as a form. Recognizing fact from fiction in the *blivitous* media, or truth from propaganda, has in these days become largely a semiotic activity of learning how to recognize what regime of truth is in play at a given moment. This means, of course, that reading (and viewing and listening – the term 'reading' will be used to cover all cases) is still a highly political activity.

As is well known, war is the continuation of politics by other means. In these days – the days of Tripoli, Port Stanley, Nicaragua, Grenada, *Rainbow Warrior*, the Gulf – warfare is more than ever a continuation of domestic political rhetoric. Without the benefit, or embarrassment, of official institutions of propaganda, strong governments nevertheless maintain a militantly pedagogic attitude towards their citizens, and necessarily rely on the news media to popularize their truths. To supply the occasional war is to make to citizens and media alike an offer of truth that they cannot refuse.

This is what makes the politics of reading so important, since a truth is not produced by the mere act of utterance, by whatever authority, in whatever medium. A truth is produced in the act of reading. Even if there are authorial intentions, authorized versions, official manipulations or preferred readings inscribed into those utterances (all contentious claims in these days of high theory), there is still no guarantee of the semiotic, let alone the political, outcome. So it is not enough simply to maintain that all texts are polysemic, that they don't determine what sense will be made of them, that authorial intentions are irrelevant to meanings, or even that both authors and readers are mere epiphenomena of impersonal textual and discursive processes. The politics of reading arises from the power of certain discourses, in the teeth of all this, to command assent, to mobilize social and individual action, to allow governments to burnish their truths in the glare of the television lights and then hurl them, on everyone's behalf, at the current opponent. In these days of mass democracy and mass communication, everyone is made complicit with the militant, pedagogical, adversarial, authoritative truths of the day. But these truths are also the lies of professional storytellers, and they display similar logic: 'the fatal premise of *A Connecticut Yankee [in King Arthur's Court]* remains a chief premise of Western civilization, and increasingly of world civilization, to wit: the sanest, most likeable persons, employing superior technology, will enforce sanity throughout the world.'[17]

The fatal premise of news is this: that it simply imitates reality or nature; it is transparent, representational and unconstructed. Therefore, so long as it avoids bias, remains impartial and sticks to plain facts in plain language, it is true, and can enforce its truth throughout the world.

* * *

How is it possible, then, for sane, likeable readers to recognize propaganda? Generally speaking, as far as readers are concerned, propaganda is more honest than news – it makes none of the truth-claims of news; it is the antithesis of news, precisely because its form invites a different politics of reading. Whereas news has taken the path of realistic fiction and referentiality, propaganda has taken a different path.

News is diegetic; propaganda is dialogic. News uses narrative storytelling, employing the oldest three-act plot scheme in the book: Act 1 – get a man up a tree; Act 2 – throw stones at him; Act 3 – get him down.[18] Like all storytelling forms, news is based on conflict, confrontation or struggle. The newsworthiness of an event depends on its suspense value, on how it might turn out. News uses the other staples of fiction – action and character – though the characters are presented as playing themselves and the actions are presented as unconstructed (though rarely spontaneous).

Propaganda is not confined, however, to the restricted, dull, authoritarian aesthetics of news, nor to the conventions and politics of a closed, diegetic world. Whereas news and realist fiction draw readers' attention *into* the text, propaganda directs their attention *beyond* it. Where news and realist fiction resolve conflicts diegetically, within the text, propaganda provokes conflict dialogically, within the reader. News and realist fiction align the reader to the past, in which the actions portrayed have already been completed. Propaganda aligns the reader to the present and the future, towards action yet to occur. News and realist fiction position the reader as a judgemental, impartial, omniscient, voyeuristic spectator; propaganda orients the reader towards engagement or participation in an action. News, unlike realist fiction, presents itself on television as unauthored, and it uses direct address and eye-contact – these being among the semiotic devices used to set the 'real' apart from the 'fictional'. But propaganda does not seek to produce in its readers a recognition of an abstract, unauthored truth. It seeks first and foremost to produce recognition of a relationship between the addresser and the addressee, a relationship ideally of faith, allegiance, loyalty to the cause: old-style truth. News and realist fiction are enslaved to representation, to the notion that a sign stands for a referent and that's that. Propaganda is able to exploit the postmodernist repertoires of signification, rhetoric, pleasure and celebratory self-awareness; its skills are devoted to presenting its techniques not as 'not there', but as *here*. Both news and realist fiction seek to capture and colonize the future, filling it with the meanings and social relationships of the past. Propaganda, on the contrary, is always an ephemeral and instrumental art, seeking not to fix the future but to challenge and change it.

* * *

Even so, propaganda continues to have a bad name, perhaps because its techniques have proved so popular in publicity, advertising, pop music (video clips and promos), and in the jingles, station idents and promos, trailers, continuity and 'sniplet' shows that together stitch the *blivitous* texts of television (and other media) into readability. However, despite its good name for impartiality, facticity and unbiased access to unarguable truths, news still has to win readers. And in order to do this it has necessarily to compete with the pleasures, genres and distractions that surround it.

News has never been exempt from the need to con with entertainment a readership otherwise likely to be indifferent. Witness merely one of the titans of the first phase of popular newspapers, the radical 'pauper press' of the early nineteenth century. Henry Hetherington, founder of the *Poor Men's Guardian*, announced a successor to that paper in 1833. The *Twopenny Dispatch* would be 'a repository of all the gems and treasures, and fun and frolic . . . news and occurrences' of the week. 'It shall abound in Police Intelligence, in Murders, Rapes, Suicides, Burnings, Maimings, Theatricals, Races, Pugilism, and all manner of "accidents by flood and field". In short, it will be stuffed with every sort of devilment that will make it sell.' This despite the fact that 'our object is not to make money, but to beat the Government'.[19] More recently, and on the other side of the political barricades, one of the archetypal press barons of the twentieth century told the same story. Lord Beaverbrook said of his *Daily Express*: 'My purpose originally was to set up a propaganda paper. . . . But in order to make the propaganda effective the paper had to be successful. No paper is any good at all for propaganda unless it has a thoroughly good financial position.'[20]

Despite Lord Beaverbrook's brave words, straightforward party propaganda did not survive the era of the press barons and the rise of mass-circulation newspapers. The paradoxical legacy of the influential barons is a newspaper business that is wholeheartedly dedicated to being 'successful' with a 'thoroughly good financial position' – a business dedicated to entertainment, not to government. Where the barons were consistent, and where they laid the framework for their modern unennobled successors, was in maximizing circulation with promotional, not directly political, campaigns.[21] The most important wars to the owners of the news media are now (as always) circulation wars. News, then, has developed within its regimes of truth a populist, promotional propaganda for itself – a politics of reading, and a pretty impoverished political platform at that, consisting ultimately in the slogan 'Read me!'

Truth is thus a product of the circulation and ratings wars for readers. One consequence of this in the modern media is that propaganda itself has been depoliticized, as it were. Instead of measuring success by winning the assent of their readers to the truth of this or that line of propaganda, the successors of Beaverbrook measure their success simply by winning readers. Their propaganda, consequently, doesn't appear to be propaganda *for* anything very much: the truth is not 'what we – the producers – say it is', but 'what you – the readers – know it is'. As a result, there is a declining proportion of news in the most-read newspapers. Even so, newspapers persist in so calling themselves, and in promoting themselves on their news – their regime of truth – despite their historic tendency towards contact with the world of the imaginary via stories about stars, celebrities and showbiz; their fetishization of bodies and faces; their mobilization of fantasies via competitions; and their devotion of upwards of 40 per cent of available space to non-editorial matter, namely advertisements. The 'quality' press is by no means exempt from these tendencies either, although its disproportionate 'influence' stems largely from the success of its regime of truth in not only reporting but also provoking anger and telegrams among its few but powerful readers. Similarly, news on television is privileged, and is used to promote the credibility of the station as a whole, while the daily news programmes are used to structure the schedules and to anchor the station to real time (and real life). News shows are thus normally exempt from the competitive mêlée of programming that surrounds them, despite their low ratings and their status as minority output (around 4 or 5 per cent of total air time – comparable with continuity). News on television and in the press, then, has survived both by becoming one of the entertainment media, and by claiming privileged exemption for itself as a genre that lends tone to the establishment.

* * *

Truth may be a product of wars (for hearts and minds, dollars and votes). But war, conversely, is now a branch of rhetoric, an entertaining pedagogical device which teaches the citizens of strong countries that they are not to be trifled with, and teaches the current opponent a lesson. The current opponent is usually personified by the leaders of small, unglamorous nations which profess an absolute or fundamental truth of their own – a nationalism rendered ludicrous by the espousal of, say, Islam (Gaddafi of Libya), communism (Ortega of Nicaragua, or so says the White House), even territorial integrity (Galtieri of Argentina). What better than to wallop such dangerous, threatening truths, to prove that the inability, for 45 years, to wallop the Russians isn't *really* impotence?

* * *

The largest single piece of equipment in the technology of truth – of the kind that was dropped on Hiroshima – displaces 95,000 tons, has a 4½-acre top and is called the *Carl Vinson*. The *Carl Vinson* is the largest aircraft carrier in the world. But its role, in these adversarial days, isn't so much propaganda as propagation: it is the flagship not for any particular truth, but for technological and bodily potency.

Kurt Vonnegut claims that 'the first story in the history of literature to have "fuck" in its title' was his own short story 'The Big Space Fuck'. It was about an American rocket ship loaded with human sperm, and sent off to Andromeda in an effort to propagate the human species: 'to make sure that human life would continue to exist somewhere in the Universe since it certainly couldn't continue much longer on earth', what with 38-foot lampreys in Lake Erie, living on 'shit and beer cans and old automobiles and Clorox bottles'.[22]

The Big Space Fuck is, of course, a mere fiction. What actually happened was reported in the *San Francisco Chronicle* (25 May 1985). 'Sailors dotted the flight deck' = spermatozoa; 'the world's largest warship' = the world's largest penis; 'passed beneath the Golden Gate Bridge on the way to its home' = fucked. 'The sailors on the Navy's newest carrier – recently adopted as "San Francisco's Own"' = legitimate marriage; 'received an enthusiastic welcome from families, sweethearts and friends as the ship eased into her berth' = the earth moved for me too, dear.

Part of the politics of reading is, of course, to persuade readers to turn the page, to the 'Story and another photo on Page 2'. The act of turning, a pregnant pause, reveals instantly the fruits of the union of warship and city: a photo of an infant held triumphantly aloft – *Ecce homo!* The *San Francisco Chronicle* succeeds where nature has failed – simultaneous consummation and confinement.

'The huge carrier . . . made a dramatic entrance . . . after nosing through a 200-mile-thick fogbank that clung to the coast like whipped cream.' God is on hand to bless the union, dispersing the spermicidal whipped cream: 'As if on cue, the fog dissipated and the sun warmed the vast flight deck like a benediction.' The climax comes at 9.15 a.m., 'exactly on time': 'A lusty roar exploded from the 5000 homesick sailors.'

Like the readers, the sailors too can instantly enjoy the sight of the fruits of their wives' labours: one 'stood on the 4.5-acre flight deck and strained to see his pregnant wife'; another 'wore a big grin but could not stop his tears as he met his 2-month-old son Christopher for the first time'; indeed, there were 'about 50 new fathers who met their children for the first time yesterday along Alameda's Pier 3, where wives and families began gathering at dawn for the arrival'. If the best end of marriage is indeed the propagation of the species, then those fifty must be counted the lucky ones – or at least the ones whose photos are taken whose words are quoted. For the rest of the lusty 5,000, however, there are hints of propagations to come: 'Some 3000 wives, sweethearts, children and other family members . . . laughed with delight as the big gray ship was pushed into her berthing spaces by straining tugboats. "Awwwriiight!" howled a gang of sailors . . . admiring the women waiting ashore.'

By Eric Luse

View of the Bridge — From the Bridge

Sailors dotted the flight deck of the aircraft carrier Carl Vinson yesterday as the world's largest warship passed beneath the Golden Gate Bridge on the way to its home at the Alameda Naval Air Station, completing a 7½-month, 65,000-mile voyage in the western Pacific and Indian oceans. The sailors on the Navy's newest carrier — recently adopted as 'San Francisco's Own' — received an enthusiastic welcome from families, sweethearts and friends as the ship eased into her berth at the naval air station's Pier 3. This photo, taken from the carrier's bridge, shows lights (foreground) used to direct planes. Story and another photo on Page 2.

But for them all there is a significance beyond pleasure. Their potency signifies that of the 'big gray ship': 'A couple of hundred tossed their sailor hats like Frisbees into the waiting crowd.' And the potency of the carrier matches theirs: 'last Sunday they put on a terrific live fire exercise that you wouldn't believe. Bombing and strafing. It was very impressive. The firepower of this ship is awesome.'

* * *

The firepower of this story arises from its status as truth. Truth is easy to recognize. The event happened 'yesterday', and makes the front page in several local newspapers. In this sixteen-paragraph story there are twenty-four numerical facts, ten place-names, seven named people and six direct-speech quotations. But there are attributes to these facts too – just as true, only more entertaining. There are thirty-odd adjectives, applying mostly to the *Carl Vinson* (mighty, huge, vast, largest, newest, big, gray, dramatic, exactly, straining) or to the sailors and their families (lusty, homesick, pregnant, crowded, rowdy, big, red-faced, new, male, civilian). And the similes – 'like whipped cream', 'like a benediction', 'like Frisbees' – are just the sorts of visual image that together with the photographs themselves are already clichéd in pop videos: the familiar correspondences between technology and sex, the divine and the domestic, don't have to be stated. They can be seen to be true. But they are more important than the facts in producing an agreed meaning for the event. The *Oakland Tribune* (25 May 1985) also reported it, with different facts (ninety-nine new fathers, not fifty, and different individuals), but with the very same signification.

Neither story mentions an actual or potential adversary against whom the 'awesome firepower' might be directed, and neither says anything about nuclear weapons. The purpose of the 7½-month, 65,000-mile 'cruise' is restricted to a passing reference in the *San Francisco Chronicle* to 'one uninterrupted stretch of 107 days at sea and rowdy liberties in the Philippines, Australia and Japan'.

This was not the first visit of the *Carl Vinson* to Australia. In July 1983 there had been another 'rowdy liberty' in Fremantle, and the Australian press had understood it in just the same way as the Californian press understood the *Carl Vinson*'s 1985 return. The Melbourne *Age* (4 July 1983) reported that John Curtin High School in Fremantle had instituted eight daily truancy checks, one every forty minutes, to stop 'scores of girls' being 'away for days on end with newly acquired American boyfriends, many of them met through the "Dial a Sailor Service" organised by the US Navy and given wide publicity in the Perth media'. However, the same story does contain a reminder of other, popular, truths: 9,000 people, in the 'biggest anti-nuclear demonstration ever seen' in Western Australia, 'linked arms . . . to form a human chain more than two kilometres long' to

By Chris Stewart

Lieutenant Commander Sam Locklear held his 15-month-old daughter Jillian after arriving in Alameda aboard the Carl Vinson

The Carl Vinson Comes Home to the Bay

Best Part of a 65,000-Mile Voyage

By Kevin Leary

The mighty aircraft carrier Carl Vinson came home to an emotional and patriotic welcome yesterday after a 7½-month, 65,000-mile cruise in the western Pacific and Indian Oceans.

The huge carrier, newly adopted as "San Francisco's own," made a dramatic entrance into San Francisco Bay after nosing through a 200-mile-thick fogbank that clung to the coast like whipped cream.

As if on cue, the fog dissipated and the sun warmed the vast flight deck like a benediction as the Vinson steamed under the Golden Gate Bridge at 9:15 a.m. — exactly on time.

A lusty roar exploded from the 5000 homesick sailors aboard the 95,000-ton flattop, the largest warship in the world and the Navy's newest carrier.

"I'm gonna go home to Merced and be a husband to someone I've really missed for 7½ months and be a father pretty soon," said Airman Bill Lampley, 22, as he stood on the 4.5-acre flight deck and strained to see his pregnant wife waiting on the crowded pier at Alameda Naval Air Station.

"The cruise was long — really long — but there were adventures and beautiful ports most people will never get to see," said Lampley. "It's been worth it."

The voyage included one uninterrupted stretch of 107 days at sea and rowdy liberties in the Philippines, Australia and Japan.

When the ship tied up at Alameda Naval Air Station, Airman Vincent Ayule, 22, wore a big grin but could not stop his tears as he met his 2-month-old son Christopher for the first time.

"Big, ain't he?" said Ayule after inspecting the red-faced, 10-pound baby. "I love him. I've been dying to see my baby. He was born on March 30 when we were in the Indian Ocean. It's tough having your first son born when you're so far away."

Ayule was one of about 50 new fathers who met their children for the first time yesterday along Alameda's Pier 3, where wives and families began gathering at dawn for the arrival.

Some 3000 wives, sweethearts, children and other family members stood on the pier and waved "Welcome Home" signs and laughed with delight as the big gray ship was pushed into her berthing spaces by straining tugboats.

"Awwwriiight!" howled a gang sailors hanging over the port side the ship admiring the women waiting ashore. A couple of hundred tossed their sailor hats like frisbees into the waiting crowd.

Also aboard the ship yesterday were 1200 civilian relatives — all male — whom the Navy invited aboard in Pearl Harbor for a free six-day trip aboard the Vinson for the last 2398-mile leg of the voyage home.

"We had a wonderful time," said Carlton Da Vega, 54, of Santa Rosa, who joined his 21-year-old son, Flight Crewman Eric Da Vega, on the trip from Hawaii to San Francisco.

"Everything was great," said the senior Da Vega, obviously proud of his sailor son. "Then last Sunday they put on a terrific live fire exercise that you wouldn't believe. Bombing and strafing. It was very impressive. The firepower of this ship is awesome."

The Vinson will be in port for three months for refitting. She is expected to take another extended cruise next fall.

protest against the presence of 'nuclear armed American vessels in their port, including the . . . Carl Vinson, the newest, most sophisticated warship in the US Navy'.

Even so, 9,000 protesters did not get the last word. That went to Lieutenant-Commander John Whittaker, senior Australian recruiting officer in Western Australia, who warned the 5,000 US sailors to 'be prepared for these clowns', since 'one of the problems of democracy is that every idiot will have his say'. The Brisbane *Sun* (2 July 1983) also reported his speech, adding: '"You'll get what you want ashore in Perth, whatever that may be," Cdr. Whittaker assured the cheering crew of the USS Carl Vinson . . . "the birds will be interested. Everyone in Perth will be interested and friendly except one group"' [the anti-nuclear protesters]; but 'You'll meet a bird and all you'll be interested in will be indoor sports.'

* * *

One of the problems of democracy is that it is all too easy for some idiots to have their say. For others it is much more difficult. It is the teachers, not the taught, who do most of the talking in the pedagogic modern media; 9,000 'people' are no match for one lieutenant-commander. The consequence of this arithmetic is that when a producer or reporter tries, as Ken Loach did in his British series *Questions of Leadership* (1983), made for Channel 4, to show people who have 'rarely, if ever, been seen on national television, putting views that are never acknowledged',[23] then such stories are accused of bias, propaganda, half-truth – and they are banned. Who were the dangerous 'people' in Loach's films? They were trade-unionists, not the leaders but the led. And what, asks Loach, caused the Independent Broadcasting Authority to shelve the films?

> I believe it was because we touched on the most sensitive political nerve. . . . Working people explain in the films how their leaders have confused, demoralized, and sabotaged the struggle to prevent closures and defend living standards. . . . Union leaders have failed to organize the strength of the labour movement. They have, in effect, kept the Tories in power.

Thus a series that 'enabled trade unionists to recount incidents and experiences that provoked questions about the political directions of their unions'[24] also provoked a politics of reading among the IBA administrators, who read the 'message' on behalf of an untrustworthy audience, pronounced it 'unbalanced', and scuppered the series.

Of course, Loach's series wasn't exactly banned. Its effective censorship was achieved, 'not by an outright ban but by delay and inaction, by passing the item from one desk to another, so that the programme gradually loses its topicality and relevance'.[25] The most notorious example of a victim of this process is Peter Watkins's film *The War Game*, made as a documentary for the BBC in 1965. Despite the opinion of senior BBC executives – Grace Wyndham Goldie (head of television talks) and Huw Wheldon – at the time that 'so long as there is no security risk and the facts are authentic, the people should be trusted with the truth',[26] they were not so trusted by the BBC until 4,400,000 of them watched it twenty years later, in August 1985 (the fortieth anniversary of Hiroshima) on the minority channel BBC2.[27]

* * *

One that got away was the Australian Broadcasting Corporation's film report called *Black Death*, dealing with the deaths of Aborigines in police or prison custody in Western Australia, and screened in the ABC's *Four Corners* slot in September 1985. According to the Perth *West Australian* (25 September 1985), the programme was welcomed by the Aboriginal Legal Service, who 'said it was an accurate reflection of concerns felt by Aborigines over prison deaths'. In the wider political community, its truth was deemed sufficiently probable to precipitate the setting up of a Royal Commission to investigate over 100 black deaths in custody throughout Australia. However, the police and prison officers' unions, and their legal representatives, said *Black Death* was nothing but lies; their barrister 'said the program was the most disgraceful example of biased, unfair and untrue reporting that he had ever seen', while the secretary of the Western Australian police union 'said there were blatant untruths throughout the program'. As a result, the police banned ABC-TV reporters from their briefings on all other matters in Western Australia, and refused their crews admittance to police premises – a bizarre procedure that the crews duly filmed for the ABC's *National* news programme. There were moves to have the reporter responsible for *Black Death*, David Marr, extradited from New South Wales to Western Australia to face charges of criminal libel, and various civil cases were initiated. Both the police and prison officers' unions lodged complaints with the Australian Journalists' Association, claiming that Marr had breached the first standard of the AJA Code of Ethics. This move had the curious effect of ensuring that the relevant part of the code was quoted in full on the front page of the *West Australian*, a rare example of self-reflexivity, giving readers a glimpse of the paper's regime of truth from the professionals' own point of view.

* * *

Thus do the police and prison officers, upholders of public truths, defend themselves. Their wrath was directed at a television corporation and a very senior reporter (Marr was former editor of the *National Times*) – certainly both well able to defend themselves in turn. But the occasion of that wrath, the 'biased, unfair and untrue', was simply another kind of truth; not natural, unauthored, eternal or 'representative', but the truth of some of those people who have rarely, if ever, been seen on national television, putting views that are never acknowledged. The strong and no doubt honestly held idea that such truths are not only propagandist and biased, but actually untrue, is itself a product of the prevailing regime of truth in the popular media. While the 'meaning' of the largest nuclear weapon in the world is 'naturally' to do with propagation, and goes unchallenged, the truths of such groups as nuclear disarmers, trade-unionists, workers, Aborigines and even mere 'people' are inadmissible; capable of being reported, if at all, only as the wild ravings of clowns and idiots on the lunatic fringe. And such groups rarely have the organized power or institutional clout to hit back at the media, whereas politicians, police and other representatives of the world of anger and telegrams do.

Thus the forces of truth are unequally balanced. As a result, journalists have arrived at a set of restrictive, defensive rules about 'balance' which are designed primarily to keep politicians off their backs. Commenting on this situation, the then political editor of the London *Sunday Times*, Hugo Young, argued that in these days of political and audio-visual fragmentation, with multiple political parties and more screen outlets, the preservation of balance 'won't make for stimulating television. Nor do such defensive rules of journalism have much connection with arriving at truth.' However, Young concludes that these rules of balance are not a result of journalistic criteria at all, but are based on politicians' interference with the media, an interference that is 'rooted in terror. They are frightened of what they conceive to be television's power, and of what effect unorthodox opinion on the screen (about nuclear disarmament, for example) might have on the untutored populace.'[28]

In the examples cited by Young, it becomes clear that it isn't even the opinion of the 'untutored populace' as such that so scares their political teachers, but rather the 'unorthodox opinions' of critical individuals within their own ranks. Thus, said Young, the producer of the BBC's flagship current affairs programme, *Panorama*, was 'called a traitor and the BBC chairman almost torn limb from limb' after part of one *Panorama* programme was given over, not to the lunatic fringe, but to Members of Parliament critical of the Falklands War. 'The pressure', wrote Young, 'was effective. Very little was televised from the critics after that. It was also shocking. It showed . . . how unable they [politicians] are to accept a deviation from the orthodoxies they define.'[29]

* * *

Orthodoxy in the realm of public affairs doesn't even extend to the limits of the two major parties, let alone beyond them to the opinions of the 'untutored populace' at large. Meanwhile, party and national leaderships themselves assiduously cultivate their own particular, partial home-truths, exploiting the media, especially television, to such an extent that there surely can be no such thing as an 'untutored' populace any more, if there ever was. It is only untutored in very specific areas of the political curriculum: areas of unorthodox truth generated from unofficial sources, especially from among sections of the populace itself. But in these days of representative democracies and balanced television, such areas appear as unrepresentative, therefore undemocratic, therefore propaganda, therefore untrue. This dangerous logic makes representative (authorized) truth into a weapon in the constant war against 'unorthodox' (popular) opinions; it is a pedagogy for an over-tutored populace who cannot be trusted with any other kind of truth because they never have been.

* * *

It is time – in these days of *blivitous*, simulated, selected, constructed, warlike, Protestant, pedagogic, representational, diegetic, representative, entertaining, numerical, impartial, godlike and terrified truths – it is time, as Hugo Young put it, 'to be unbalanced'. It is time to promote the 'disgraceful' ('displeasing to God') example of 'biased, unfair and untrue' reporting of the voices and faces of the idiots and clowns on the lunatic fringe. Otherwise, as Kurt Vonnegut feared, sanity may well be enforced throughout the world, by the *Carl Vinson*, but there may be no world left to applaud the result. It is time, in short, for propaganda to be taken seriously – which entails trusting the untutored populace to engage for itself in the politics of reading. In days such as these, the truth media should admit that their notion of truth and their means of arriving at it are incommensurable; they should admit the secret of the *blivit* and follow Vonnegut's lying but honest storytellers, whose premise is not 'this is God's truth', but merely the much less fatal 'Keep your hat on. We may wind up miles from here.'[30]

Chapter 4

Consciousness razing*

In April 1982, as the British government assembled its Task Force in readiness for the assault on the Falklands, it soon became clear that the real casualty of the war was the credibility of any opposition to it. National consciousness, as well as the fleet, was mobilized in support of Tory High Command. Within days, unthinkable acts and unspeakable attitudes were commonplace; the early sense of amazement, high-risk politics and the imminent fall of the Prime Minister quickly dissolved into pub talk about military tactics, the gallantry of 2 Para, biffing the Argies and the impact of Exocets on aluminium superstructures.

War aims were taken out of the domain of policy and replaced by the familiar unfolding of a suspense narrative. The spectator–nation could only judge the war on the criteria of fiction: Will they? Won't they? She biffs them; she biffs them not. Caught up in the successive enigmas, disclosures and cliffhangers of the action series, we hardly had time to notice how effortlessly the old ways of expressing patriotism and national solidarity had been reinstated. A rhetoric that had been in continuous retreat since Suez (and seemingly finally laid to rest in Anguilla) was suddenly elevated to the status of national policy: what we must do is kill foreigners and humiliate their state. At last, we had a real enemy, and the news from the front was good.

Where in all this was the voice of opposition? Who would give access to those who denounced this dress rehearsal for Armageddon? As things stood, all that we knew about the war was what we were told by the media; and the media, following their ingrained professional habits, could only make sense of it for us by naturalizing it. For over a generation broadcasters have striven to make the news into good television. So their response to the war was to get the best pictures, the most dramatic dispatches, and to tutor us in the maps and minutiae of military planning. They worked very hard to make it all realistic (like fiction); and we were

* Originally published as John Hartley, Holly Goulden and Trevor Wright (1982) 'Consciousness razing: Channel 4 news and current affairs', in Simon Blanchard and David Morley (eds) *What's this Channel Four? An Alternative Report*, London: Comedia.

certainly informed, educated and entertained. But meanwhile, the war was steadily made acceptable to the British public.

Just as the fleet set sail, the High Command of Charlotte Street, Channel 4's HQ, also announced the launch of a rather different task force; the news and current affairs line-up, complete with a flagship aptly named Broadside, that was being assembled for the channel's own 2 November opening. Suddenly, these plans took on a new and dreadful import. Was *this* the face that could stop the launch of 27,000 men? Once a task force has been assembled and sent on its way, it is virtually impossible to stop, except by missile, bomb and torpedo. The mobilization of national popular consciousness in support of the Falklands war looked uncannily easy. So would Channel 4, planning its launch as the first new national TV network in Britain for nearly twenty years, prove to be a resource for contesting the rhetoric of government, and a force for making the unthinkable stay that way? Given its much vaunted innovative and mould-breaking specifications, would Channel 4 be any use for naturalizing not state but oppositional or alternative popular consciousness, and could it discipline the state?

TASK FORCE CHANNEL 4

Like most task forces, this one was designed to fight the last war. The news values which Channel 4 inherited from professional journalism have survived from periods like the 1930s and the 1950s, when part of the standard procedure for explaining what's what in the world was to contrast us (Britain) with them (totalitarian states like Nazi Germany in the 1930s or the USSR from the 1950s onwards). In this conventional wisdom, we don't have dissidents – only the Russians (and the Czechs and the Poles) do. We have a prevailing consensus in which no account need be taken of dissidence, since dissidents are in fact deviants – mad, malicious, mindless or bloody-minded. In those good old days, which are still with us, the lesson is clear: home-grown opposition is foreign to the national character.

According to this conventional wisdom, minorities are not created by unequal power relations but by individual preferences of taste – for example, a taste for serious as opposed to popular (trivial) entertainment on television. And minorities in the field of politics are merely those who lack something – the underprivileged, the under-achievers, the disabled, the disadvantaged, the misfits.

In the good old days, the audience for news was a mass of common-sense family men and their wisely consuming wives who weren't disadvantaged, deviant or dissident. In those days, a fact was a fact, and the news was a recent conflict involving well-known personalities representing us who were threatened with negative action by them. And news was produced by non-political professionals in conditions of routine panic, requiring unreflecting reproduction of these established news values and practices which –

except for occasional MoD-ifications, when the news editor of the national media became, for a while, the Ministry of Defence – cannot be interrupted by stated policy objectives or outside accountability.

The very idea that news might be subject to policies of accountability that attempted to be fair to oppositional stances is itself hard to grasp. For just as newsmakers can render the unthinkable commonplace (war = drama), so can professional wisdom make what ought to be normal into the unthinkable. *Be fair* to the likes of mineworkers' leader Arthur Scargill, railway union ASLEF or Argie Galtieri? Unthinkable! *Be fair* to women, workers, Wales, Russia? Unheard of! If such pressures were to succeed, claim the pros, the news would become biased. So credibility for the broadcasters is to operate on the notion that if they don't take sides between the cat and the mouse then both parties are protected and it's hardly their fault if the mouse gets eaten. And since news is only credible if it's new, they can't always be looking over their shoulder (to the spectre of the Commissar) to check who they've travestied today.

The problem with professional newsmaking designed to these criteria (and refitted for popular entertainment on television) is that its consensual, middle-ground ideology and airy disregard for minorities looks, in the wake of the departing task force, not so much like an accidental congruence with dominant values but more like open complicity with the state. By the outbreak of the Falklands war, the big broadcasting organizations had still not come to terms with the explicit rejection of consensual politics that Margaret Thatcher had announced soon after her 1979 election victory. Under the old consensualism, legitimate opposition extended at least to the boundaries of the two major parties; but under adversarial Thatcherism, 'there was no alternative'. Treating such a narrow definition of the legitimate as if it were still 'the middle ground' inevitably meant that broadcasters marginalized and travestied opposition to it, pushing previously respectable positions beyond the framework of the legitimate.

As the fleet set sail, non-parliamentary opposition and resistance were incomprehensible to the media, whether they came from the women's movement, the so-called far left or the citizens of Toxteth, scene of 1981 riots. The only politics media organizations did feel at home with paradoxically made their senior executives feel very uncomfortable. For the middle ground could no longer pose as apolitical or ideologically inert. As the London *Guardian* reported (January 1982):

> One senior BBC man said: 'I think the BBC employs the kind of people it has always employed: educated, middle-of-the-road people. But since the SDP, the middle ground has become an identifiable political identity. And that makes it very difficult.'

No doubt Channel 4 faced similar difficulties. The liberal–pluralist centre politics that spawned the SDP (Social Democratic Party) was the very same ideological pond that nurtured Channel 4. But the trouble with centre politics and middle-ground broadcasting alike is that neither can cope with opposition: the whole idea of the SDP was to smother it with a wished-for (imaginary) unity within the nation, and to break the mould of (i.e. discredit) the old adversarial structure of British politics.

Similarly, Channel 4's response to the challenge of breaking the mould of broadcast news was not to give form and structure to the opposition of contending interests and powers, but to cling on to the outmoded notions of consensus and pluralism. In the face of an authoritarian government which had rejected the consensus and proudly went to war (with Argies or ASLEF), Channel 4 was hopelessly outmanoeuvred from the start. It became at best the urbane and civilized voice of the social group from which its own and the SDP's support had been mobilized.

It was not interested, apparently, in opposition or resistance, and was not prepared to defend the voices of contestation, much less to promote forms of consciousness which were being hammered out in every medium except television. Pluralism simply meant variety; and variety of opinion was fine as long as it didn't challenge anything. In a revealing interview in The *Guardian* (December 1980), Channel 4's chief executive Jeremy Isaacs talked to the editor of the woman's page, Liz Forgan, whom he subsequently went on to appoint as commissioning editor for actuality – the news/current affairs supremo. Isaacs was very clear:

> We must find room for a variety of opinion and if that means a variety of types of programmes so much the better. But if people try to blow the transmitters by their rudery they are going to make life very difficult for themselves and for the Channel. That's where I would put my foot down if I think it's going too far.

He went on:

> If all I get offered is agit-prop I'm not likely to be terribly responsive to it. The people who are going to write and produce for this channel will have the freedom to write for particular audiences instead of always for the mass, but they are going to have to do it – I won't say in acceptable ways – but in subtle, amusing and stimulating ways.

This kind of insistence on style was no doubt a proper concern for a producer, but it was used to reinforce the notion that unfamiliar topics are unintelligible, and that oppositional television is by definition heavy. Isaacs may have been right to worry about *how* new television addresses its audience, but as we can see, the line between that and prescribing *what* is said (no rudery or agit-prop) is narrow. The problem is of course deeply rooted in the confusion about pluralism. You want lots of different voices, but no fights; the cat and the mouse in the same cage, but the mouse mustn't bite the cat. So Isaacs merely reiterated the position adopted in the quasi-official Annan Report, which marked one of the major milestones in the prehistory of Channel 4:

> the next requirement for good broadcasting in future is diversity. Our society's culture is now multi-racial and pluralist: that is to say, people adhere to different views of the nature and purpose of life and expect their own view to be expressed in some form or other. The structure of broadcasting should reflect this variety.[1]

It also expressed its own view on the fourth channel:

> So we do not see the fourth channel merely as an addition to the plurality of outlets, but as a force for plurality in a deeper sense.[2]

Whatever that means, it doesn't recognize that opinions come from conditions and discourses which compete for dominance, and compete on unequal grounds. *This* kind of pluralism has winners and losers – and Channel 4 is backing winners whilst appearing, for the sake of diversity, to be hedging its bets.

BATTLESHIP ITN

What were the specifications of the task force that Liz Forgan and Jeremy Isaacs assembled? The naval analogy is appropriate, especially for the ageing battlecruiser in the shape of big, unmanoeuvrable ITN (Independent Television News, the news-provider for commercial TV in the UK). As the *Guardian* put it:

> ITN's new mid-evening, hour-long news background programme on Channel Four could be very important. It could be the best chance to break the mould of television news since BBC-2 muffed it.

ITN was in fact central to the whole Channel 4 news/current affairs issue. It got the lion's share of programme time – four-and-a-half peak-time weekday hours out of a weekly total of eight hours. This disproportionate allocation was even more marked when it emerged that Channel 4 did not effectively challenge the traditional news/current affairs split. The other contender for news was the group which got the odd half-hour on Friday nights – Diverse Productions – but all the other offerings were clearly designed as current affairs, of which ITN has no direct experience.

Despite its size, ITN was less well equipped for mould-breaking than first appeared. The 'distinctively different' approach it promised was based on the more-of-the-same principle. The difference was not in policy or presentation but in the time given to items, in the range of topics deemed newsworthy – these would now include the arts, science, technology and business – and in the use of presenters who also led specialist teams to produce stories. The presenters, Peter Sissons and Sarah Hogg, were mainstream journalists whose previous specialisms were industrial affairs and the economy. There was also a promise to increase foreign news coverage to up to one-third of air time, with maybe even clips of foreign TV's own versions of events.

All this indicated a willingness on the part of ITN to gear up to a new professional and commercial initiative. But it is also clear that the thinking behind it was inward-looking, not a response to perceived changes in the world beyond the media. In line with Jeremy Isaacs's own notions about the new direction TV news should take, ITN modelled its new news on the old inside pages of the quality press: mould-breaking innovation came down in the end to aping the *Guardian* or the *Sunday Times*.

This insider's definition of a new model for the news was then doubly compounded. First, ITN's recruiting policy reinforced the link: Sarah Hogg, the new presenter, was ex-*Sunday Times* and ex-*Economist*. Derrick Mercer, ITN's associate editor (the boss), was ex-*Sunday Times*. David Nicholas, CBE, ITN's editor and chief executive, came to ITN originally from the *Yorkshire Post* and the *Daily Telegraph*. And of course Channel 4 itself recruited from the same source – most notably Liz Forgan from the *Guardian* and previously the *Evening Standard*.

Second, and more important, the very practice of newsgathering was less outward-looking than its name implied. Most news stories are deemed newsworthy only to the extent that they are being covered by the other news outlets, and a great deal of the news actually comes straight from those outlets: the Press Association (domestic), Reuters (foreign) and the radio and newspapers which are the starting points for daily editorial decisions. ITN is not a world leader, despite its claims, in originating news. In 1982 it had only one resident foreign correspondent (in Washington) while the BBC had nearly thirty, and ITN takes much of its domestic film coverage from the regional ITV (commercial TV) companies. Like most industrialized news organizations, ITN is geared to a well-established diary of highly predictable events and topics. Its primary function is to take already existing press reports, press releases, official and other documents, and put these together with vision (much of which is not its own) in an account that is supposed to make sense of the whole business for the supposed viewer. And sense, in this context, means breathless present-tense narration of a story that must entertain by rendering the new in as familiar a form as possible – the form of fiction.

However, as long as the ratings hold up, the unseen viewer isn't an everyday presence for the professionals of ITN's Wells Street HQ. Other professionals are, however, so effective discipline or accountability comes not from attention to any obligations to the viewing constituencies but from what other insiders are doing, and how. Competition is therefore based on fear of missing what the other lot have, producing ever more similar news on competing channels. If by chance the ratings don't hold up, the answer is to present the same second-hand stuff, only more entertainingly.

But if ITN were to go even as far as honouring its commitment to more of the same, it would have had to increase its staffing levels dramatically. Investigative reporting is notoriously labour intensive, and with only one resident foreign correspondent and only one resident crew outside London (in a geographical nonsense ITN called North of Britain), it needed an awful lot of so-called 'firemen' to react to the unpredictable news. ITN's total staff numbered nearly seven hundred in 1982, but its Channel 4 news was to be produced by a separate unit of just ninety. Of these, two were presenters, with four live reporters, twenty-four other journalists and sixty technical staff. Enough just to clip the *Guardian*, maybe, but then ITN had the advantage that it could recycle material from ITV's *News at One*, *News at 5.45* and *News at Ten*. The result was news for Channel 4 at less than the channel's modest overall budget allowance of £30,000 per hour average for 1982–3, but then it is important to realize that the production costs of a five-minute item (of news background) can cost the same as a one-minute item (of news) – making the innovatory surprisingly cost-effective.

There was no cost benefit, it seemed, in breaking the mould where it really mattered. ITN was still committed to the professional presentation of the fetishized fact – the name, rank and serial number approach which tells us how many arrests but not the case being demonstrated for – a commitment reflected in the remarks of Channel 4 presenter Peter Sissons in commercial TV's house magazine *Independent Broadcasting*:

> Frankly I think that a lot of what's been written about the balance of TV reporting of industry and its problems is itself far from impartial. It invariably comes from people of particular political beliefs, writing little more than political tracts about the way they believe the media should be organised. But some of it's persuasive – half-truths often are – part of it may be valid, sometimes.

This grudging concession to the 'persuasiveness' and 'validity' of critiques of professional balance is clearly disingenuous. It presumes that professionals are free of 'particular political beliefs', that ITN bulletins are not 'little more than political tracts' and that politics is merely a matter of 'personal belief'. Sissons countered the criticism by insisting ever more firmly on the very practices that had given rise to the problem:

> It will be a sad moment for us all if any strong, independent news organisation backs off from putting its faith unreservedly in its personnel – talented journalists, backed up by the best technicians, using their judgement to pursue accuracy, impartiality and truth in reporting an increasingly complex world.

In other words we can leave the professionals, like the police, to keep their own house in order; we need 'faith'. We don't need critics such as the Glasgow Media Group,[3] to whom Sissons silently refers, and their 'far from impartial' stuff, even for the sake of variety. Of course, Glasgow Media Group's significance is that, in common with others who have been less successful in provoking professional paranoia, they don't trust the personal talent of professionals who have been socialized into mainstream journalism to defend the rights and visions of such as the women's movement, blacks, Glasgow dustmen or even the organized left. But ITN ideology does share one thing with its sharpest critics in the Glasgow Media Group: a failure to recognize that 'balance' isn't possible in principle, and that there is no ready-made truth lurking under the surface waiting to be dug out by professionals or their critics. Truth is what results from the processes of newsmaking and argumentation, it is not a pre-existing quantum found in nature. There are contending ways of making sense, and whilst the powerful get fair coverage, the rest are either undefended or absent from the news.

The pursuit of truth always raises the question of who is pursuing it, on behalf of whom. This is not a question of, for instance, preferring the British view to the Argentinian view, because there is no one 'British' view, and the truth or otherwise of reporting the events of the Falklands crisis is an effect of the reporting, not the event. It would have been equally possible, equally truthful, to have campaigned actively against sending the Task Force, to have contested the inevitability of military aggression aimed at unconditional restoration of British supremacy, to have reported each and every event of the crisis from the point of view not of the military tacticians at High Command but from that of a Britain that has no access to, no interest in and no desire to be complicit with this course of action (for instance, the British news could (conceivably) have reported the invasion of the Falklands in the same way as it reported the Soviet invasion of Afghanistan the previous year). Such an approach would have been 'accurate, impartial and true' in Sissons's terms, but with news like that the course of events itself could have been truly different. But the *ideology* of impartiality renders such an approach as biased opinion. Channel 4, meanwhile, was not only aware of these difficulties but actually valued the presence of familiar old ITN to fend off the charges of esotericism which would undoubtedly greet any output not produced according to the conventional wisdoms of metropolitan, professional and male thinking.

Alternatives to such news values don't even have to be radical in the usual political sense of that word. For some of the many disenfranchised viewers to whom news is 'his and boring' or 'always too depressing' or 'everybody bickering', for example, there are existing programmes which, despite their popularity (despised by the professionals and critics alike) and despite the careful professional distinctions between categories (especially fact and fiction), nevertheless are newsy and do show what other people are like and how they live. Even in extreme cases like *That's Life* or *Game for a Laugh* there are glimpses, behind the presenters' inane smiles, of the submerged worlds of unstereotyped people and families acting (the goat) in the context of recognizable streets and estates. If you like to hear about people's lives, they can be found in quizzes, serials and plays. There are plenty of places where news can be found on TV; it doesn't have to be labelled and distinguished by a serious tone and a talking head. But far from seeking to enfranchise those whose news currently comes from light entertainment, it is clear that Channel 4's ITN news was not designed to benefit any audience constituency not already over-represented on television.

NEWS DESTROYERS

In the name of diversity, however, Channel 4 shamelessly hedged its bets. For just in case battlecruiser ITN proved to be as much use as the *General Belgrano*, Channel 4 provided it with a couple of racier escort destroyers; Diverse and Broadside. Their function seemed to be to fend off the flak and provide the battlecruiser with a smokescreen of credibility.

On the more exposed news side of the news/current affairs divide, the escort was the independent production company Diverse; on the current affairs side of it two companies were commissioned: Broadside, staffed by women, and Gambles–Milne (named after the two women journalists who headed it).[4] Even such potentially hopeful and innovative outfits were regarded by Channel 4 not as a political but as a professional experiment. The danger was that if they were judged by traditional journalistic criteria and found wanting, they would be ditched. Hence they would be driven to reproduce ever more slickly the very practices they ought to have contested. In short, they had to contend with the professional demands of Channel 4 as well as the political demands of the disenfranchised. But to succeed in what Liz Forgan, in the launch press release, insisted was a '*journalistic* experiment' would seriously jeopardize the more political possibilities offered by Channel 4; conceding the glittering prize of adversarial politics, and settling for the cosy confusion of pluralist professionalism.

The rest of the escort flotilla on the current affairs side may be disposed of quickly. Its specifications, as gleaned from the launch press release, were:

1 A monthly two-hour 'social audit', *Report to the Nation*, which 'will offer us, the shareholders (and customers) of a range of nationalised industries', a public annual meeting in which 'informed experts' will cross-examine 'managers' on our behalf. This supposedly public-spirited prestige slot was to be produced for Video Arts by Paul Ellis, ex-editor of *The Money Programme*. The idea was devised by Video Arts' managing director, Michael Peacock, who launched and was controller of BBC2.

2 A weekly forty-five minute politics programme centred on Whitehall and Westminster, 'at a time of heightened public interest in the possibility of change within the parliamentary political system'. The executive producer was David Elstein, ex-editor of *This Week*, and the programme was to be produced by Anne Lapping, ex-labour correspondent of the *Economist* and previously a reporter for Thames and the BBC and producer for *Weekend World*. She said the programme 'will cover the political how and why, as well as what', and the programme was intended also to cover local government, grassroots political activity and something called 'Europolitics'.
3 A promised 'weekly slot for industry, filled by several series (to be announced later) representing both unions and management, workers and entrepreneurs'.
4 The oldest current affairs show on ITV, *What the Papers Say* from Granada (produced, way back in the late 1950s and early 1960s, by none other than Channel 4's chief executive, Jeremy Isaacs). (Later this show was sold by Channel 4 to the BBC.)
5 *Face the Press* from Tyne Tees, which had never been regularly networked, except as a summer replacement for *Weekend World*.
6 A nightly five-minute editorial in ITN's time but not under their control. The speaker and the topic would be chosen by Channel 4 – initially under Liz Forgan's direct charge.

This package (excluding ITN) was budgeted at £6 million annually at 1982 prices, and with the exception of Broadside and Diverse was made up entirely of traditional ideas in the hands of mainstream professionals, whether they appeared in the guise of independents or not.

No doubt Channel 4 congratulated itself on assembling such a varied package for so modest a sum – and no doubt some interesting television came out of it. But it is clear that the extension of the old monolithic consensus to include pluralism, variety and diversity did not extend as far as recognizing that the variety of ways of life are also contending ways of life. It is also clear that Channel 4 held on to a notion of news and current affairs which reproduced directly the characteristics it should have contested most vigorously: professionalism, insularity, metropolitanism and the tyranny of established news values. In a partnership with ITN, which only makes sense in terms of commercial and institutional expediency, Channel 4 launched a task force which was seriously disabled from the outset. In the event it was launched to zero ratings – a UK TV first.

To end with, a quiz. ITN told the Annan Committee that 'it is our duty to keep in touch with everyone who has a television set',[5] and the *IBA Handbook* for 1982 described how ITN set about doing this:

> ITN's twin aims, to get the facts right and to give both sides of the story, are more than a matter of professional pride or statutory requirement.

> On them depends ITN's credibility as a prime service of information to the public.[6]

In February/March 1982 I undertook a research project with a student, Trevor Wright, which tried to find out how much weekday ITN 'kept in touch' with, for instance, women, workers, Wales and blacks. We were interested in what facts ITN got right and which two sides of the story they gave. In that month, stories with women in were either about well-known people close to the political heart of the British state – Lady Di, Princess Anne, the Queen (plus Mother) – or about show-business personalities like Elizabeth Taylor, or Julie Goodyear from *Coronation Street*. Less well-known women who rated a mention were either mothers (of Blair Peach), wives (of Lech Wałesa) or daughters (of Leonid Brezhnev), or else they were the reported victims of crime. Blacks were easier to spot. In the entire month the only stories that included blacks were crime stories. Wales got four mentions that month. (1) A memorial to Welsh writer Dylan Thomas was unveiled in Westminster Abbey in London; 1 minute 59 seconds. (2) Michael Foot (ex-leader of the Labour Party) was reselected for the Welsh parliamentary constituency of Ebbw Vale; 8 seconds. (3) Irish seamen blockaded Dun Laoghaire in Ireland to stop the Holyhead (Wales) ferry from docking; 1 minute 44 seconds. (4) The Home Secretary extended stop and search laws to England and Wales (England-and-Wales is a legal unity, differing from Scotland); 2 minutes 8 seconds. So Wales's four mentions were all in the context of stories about something else. As for workers, they started strikes.

Now the quiz. See if you can find any evidence that ITN is keeping in touch with you. Send your answers to Channel 4.

Chapter 5

Home help for populist politics: relational aspects of TV news*

In the kind of country we live in there cannot be any 'we' or 'they'. There is only 'us'; all of us. If the Government is 'defeated', then the country is defeated, because the Government is just a group of people elected to do what the majority of 'us' want to see done. That is what our way of life is all about.

It really does not matter whether it is a picket line, a demonstration or the House of Commons. We are all used to peaceful argument. But when violence or the threat of violence is used, it challenges what most of us consider to be the right way of doing things. I do not believe you elect any government to allow that to happen and I can promise you that it will not be tolerated wherever it occurs.

(Prime Minister Edward Heath in a ministerial broadcast after the 1972 miners' strike)[1]

This chapter is a revised version of part of a paper I wrote with Martin Montgomery on the way news constructs both *representations* of events and *relations* with the viewer or reader of the news. In this version, I concentrate on the relational aspect; how TV news positions itself and its stories in relation to the viewer. The news text under analysis was part of a main evening bulletin on BBC-TV during the so-called 'winter of discontent' in Britain in February 1979, just three months before the general election which saw the first Thatcher government sweep Labour from power. The story concerns one of the industrial disputes of which that 'discontent' was comprised. The purpose of the analysis is to show how large-scale issues, such as ideology and power, may be connected with small-scale processes within texts.

It would be silly to suggest that a single news story was instrumental in

* Originally published as John Hartley and Martin Montgomery (1985) 'Representations and relations: ideology and power in press and TV news', in Teun van Dijk (ed.) *Discourse and Communication: New Approaches to the Analysis of Mass Media Discourse and Communication*, Berlin and New York: Walter de Gruyter.

changing the political map of Britain, but single news stories are still worthy of analysis as complex texts which indicate, at the very least, what discursive mobilizations and textual strategies were in fact deployed at a time of political instability; they are empirical evidence of a cultural climate. In this case, it is striking to observe how, in the internal (textual) struggle over the meaning of its verbal, visual and sound elements, the story prefigured the election result: Prime Minister Callaghan was discursively defeated, and Margaret Thatcher was helped. Even more striking is that this outcome was achieved in an impartial news story which was not about parliamentary politics as such. It is certainly not my contention that the story was biased or distorted; on the contrary, what makes it interesting is that it was produced by an organization committed to impartiality, neutrality, balance and truth. That these are impossible to achieve is not a result of political bias or union-bashing but of semiotic imperatives.

As the quotation from Edward Heath at the beginning of this chapter indicates, the question of relations – of we and they – is highly charged politically. Heath's 'one nation' rhetoric goes back to Disraeli, but it did not survive his defeat, first at the hands of the miners and the electorate in 1974, and then at the hands of Margaret Thatcher in a contest for the Conservative leadership in 1975. Thatcher's own political rhetoric was, and remained, much more combative and divisive, while simultaneously appealing to populist sentiments which she cultivated directly, over the heads of parliament and party. But the ideological ground she tilled, that of populist common-sense discourses, is also the ground upon which television news establishes its intelligibility. While television news must, for reasons of its own survival and popularity, endorse the 'one nation' view of its audience, Thatcher herself did not. She explicitly abandoned the consensualist tradition invoked by Ted Heath, and had no qualms about creating 'they' identities for all who did not agree with her.[2]

In this context, the way in which the news semiotically sorts out the participants in a story into we/they identifications,[3] and how it positions the viewer in relation to them, is significant politically.

EYE CONTACT

Television news exploits one of the most distinctive features of TV in general, namely the representation of people, and in particular of people's faces, expressive features and eyes, in the process of narration. But whereas by established convention TV and cinema fiction rarely make use of direct eye-contact with the camera/viewer, television news has instated this form of address at the centre of its textual strategy. Thus, without verbalizing it, television news operates on a first person (I) to second person (you) axis, in the form of the newsreader's relation to the viewer via direct address and eye-contact.

In addition to the relations between viewer and newsreader/reporter there is a textual relation between viewer and news story; that is, between the viewer and the characters whose stories are narrated. In this case there is a choice as to whether the relation is constructed as 'we' (including the viewer with depicted characters), or as 'they' (excluding the viewer from identification with them). Television news activates a full circuit between first (narrator), second (viewer) and third (depicted) persons, being able to align the viewer to the newsworthy people represented in the story (as either we or they), but also being able to address the viewer over the heads, literally, of such people. It can do this without verbal intrusion; eye-contact alone establishes an I/you axis between newsreader and viewer, without, apparently, any unwanted editorializing interventions.

INSTITUTIONAL VS. FORMAL RELATIONS

However, television news is not simply a matter of newsreader addressing viewer. Beyond this basic relation are (at least) two other kinds of relation that TV news has to accommodate in its routine practices. These are extra-textual relations, and it so happens that they make mutually exclusive, and thus contradictory, demands on TV news. The first may be called TV news's *institutional* relations. Foremost among these is the statutory requirement laid on broadcasters that TV news be impartial. That is, events must be narrated without the news adopting the point of view of any one faction, party or person. The second relation, which may be called *formal*, contradicts the first because news cannot escape the television/cinema codes of visual representation that it uses. To put it bluntly, the first problem news camerawork faces is where to put the camera. In fiction-filmmaking, a conventional distinction has arisen between what are known as p.o.v. (point of view) shots and neutral shots. A p.o.v. shot is one that shows the scene or characters from one of the characters' point of view. Often the point of view is visually *motivated* by including part of the observer's figure (shoulder, side of head) seen from behind, in the frame. Such shots are often used to show dialogue between two characters, with the point of view of each seen in alternate shots (a sequential strategy known as shot–reverse-shot). The viewer is thus positioned as the character whose point of view is shown. However, the viewer is not limited to this point of view, since that of several different characters may be shown, as well as neutral shots. Hence, during the course of a film, the viewer achieves a kind of composite point of view; one which is privileged over the point of view of any one character since the viewer knows more, from more points of view, than anyone in the film. In fact, television/cinema codes position the viewer as that point from which all the different characters, scenes, actions and plot developments are *intelligible*, and this totalizing position is denied to the characters themselves.

This discussion leads to two conclusions about news camerawork. First, the conventionalized distinction between p.o.v. shots and neutral shots does not stand up to close inspection. All shots have a point of view, whether *internally motivated* by the placing of a character, or *externally motivated* by the positioning of the imaginary observer (viewer). Furthermore, shots presented as neutral are unable to stand alone – they are only ever seen in contrast to p.o.v. shots. Thus, at the very least, neutral shots signify a point of view which is not that of the participants. When set against other shots that do offer a participant's point of view, such neutrality becomes, ideologically, very productive.

Second, news camerawork solves the problem of where to put the camera in a very similar way to the way fictional conventions have dealt with it. That is, the news also constructs an imaginary viewer, positioned as it were behind the camera, from whose point of view the partial and disjointed fragments of picture, sound and story can cohere into intelligibility. As in fiction, so in news; there is no point of view from within the news where it all makes sense. None of the institutional personnel (newsreader, correspondent, reporter, etc.) and none of the accessed characters whose faces and voices appear in the news are in a position to see the whole. Indeed, all the people who are seen, and all the textual deployments of sound, picture and sequence, are subordinate to the imaginary viewer, who thus takes the place of the omniscient author/narrator of realist novels.

Here the force of the inevitable contradiction between TV news's *formal* relations and its *institutional* relations can be sensed. News has to be impartial; that is, it must narrate events without a point of view. Since that is impossible, there is a contradiction between (required) impartiality and (unavoidable) point of view. The construction of an imaginary viewer as the point of intelligibility actually makes matters worse. This is because, in the first place, there is no viewer at the point(s) of production who can offer advice on what an appropriate point of view might look like; broadcasters work to a fictionalized image of the viewer (see chapter 6). Second, there is no unified point of view among those who actually watch the news at the point(s) of consumption. Quite the reverse, in fact.

Nevertheless, the news institutions have not only accepted the requirement of impartiality, but (even in the face of widespread doubt and criticism) they continue to assert that they have achieved it. Thus the news is presented with an assurance not only that it is intelligible to the viewer, but also that it is true. So the contradiction is erased in the relation the news proposes with its viewers – the type of intelligibility that is offered textually seems to escape the problem of point of view, since it is the only point of view that allows no alternative – the point of view of impartiality, namely truth.

IT'S A PLOT

At this point it is useful to turn to detailed analysis of the news text, from the BBC *Nine O'Clock News* of 1 February 1979.[4] A transcript of the story, which lasted eight minutes forty seconds, is given as an appendix to this chapter. It was the second item of its bulletin, being preceded by a foreign affairs story from Iran about the return of the Ayatollah Khomeini from exile. The story was divided up into seven sections, of which two (sections IV and VI) were film reports. This analysis concentrates largely on these two sections. Overall, the story used thirty-two different shots, as shown in the transcript – particular sequences are referred to by their shot number.

The most obvious means by which the viewer is positioned in relation to the event is through what can be called the plot of the story as a whole. The plot is a simple affair of cause and effect. It is initiated verbally (shot 1):

> Here at home the dispute by public service workers is still spreading. *(Cause)*
>
> Half the hospitals in England and Wales and some in Scotland can now open their doors only to emergency cases. *(Effect)*

Both the film report sections (IV and VI) reiterate this cause–effect movement. They open with almost identical shots (9–11 and 19–20) showing the picket lines of strikers (cause), and then spend most of their time on the effects on patients and medical staff. Whilst these effects are being shown visually, the voice-over commentary ascribes causes to them, as in shots 13–14:

> Only two cooks were allowed to remain, so lunch was a little late today for nearly three hundred young patients.

This is over a shot of nurses and a young boy (patient?) trundling food trolleys into a lift. Hence, it follows, the cause of the event is the negative action initiated by the strikers; its effect is on medical staff and patients.

INTERNAL VS. EXTERNAL POINT OF VIEW

Within the cause–effect plot, the camera is used to establish point of view in different ways for the different participants. As far as the picketers are concerned, the point of view of the shots of them can be established by asking whether the camera point of view is that of the strikers themselves. For this to be so, the scene would have to be shot from their point of view; that is, looking *out* of the picket line (across the street or into the entrance), or else looking *inside* the picket line, sharing the talk and seeing the faces of the others there. Such shots would, in fact, differ considerably from what is shown (shots 9, 10, 11, 19, 20). These are filmed from a distance outside the picket line, usually from across a road, and the picketers are only seen as a collectivity, in long-shot, never as individuals. These shots, then, display an *external* point of view, orienting the viewer along the third person to second person axis of relation (they/you): the point of view is the viewer's.

In the film sequences showing the effect of the action inside the hospital the point of view is different. They are framed more tightly than the shots of the pickets, showing fewer people at a time on screen, usually no more than two, and more of their facial and expressive features are identifiable than are those of the strikers. Participants move towards the camera and even past it (shot 13), including it within their action. These shots, then, display an *internal* point of view, orienting the viewer along the third person to first person axis of relation (they/we). This positions the viewer *as* one of the participants, and is comparable to proper p.o.v. shots in cinema.

DEFERENTIAL VS. UNMOTIVATED CAMERA-MOVEMENT

A further set of differences that compounds these point of view distinctions is associated with movements of the camera itself, as opposed to the participants moving in the frame. Here again the differences are organized about the strikers on the one hand, and the patients and medical staff on the other. Where there is camera-movement in the shots of the picketers, it is *unmotivated* by their movements. There are reframings from close-ups of details (an entrance sign, a placard, a banner) to long-shots of the nearby pickets. If this is compared with the shots of patients and medical staff, it is clear that in these the camera-movements are motivated by action. The camera is *deferential*; it follows the actions of the people in shot, usually panning. The only shots in the 'effects' sequences where this doesn't hold true are those that show inanimate objects (rubbish, shot 16; equipment, shot 22).

It may be argued that these differences are determined by the fact that the two sets of shots are literally outside and inside buildings. But there are also shots showing effects, this time on patients, which are exterior shots. In both film reports, these are the last shots, and in both the camera is deferential – it follows the movement of a man and a child (shot 17) and of a baby and car (shots 29-30). In both there is subject movement toward the camera, which pans to follow it, and although the framing of the first remains relatively wide, the child gazes intently at the camera/viewer. In the second, the baby is carried towards the camera by a nurse, and then handed into a woman waiting in a car. At this point the framing is quite tight, and the nurse can be heard (saying 'Bye-bye, mind how you go'), as can the car door closing, and the car's motor as it is driven away. Thus these exterior shots are both from an internal point of view and deferential in their camera-movement.

In summary of this section it is possible to set out how the relational dimension of the camera point of view has sorted the strikers and the nurses/patients into a they/we position:

cause :	effect
external point of view :	internal point of view
unmotivated camera-movement :	deferential camera-movement
long/wide frame :	mid/close frame
strikers/picketers :	nurses/patients/employers
they :	we

NARRATIVE POINT OF VIEW

While the pictures are busy sorting out the strikers from the nurses and patients, the verbal component of the film reports is adding its own relational dimension to the story. It too offers a point of view from which the viewer can make sense of the story. It is possible to use a simple analytical procedure which may be called *reversal* to try to identify a narrative point of view. Here is a version of the opening sequence of section IV (shots 9–12). But the 'they' pronouns and cognates, and the names, have been reversed for the sake of analysis to read 'we' instead (in italics). Having done this, it is possible to look for any strain to the syntax, or any disruption of the popular idiom in which the voice-over is delivered:

> *We* didn't give much warning about *our* strike – just five minutes' notice. *We* then walked out to join the picket line and stayed out for four hours. Now further action in other departments of the hospital is planned [*by us*], though *we* claim the children themselves won't suffer.

The two most striking misfits are the agentless passive 'is planned', which is very hard to render with a 'we' agent; and the 'we claim', which is idiomatically suspect. Beyond this, a 'we' identity that made such a point of giving little warning before walking out and staying out would be representing itself as a bloody-minded identity, to say the least.

After an interview with a union shop steward, the film returns to voice-over. Once again the narrative point of view has been reversed (shots 13–14):

> Inside the hospital the disruption was more than just the minimum *we* had promised. Only two cooks were allowed to remain [*by us*], so lunch was a little late today for nearly three hundred [of] *them*.

There is a reiterated agentless passive ('were allowed'), and further oddities are the unconventional way 'we' announce that we have broken our 'promise', and the numerical disproportion of 'two cooks' and 'nearly three hundred' of 'them'.

Moving on to section VI, the voice-over covering its opening (shot 19) can also be reversed:

> *We* refused to supply any cleaners, because *we* say that's not part of *our* emergency service.

Apart from another bloody-minded 'so there!' refusal, the 'we say' seems ill-fitting because it is a hang-over from the reported speech of the original, and is unlikely in direct speech. But it does raise the question of exactly whose speech was being reported. In the original the 'speakers' are given as 'this hospital's strikers', but it is hardly likely that they actually said what is imputed to them here – the idiomatic turn of phrase 'they say' not only resists reversal into a 'we', but is strictly speaking inaccurate too. Thus it cannot easily be understood from a 'we' point of view.

These points of view of the strikers can be compared with those of other participants to see if there are any significant differences. In section IV, the strikers are followed narratively by 'senior nursing staff' (shot 15), and once again the point of view is reversed:

> *We* had to help out sorting dirty linen from the wards; it took up much of *our* valuable time.

Here the oddity is actually in the original – this idiomatic phrasing fits a 'we' identity so well that the original 'it took up much of their valuable time' is the surprising version. In section VI there are further references to medical staff (shots 21–2 and 24):

> Every day *we* [doctors] treat up to a hundred patients who are suffering from everything from cuts and bruises to heart attacks and appendicitis.
>
> Until unpaid volunteers like her came along, *we* [the nurses] had to dust and vacuum.

These too fit easily into an idiomatically plausible 'we' form, as do references to the patients, who can be found in shots 27–30.

A control of the reversal strategy can be derived from the bulletin. The union shop steward interviewed in section IV (shot 12) actually uses 'we' forms through his answers. If these are reversed into 'they' forms, the results can be compared with the voice-overs directly:

> Yes *they* can guarantee . . . *they've* told the unit administrator that if, during *their* action, children were at risk, *they* would immediately leave the picket line and go in and help . . . *They* believe *they've* shown responsibility . . . *they've* been traditionally a very passive workforce, and *they* hope that by workers at this world-famous hospital taking action it will bring public sympathy to *their* side.

In view of the marked differences between this and the voice-over presentation of the strikers, and the differences between them and the medical staff and patients, it is possible to conclude that the narrative point of view confirms the camera point of view by verbally sorting out these two classes of participants into 'they' and 'we' identities. Thus, the viewer is positioned differently in relation to the strikers and to the doctors/nurses/patients respectively, and cannot so easily adopt the strikers' point of view.

PICTURE AND SOUND RELATIONS

The separate components of picture and sound work in their own ways, but they also work together, and this provides a further, distinct area of analysis. In general, TV news conforms to the realist relationship between picture and sound tracks. That is, each is taken to motivate the other, and the sounds heard are understood as being synchronous ('in sync.') with the picture. Thus, ambient sound is confined to that which occurred at the moment of shooting – TV news does not generally avail itself of the possibilities offered by music, wild-track sound, etc. (though the realist relation between picture and sound can be *manufactured* by using sounds from the effects library to cover mute pictures, for instance, although there is no evidence of this practice here). Ambient sound itself may be significant, but it is subordinate to voice-over commentary, so it tends to get faded up and down according to the voice-over's prior claim to audibility.

The apparent mutual motivation of picture and sound in TV news is very important ideologically, not because it actually occurs, but because it doesn't. The paradox is caused by voice-over commentary, which benefits from the genre-expectation that picture and sound are synchronized, even though it is in fact quite separate in origin from the footage it comments on. Voice-overs are not unmotivated by the picture/ambient sound, but they are external to them, and just as voice-overs are always more audible than ambient or synchronized sound, so they claim a 'higher' level of correspondence to actuality than mere synchronicity. Because they 'helpfully' explain the pictures, voice-overs both encourage and benefit from the viewer's sense that there is a unity of picture and sound. This 'unity' is then cashed in ideologically, as it were, since the explanations appear to arise 'naturally' from the pictures with which they are united.

Section VI (shots 21–4) offers a good example of the way the relations between picture and sound track are handled in practice to produce an effect of apparently seamless unity. The sequence opens not with voice-over commentary, but something even more imperative; that is, the reporter on screen, facing the camera and addressing his remarks directly to the viewer. He signals his presence deictically (shot 21): '*This is* the hospital's accident and emergency department.' As he speaks, in long-shot, the viewer can observe the difference between what he says and what is seen. He says: 'It's normally the busiest place in a hospital', whilst the picture shows empty beds and absence. What happens next is representationally quite simple (it's a story of emptiness, caused by industrial action), but textually quite complex. The reporter says, looking directly at the viewer (shot 21):

> Every day doctors treat up to a hundred patients who are suffering from everything from cuts and bruises to/

At this point there is a picture-edit [such cuts are signified herein by a slash (/)] to shot 22, and a sound change from direct address to voice-over commentary. The picture changes to a piece of equipment, behind which is a chart headlined 'The Treatment of Cardiac Arrest'. The picture itself is mute (there's no ambient sound). And the voice-over is saying:

> /heart attacks and appendicitis. But since yesterday it's been completely empty./

The picture changes again, to a wide shot of an empty ward. Once again the emptiness is signified by a presence, this time of a nurse who walks across (and so defines visually) the space in front of the camera. The voice-over continues (shot 23):

> /The hospital authorities closed it down because of a lack of/

Another picture-edit reveals an active ward, shown in diagonal long-shot, with a glimpse of a patient with a nurse at the bedside in the left foregound, and more patients in bed in the right background. In the middle (middle-distance and mid-screen) is a woman vacuum cleaning between the beds. The camera zooms in to find her in mid-shot. Meanwhile the voice-over is saying (shot 24):

> /clean wards for patients to go to after their treatment here.

At this stage the voice-over is of ambiguous status, since it is not voice-over proper, but a continuation of the words the reporter began as direct address. But the viewer is shifted progressively away from that context by the succession of picture-edits, each one of which is explained or anchored by what the voice-over says. Thus, 'heart attacks' = cardiac arrest machine (though the more mundane equipment used for cuts and bruises is not shown). 'Completely empty' = an empty ward; 'clean wards' = a ward being cleaned. But that 'clean' is a point at which the picture-sense and the verbal-sense go out of sync. The voice-over is telling about 'a lack of/clean wards', but the picture cuts to a cleaner working in a full ward. This is a micro-semiotic instance of narrative enigma,[5] setting up a kind of suspense that will be resolved later. Meanwhile, the voice-over signals the difference that exists at this point between the picture and sound tracks by the final phrase: 'after their treatment *here'*. This deictic can only be understood by reference to the earlier shot of the reporter talking directly; 'here' corresponds to the opening 'This is'. As he says 'treatment here' the sync. of the vacuum-cleaner being faded up momentarily can be heard, and by the time he's finished speaking the zoom-in has found Mrs Munns in mid-shot. The voice-over resumes almost immediately, but there has been a change in sound-quality – it has gone into proper voice-over. The next stage in the story is the description of Mrs Munns, the volunteer who came along to help. At this point the narrative enigma (of a *lack* of clean wards vs. a ward being *cleaned*) is resolved, and picture-sense is reunited with sound-sense.

So in the space of a few seconds the picture and sound tracks have gone from direct lip-sync. through the overlap of speech and picture (mute cutaway) to sync. sound (the vacuum-cleaner) to picture-with-sync.-sound + voice-over. The only point from which this complex interplay of picture, sound and speech is intelligible is the viewer's point of view, and further, its intelligibility depends upon the acceptance of the different elements as comprising a unity. Otherwise the narrative confusion of referring forwards to the volunteer, and back to the empty emergency department, whilst looking at a busy ward would not make any sense at all.

THE EMPLOYERS: AN ABSENT 'THEY'

Having seen how textually complex the relations between picture and sound can be at a given moment, it is useful to return to the main topic of the story, namely the industrial dispute itself, to see if these relations contribute to its signification. Here the apparent unity of picture, speech and sound is ideologically productive, because there are significant points at which the sense of the speech and that of the picture go out of sync. These are the points when the employers are brought into the story.

As a matter of fact the employers are never named directly as such, and no employer's representative is interviewed or shown. This is a significant absence, given that there is an interview with the shop steward, there are pictures of strikers, volunteers, patients and nurses, while doctors, the government and the opposition are mentioned verbally; every party to the dispute gets a look-in except the employers. But they do make their shadowy presence felt (shots 16–17):

> Because of the unpredictable/nature of the strike action consultants at the hospital *have now been instructed* to admit only emergency cases.

The employers, then, are deleted as agents from the passive 'have now been instructed'. Verbally, the instruction seems to flow from the 'unpredictable nature of the strike action' rather than from the employers. Visually, the instruction is signified not by reference to those that issued it, but to its effect. Whilst the voice-over says what the instruction 'means' ('It means that children . . . are being turned away'), the picture shows a man and child approaching the camera, crossing in front of it to stop at the hospital entrance, where the child continues to gaze back at the viewer. Thus the employers cannot be mapped into any position or point of view with respect to the viewer – there is no point of view from which to observe an absent 'they'.

In section VI the employers figure again, but this time they are first encountered not in the context of the strike's effects, but of its ascribed (plot) 'cause'. The voice-over tells about the strikers' reported refusal to supply any cleaners, whilst the picture shows the strikers in question – here there is sense-synchronicity between picture and sound (shot 19) The next shot opens with a close-up of a banner being held by the picketers, which reads 'NUPE [the union] Say: Even Dragons Must Eat'. This is in fact the closest the viewer ever gets to an unmediated presentation of the strikers' own point of view, apart from a placard shown in shot 10 which states the wage demand ('£60 a Week Basic'). But whereas the placard is shown whilst the voice-over describes the strikers' actions, and can thus be understood as sense-synchronized, the banner is shown at the very moment when the employers make their very indirect appearance. So the juxtaposition of picture and sound at this point actually gives:

> Picture: Even Dragons Must Eat
> Sound : The authorities think differently

Although the juxtaposition can hardly be read as showing what the authorities think of NUPE's enigmatic message, there is sufficient force in the conventional assumption of a unity between picture and sound for a correspondence of some kind to be proposed. It seems that the relationship here is one of cause and effect: the strikers cause (cleaners aren't part of emergency service) and the employers are affected (they think differently). Thus according to the relationship between picture and sound it is the strikers who cause the closure of the hospital directly, not the 'authorities' whose decision it actually was.

Moments later the employers figure again, but this time in the same context as in section IV. Whilst the screen shows the effect of the action (empty emergency department and ward), the employers are encountered verbally (shots 22–3):

> since yesterday it's been completely empty. The *hospital authorities* closed it down because of a lack of clean wards . . .

Thus when the employers figure in the actuality sequences they are displaced verbally into 'instructions' and 'authorities', and visually into the strike's effects rather than its causes. Because of this, it seems in the end that a point of view is established for the employers; they are collapsed into the other groups who are represented as the bearers of the strike's effects: the patients, doctors and nurses. To the extent that this is so, and because they are presented in opposition to the strikers (they think differently), the employers are aligned with the 'we' side of the we/they opposition.

RELATIONS BETWEEN SPEAKERS: WHO'S TALKING?

News is often described as being about events, but it isn't. News is a complex mixture of voices, some of which speak for themselves, whilst others speak professionally. Some of the speakers are 'institutional voices', and others are 'accessed voices'; that is, some speakers are employees of the broadcasting institution (newsreaders, correspondents, reporters), whilst others are accessed by it (these include anyone who isn't a news-person, from prime ministers to vox pops, but it may include professional voices in the form of 'experts', and these are often broadcasters and journalists themselves). The way in which this variety of voices actually appears in the news is complex. They may be present in both picture and sound as they speak, or accessed by sound but not by picture (as in recordings of parliament) or vice versa (as in the picket-line talk). Otherwise, the things people say may be quoted directly or indirectly, with or without attribution, by the institutional voices. Such quotations may be reinforced visually by being spelt out in a caption, often with an accompanying picture of the original speaker (see shot 2).

Thus it is not always easy, in the course of a news story in which all of these possibilities are deployed in one place or another, to identify exactly who is speaking at a given moment, or what relation between the speakers is being proposed. But the multiplicity of voices and speakers does not appear at the time as mere confusion, since each speaker is subordinate to the overall discursive unity of the bulletin. At this higher level of unity, the variety of voices contributes to the flow of sense. No matter who is speaking, certain terms, concepts and registers are brought into play, and in the course of the story as a whole they are either taken up, confirmed and endorsed, or set in opposition to others, or left unexploited and neglected. But once such a discursive unity has been achieved, it is useful to return to its textual sources to see which of the voices, if any, have won. Such textual gains and losses may turn out to have political implications.

'HOME HELP': A DISCOURSE OF DOMESTICITY

A good example of a unity which transcends the voices that contribute to it but clearly works to the benefit of some of those voices as against others is what may be called the discourse of domesticity. Along the way, this discourse serves to organize the whole story into a very particular kind of intelligibility. It is first encountered in the very first phrase of the story: 'Here at home'; where 'home' is the nation as distinct from abroad (which had been signified in this bulletin by the previous story about Iran). Thereafter the discourse becomes increasingly important as the story progresses. First, it displaces the more obvious discourse for such a story as this, namely the discourse of industrial relations. Whilst very little is said about wage claims and conditions of work, quite a lot is said about dusting and vacuum cleaning. Second, it becomes associated in this story with the very fluid signifier 'help'. In actual fact the word 'help' occurs thirteen times in the story, used by different voices in different contexts to mean different things. But by the end of the story, its meaning has been fixed. Here are the places where it occurs:

1 I ask him: where does his duty lie? Is it towards the patients and the doctors and nurses to *help* them? Is he therefore prepared to encourage volunteers to go in . . .?
2 As far as low-paid workers are concerned, they must expect to get a reasonable increase in pay in order to *help* them, and . . .
3 . . . those higher up the pay scale can *help* them to do so.
4 I've told the unit administrator that if, during our action, children were at risk, we would immediately leave the picket line and go in and *help*.
5 Senior nursing staff had to *help* out sorting dirty linen from the wards; it took up much of their valuable time.
6 Jenny Munns left her own housework to *help* clean a priority ward. Until unpaid volunteers like her came along, the nurses had to dust and vacuum. What made . . .
7 . . . Mrs Munns answer the appeal for *help*?
8 So I thought, w'll, you know, erm, I'm at home in the morning, it's probably a good idea to *help*.
9 Well, actually, I've been washing up and, er, *helping* out generally.
10 No patients grumbled about the paper plates, or having to *help* with the washing up afterwards. And when this tiny baby, only 30 hours old, was discharged from . . .
11 . . . hospital a day early, to *help* relieve the pressure on staff and facilities.
12 The army was called in to *help* the authorities, at London's worst affected hospital, the Westminster.
13 A hospital spokesman, who called the incident 'sabotage', said the army was contacted because other breakdown services couldn't *help*.

The first speaker is Margaret Thatcher, the then leader of the opposition. Next is the then prime minister, James Callaghan (2 and 3). Use (4) is that of the interviewed NUPE shop steward, whilst (8 and 9) are those of both the volunteers. All the other uses are those of different institutional voices: the newsreader (12 and 13); and the two film reports (5 from section IV and 6, 7, 10, 11 from section VI). Thus, interestingly, almost every participant who speaks, whether accessed or institutional, uses the word 'help'. That means, of course, that the word itself cannot be assumed to belong to any speaker, party or faction. However, it can be captured, so that what 'help' means in the given circumstances is both limited and obvious.

What captures it, in fact, is the discourse of domesticity, which proves to be the means by which help can be given to the patients and the doctors and nurses who are affected by the strike. Thus, the news tells about Jenny Munns, who left her own 'housework', so that the nurses wouldn't have to 'dust and vacuum'. She herself says that what made her answer the appeal for help was a 'neighbour', and the fact that 'I'm at home in the morning'.

The second volunteer has been helping out 'generally', and with the 'washing up'. Visually the impression of domesticity is confirmed by Mrs Munns's informal housecoat (not uniform) and by her use of the vacuum-cleaner. The reporter goes on to speak of 'paper plates', and of help with the 'washing up', about which no-one 'grumbled', but which is seen in detail on the screen.

The language is not that of an industrial dispute, much less of the political conflict between government and opposition, between Tories and Labour, or between the prime minister and the 'irresponsible minority' of strikers that is quoted at the beginning of the story. Thus 'help' has displaced politics, but it doesn't escape politics. The first time the word is heard is on the lips of Margaret Thatcher, who uses it (shot 4) in the very sense the news eventually establishes for it. She calls for volunteers to help the patients and the doctors and nurses. Conversely, Mr Callaghan's use of 'help' is in a much more directly political sense. He calls for higher-paid workers to 'help' the low paid (presumably though not explicitly by moderating their own wage claims) and he says the low-paid workers must get a pay rise to 'help' them (shot 6). But neither of these senses for 'help' is taken further in the news story. Mr Callaghan's use of the term is discursively defeated. Similarly, the NUPE shop steward offers help from the picket line. Although the news shows the very workers reckoned by the prime minister to need help, and although these very workers offer to help, the drift of the story is quite contrary to such positive identifications of the strikers themselves. The upshot is not only that 'help' comes to mean domestic help, but that the volunteers who supply it are exempted altogether from any suggestion that – seen from another point of view – their action could be seen as strike-breaking, and they themselves as scabs. In this particular news story, then, the discursive victory belongs to Margaret Thatcher, since her mobilization of a particular sense and referent for 'help' is the one that the news uses, not only as a signifier for the event, but even as a determinant of its structure; that is, the selection of the volunteers for interview as newsworthy.

A way of testing just how complete this victory has been is to compare the interview with Mrs Munns with that of the NUPE shop steward. Once again, the strategy of reversal will show how different they are. For instance, given that the shop steward's reply is about coming off the picket line and 'helping', he can be given the question asked of her:

> What [would make you] answer the appeal for help?

Whereas, she can be given a reversal of the lead-in to his interview:

> Now further action [cleaning] in other departments of the hospital is planned, though [she] claims the [strikers] themselves won't suffer.

Perhaps a more plausible reversal, however, would be of the direct questions heard in the respective interviews: what if *he* were asked 'Has it been worth it, coming [out on strike]?'; and *she* were asked 'But surely this sort of action isn't going to gain a lot of public sympathy'?

CONCLUSION: THE POLITICS OF POPULIST DISCOURSES

This discussion suggests that the representional and relational dimensions of news texts mediate between textual features on the one hand and wider cultural processes on the other. The analysis shows that those wider cultural processes are not merely invoked within textual features, but rather that textual features play an active, political role in cultural relations of power. That is to say, the news is active in the politics of sense-making, even when the stories concern matters not usually understood as directly political (a wage dispute), and even when it is striving for impartiality. The common ground between news and political struggles is what can be called popular discourse. The news strives for clarity, both of representation and of point of view, and one of the most important means it uses towards this end is populism. Populist discourses (e.g. 'domesticity') and popular idioms (e.g. 'help') are mobilized to make sense of both the world and those who represent different social and political constituencies within it (e.g. both the world and such groups are sorted into we/they categories).

However, populist discourses are also the ground upon which politicians seek to cultivate support. Thus, the news enters into unwitting collusion with Thatcherism in seeking to make sense of the public service workers' dispute by means of notions of help and domesticity. For by so doing the news allows its populism to be colonized or captured by Thatcherite populism. Along the way it denies the viewer a position from which it is easy to align with the strikers, to such an extent that in the end their discourses (of industrial disputes and pay claims) become unspeakable, and the representation of 'volunteers' as scabs becomes unthinkable, which must have proved a great 'help' to Mrs Thatcher.

PAGE 2 DAILY MIRROR, *Tuesday, April 24, 1979*

'79 ELECTION SPECIAL

MAGGIE 'SHOCKER FOR THE SHOPPER'

FOOD prices would rocket under the Tories, warned Premier Jim Callaghan last night.

By MARK DOWDNEY
Political Correspondent

Family budgets would be clobbered by the Tory plan to devalue the Green Pound, the Common Market "currency" which covers food prices.

The Premier said that the Tories did not dare tell the truth about what the change would mean.

So he gave an estimate of what shoppers could expect:

Butter **UP** by 12p a lb; cheese **UP** by 11p a lb; beef **UP** by 7p a lb; bacon **UP** by 4p a lb; sugar **UP** by 3p a lb.; and bread **UP** by 1½p a loaf.

On the Tories' own admission, said Mr. Callaghan, they would be the "dear food party."

Speaking in Wandsworth, London, he attacked the Tories for failing to put a price on their plans.

Of Margaret Thatcher, he said: "People want to be sure they are not buying a pig in a poke."

Mr. Callaghan pledged that Labour's priority in the next five years would be to defeat rising prices.

The trade unions had an agreement with the Government to work together to bring the rate of price increases down to five per cent. and less.

● **The Pound in Your Pocket — Page Five**

UNIONS BOOST JIM'S HOPES

By TERRy PATTINSON

TRADE UNION leaders gave Mr. Callaghan two election boosts last night.

BOOST No. 1 came when the Scottish Trades Union Congress rejected a militant resolution on picketing.

BOOST No 2 came from Engineering President Terry Duffy who said he would oppose a double-your-money pay claim at his union's annual conference later this week.

Scottish TUC delegates meeting at Inverness turned down a call to give pickets more protection.

The defeated motion asked for legislation to prevent police from limiting the number of pickets and demanded stronger laws to allow pickets to stop vehicles.

At Eastbourne, moderate leaders of the Engineers face a punch-up over Left-wing demands for £120-a-week basic compared with the present £60.

Mr. Duffy said: "I do not believe in setting insurmountable targets."

The judge 'is an ass'

TOP judge Lord Denning got a wigging yesterday for his claim that the unions were "almost above the law."

Labour's deputy leader Michael Foot said Britain's Master of the Rolls had "made an ass of himself."

Attacking the claim as "grotesque," he added: "It's a very loose phrase

Lord Denning hit out at the unoins' "challenge" to the law

Speaking on BBC radio Mr. Foot retorted: "It's a very foolish way to talk of one of Britain's great democratic institutions."

Mrs T-party

BREWING UP: Mrs. Thatcher samples a selection of brews during a visit to a Newcastle-upon-Tyne tea factory yesterday.

Tory pay freeze still on cards

By PETER PRENDERGAST,

TORY leader Margaret Thatcher refused yesterday to rule out the pospibility of a pay freeze if her party comes to power.

But she said that it would be only a very temporary measure if it was used.

A freeze was a different matter from an incomes policy, Mrs. Thatcher told her daily news conference in London.

Too rigid

Incomes policies over the last twelve years had proved that they couldn't be operated for more than two years, she said.

After that they broke because they were too rigid and the pay differentials of skilled men suffered.

But she warned: "I do not think that any responsible government could rule out a pay freeze for a very limited period."

Similar

Mrs. Thatcher accused Labour of putting round two particular scares — that the Tories would double VAT and increase school meals by 10p.

Both were very similar to what Labour had done, she said.

Education Secretary Shirley Williams had put up school meals by 10p at one jump.

And Chancellor Denis Healey increased VAT "tremendously" in his first Budget.

'More cash for all'

TAXPAYERS would "notice the difference" in their pay packets under a Tory government, Shadow Chancellor Sir Geoffrey Howe said yesterday.

Speaking on a BBC radio phone-in, he promised a very significant change in our tax environment."

He said: "We have got to make a substantial change and we will."

He said people would feel it worthwhile working, investing, saving and changing jobs.

Sir Geoffrey also said that the Tories were not planning a great denationalisation campaign.

But he said he wanted to expose public firms to the same kind of competition and discipline as private enterprise faces.

TAX CUTS? YOU MUST BE KIDDING

LIBERAL leader David Steel called for an end to the tax cut "kidding" yesterday.

He said there could not be an overnight revolution in taxation. It would not happen the day after the election.

Reform

"Don't let them kid you," he said.

Mr. Steel, speaking on the Jimmy Young radio show, put forward his own party's plans for tax reform.

The Liberals wanted reforms spread over five years to bring income tax down to 20p in the £. To pay for these cuts, VAT would be raised to a standard rate of 10 per cent.

As Waite sees it — Page 4

Home Help for Populist Politics: Margaret Thatcher winning the 1979 General Election with a short sharp dose of domesticity. Even the Labour *Daily Mirror* (24 April 1979) seemed unable to resist giving Mrs Thatcher a 'helping' hand with icons of homeliness that were seriously at odds with Thatcherite policies.

APPENDIX Transcript of part of BBC *Nine O'Clock News*, 1 February 1979 (running time 8 min 40 sec)

Story section	*Shot number*	*Type of framing*	*Description of scene, sound, movement, names*	*Words spoken*
(I) (40 sec)	1	MS No camera-movement	Newsreader (Angela Rippon); direct address to camera, eye-contact	Here at home the dispute by public service workers is still spreading. Half the hospitals in England and Wales and some in Scotland can now open their doors only to emergency cases. Apart from the hospitals the strike is affecting more ambulance services and schools, as well as water and sewerage works. In the Commons the Prime Minister urged the hospital ancillary workers to 'go back to work' while negotiations could continue on what he called a 'proper basis'. The Prime Minister also said:
	2	Graphic	The quotation reproduced in white-on-red across screen. Words read by newsreader, VO	It is not acceptable in any community that sick human beings, whether adults or children, should have their food denied them and proper attention forbidden to them.
(II) (2 min 30 sec)	3	MS No camera-movement	Political correspondent (Rodney Foster); direct address to camera, eye-contact. Set left top, a chroma-key graphic background with line-drawing of Big Ben and the word POLITICS. Superimposed name caption	To be fair to the Prime Minister he's been among the first to condemn action by what he sees as an irresponsible minority; action which he's already decried as 'totally unacceptable to any decent trade unionist'. But what the Conservatives are so angry about is why his ministers keep insisting that the best way to deal with things is through co-operation with the unions concerned. For the Tories argue that any claim to a so-called 'special relationship' between Labour and the unions has long since been shattered. So as Mrs Thatcher did again today, they demand firm government action. 'Where's the government in that?' has become the favourite opposition response to the latest spate of ministerial statements. And despite Mr Callaghan's sharp words today about not involving the sick in industrial disputes, Mrs Thatcher wanted more:

4	Graphic	Line-drawing lower right of House of Commons with superimposed B/W still of Mrs Thatcher, left. Name caption – Mrs Thatcher: opposition leader, centre. Mrs Thatcher's voice, VO	It is precisely because the things which he spoke of are not acceptable, and precisely because many of the tasks could be done by volunteers that I ask him: where does his duty lie? Is it towards the patients and the doctors and nurses to help them? Is he therefore prepared to encourage volunteers to go in, in some hospitals they're working well. Will he make his position clear?
5	MS	(Return to shot 3)	Well, Mr Callaghan insisted this wasn't a governmental matter; of course, they wouldn't stand in the way, but it must be for the local hospital authorities to decide whether or not volunteers could usefully be employed. Labour MPs are by now of course thoroughly disgruntled with all that's going on, many of them accusing the Tories of political provocation. So a number pressed the Prime Minister to give a clear recognition of the low-paid workers' justifiable case for a decent wage. Mr Callaghan said all these disputes could be settled straight away by meeting the demands in full. But that was something which should not commend itself to anyone. Nevertheless, he went on:
6	Graphic	As in shot 4, but picture is of Mr Callaghan, and caption reads James Callaghan: Prime Minister. The words are in his voice. VO	As far as low-paid workers are concerned, they must expect to get a reasonable increase in pay in order to help them, and those higher up the pay scale can help them to do so. And I trust there will be a return to some co-operation in these matters as distinct from the, I was going to say the free collective bargaining, but it would be more true to say free collective vandalism that's going on now.
7	MS	(Return to shot 3)	Well, a parting shot which did nothing to endear him to his left-wing MPs, and certainly these troubles won't go away for the government, with MPs probably having an emergency debate on Monday night.

cont'd

Story section	*Shot number*	*Type of framing*	*Description of scene, sound, movement, names*	*Words spoken*
(III) (30 sec)	8	MS	(Return to shot 1)	The Queen Elizabeth Hospital for children in East London is threatened with a 24-hour strike from midnight. All 103 children there are seriously ill, and union officials have agreed that a limited number of staff will remain on duty during the stoppage. Another children's hospital, the world-famous Great Ormond Street Hospital, experienced two lightning strikes today by porters and kitchen staff. But the hospital authorities were able to keep essential services going for the 260 patients. A report by Christopher Morris:
(IV) (1 min 25 sec	9	CU	hospital entrance sign reading CHILDREN	
		Reframe to M–LS	Picket line gathered round entrance, their voices audible, not the words	The porters and kitchen staff didn't give much warning about their strike – just five minutes'
	10	CU	Placard with wage demand: '£60 a week basic'	notice. They then
		Reframe		walked out to join the
		to LS	Direct shot of picket line across centre; dark building and NUPE sign above; street with parked cars lower foreground. Ambient sound	picket line and stayed out for four hours. Now further action
	11	VLS	Same scene, longer shot, traffic passes between camera and picket	in other departments of the hospital is planned, though

12	MS	Interviewee (Conway Xavier; NUPE shop steward); set to screen right, looking out of frame-left to unseen interviewer. NUPE sign centre-left. Superimposed name caption. Lip-sync. speech, with reporter's VO. Ambient sound audible	they claim the children themselves won't suffer. (Xavier, lip-sync.) Yes, we can guarantee, erm, I've told the unit administrator that if, during our action, children were at risk, we would immediately leave the picket line and go in and help. (Reporter VO) But surely this sort of action isn't going to gain a lot of public sympathy. (Xavier, lip-sync.) We believe we've shown responsibility, um, we've been traditionally a very passive workforce, and we hope that by workers at this world-famous hospital taking action it will bring public sympathy to our side.
13	M–LS	Two nurses pulling trolley towards and past camera. Minor camera movement motivated by theirs	Inside the hospital the disruption was more than just the minimum the union had promised. Only two cooks were allowed
14	MS pan	Boy (patient?) pushes trolley, pan left to follow, and to reveal nurses and trolleys in lift. Ambient sound	to remain, so lunch was a little late today for nearly three hundred young patients.
15	M–CU	Linen bin; hand dips in to gather	Senior nursing staff had to help out
	Reframe	sheets, camera follows movement	sorting dirty linen from the wards;
	(Tilt) MS	finds nurse's face and action	it took up much of their valuable time.
16	MS	Grubby workbench with bucket on	And with rubbish left
	Pan	Camera pans to find rubbish pile. Mute	to pile up in the basement there's a growing risk to health. Because of the unpredictable
17	LS	Street shot, man and child walk into view and towards camera. They	nature of the strike action consultants at the hospital have now been instructed to admit only emergency cases.
	Pan	turn, camera follows as they cross in front of it to entrance. Child gazes at camera while they walk. Camera holds on child at entrance peering back at it	It means that children awaiting non-urgent operations and treatment are being turned away at least until the present dispute is over.

cont'd

Story section	*Shot number*	*Type of framing*	*Description of scene, sound, movement, names*	*Words spoken*
(V) (30 sec)	18	MS	(Return to shot 1)	It's clear that the Code of Conduct drawn up by the unions to protect emergency services is not being observed everywhere. But the National Union of Public Employees is urging local officials to 'pass the code on' to pickets. However, one NUPE official said tonight their tactics would be to 'put the screws on tighter'. More hospitals are being forced to refuse all but emergencies. Even then there's disagreement over what constitutes an emergency. From the Harold Wood Hospital at Romford in Essex, Philip Hayton reports:
(VI) (2 min 45 sec)	19	LS	Line of picketers under umbrellas seen across roadway. Ambient sound	This hospital's strikers refused to supply any cleaners, because they say that's not part of their emergency service.
	20	CU	Makeshift white banner, handwritten to read 'NUPE say Even Dragons Must Eat'	The authorities think differently
		Reframe to LS	Pull-out/pan reveals same picket line as in shot 19	and they've closed the hospital to all admissions including
			Camera steadies on long-shot	emergencies.
	21	LS No camera-movement	Interior long-shot shows reporter addressing camera, eye-contact, in empty hospital room with beds visible. Lip-sync.	(Lip-sync.) This is the hospital's accident and emergency department. It's normally the busiest place in a hospital. Every day doctors treat up to a hundred patients who are suffering from everything from cuts and bruises to

22	CU	Mute cutaway to equipment, showing instructions: ' The Treatment of Cardiac Arrest'. Reporter VO	heart attacks and appendicitis.
	Tilt	Tilt down reveals more equipment	But since yesterday, it's been completely empty.
23	LS	Empty ward; nurse crosses in front of camera. No camera movement. Mute	The hospital authorities closed it down because of a lack of
24	LS	Active ward; nurses at bedside left. Woman vacuum-cleaning centre; sync. sound. Patients in bed right background	clean wards for patients to go to after their treatment here.
	Reframe	Zoom in to find and follow movement of woman cleaning. Reporter VO	(Ambient sound of vacuum faded up momentarily.) Jenny Munns left her own housework to help clean a priority ward. Until unpaid volunteers like her came
	Reframe	Pull out to wider shot showing cleaner emerging into open space	along, the nurses had to dust and vacuum. What made Mrs Munns answer the appeal for help?
25	MS	Interviewee, centre, looking out of frame left, hands resting on vacuum handle, ward visible behind. No eye-contact, no caption, no camera-movement. Reporter's question VO	Well, I've a neighbour that's been in here, and she's been desperately ill at times, and she comes and does a lot of voluntary work, and yes'day morning she came, and she said there was only three on this ward, and would I be willing to come? So I thought, w'll, you know, erm, I'm at home in the morning, it's probably a good idea to help. (Reporter VO) Has it been worth it, coming? (Mrs Munns lip-sync.) Oh yes, yes, they're so appreciative (laughs), they really are.
26	M–CU	Woman propped on bed, looking out of frame right. No eye-contact, no caption, no camera-movement. Reporter's question VO	(Reporter VO) What have you been doing? (Interviewee lip-sync.) Well, actually, I've been washing up, and, er, helping out generally. But this morning, I had to have an X-ray, so someone else took over for me.

cont'd

Story section	*Shot number*	*Type of framing*	*Description of scene, sound, movement, names*	*Words spoken*
	27	CU	Plate with food on it, being prodded with plastic knife and fork. No camera-movement	Despite the irritations, morale on this ward was high. No patients grumbled about the
	28	M–CU	Plate being lifted into shot from washing-up bowl	paper plates, or having to help with
		Reframe	Pull out and up to reveal two nurses washing up, other figures in background	the washing up afterwards.
	29	LS	Exterior shot; nurse carrying baby towards camera	And when this tiny baby, only 30 hours old, was discharged from hospital a day
		Reframe	Nurse and baby approach to MS, pan to follow movement as she hands baby to woman waiting in back of car	early, to help relieve the pressure on staff and facilities, his parents shrugged their shoulders (car door slams sync.), did not complain
	30	M–LS	car shown driving away from camera, out of screen right	and left for home.
		Reframe	pull out to wider shot. Sync. of car motor	
(VII) (20 sec)	31	MS	(Return to shot 1)	The army was called in to help the authorities at London's worst affected hospital, the Westminster.
	32	Still	Monochrome still-photo showing army vehicle right foreground, men centre background, wheel propped against wall left	An ambulance and a van were found with slashed tyres across the delivery entrance. A hospital spokesman, who called the incident 'sabotage', said the army was contacted because other breakdown services couldn't help.

Abbreviations: CU = close-up; MS = mid-shot; LS = long-shot; B/W = black and white; VO = voice-over.

Part III

Paedocracy

Chapter 6

Invisible fictions*

PASSPORT CONTROL

Although television as an institution is dependent upon audiences, it is by no means certain what a television audience is.

However, it seems that this is not the only uncertainty facing those working in the field of television studies. Ann Kaplan, for instance, in her introduction to *Regarding Television,* remarks:

> The structure, form, content and context for British television are so radically different from those of its American counterpart that everything has to be rethought by critics in this country [the USA]. Television scholarship is simply not exportable in the easy manner of film criticism.[1]

The idea that international television criticism is a contradiction in terms is not confined to the American side of the Atlantic. In fact it has been taken even further by British writer John Ellis, who suggests not only that television scholarship is unexportable but also that one nation's television is 'incomprehensible' to observers from other nations. In the preliminaries to his *Visible Fictions* Ellis confesses that at the time of writing he had never visited the United States, and continues:

> This really demonstrates an insuperable problem with all writing about broadcast TV: unlike cinema, which in its commercial sectors has a highly integrated international aspect, broadcast TV is an essentially national activity for the vast majority of its audience. Broadcast TV is the private life of the nation-state . . . incomprehensible for anyone who is outside its scope.[2]

Neither Kaplan nor Ellis qualifies these remarks with customary scholarly

* Originally published as John Hartley (1987) 'Invisible fictions: television audiences, paedocracy, pleasure', *Textual Practice*, 1(2), 121–38. Published in the USA in Robert J. Thompson and Gary Burns (eds) (1989) *Television Studies: Textual Analysis*, New York: Praeger.

caution. Both write in absolute terms: television is incomprehensible for those outside its scope; television criticism is simply not exportable; everything has to be rethought; the problem is insuperable; it applies to all writing about broadcast television; television is essentially national. Furthermore, their remarks are not isolated. Quite a lot of media criticism in recent years has been conducted around a perceived gulf, as wide as the Atlantic Ocean, between American and Anglo-European perspectives.[3] This gulf, once invoked, is made to explain such divisions as those between empirical and theoretical approaches; so-called transmission and ritual models of communication; liberal–pluralist and Marxist theories; even the disciplinary location of media studies – in America it's a social science, in Britain it's in the humanities.

If these divisions really constitute an insuperable problem, then of course international television scholarship does become impossible. Or, more accurately, the kind of criticism that constructs as its object an *essential* form, on the model of 'cinema' or 'literature', becomes impossible. What the uncertainties noted above do imply is that there is no such thing as 'television' – an abstract, general form with invariable features. Neither does television have any *essential* mode of production, distribution and consumption, despite the very obvious fact that many television shows, series and formats display exactly that 'highly integrated international aspect' claimed by Ellis for cinema.

As for television studies, a certain uneasiness with the erection of essential, national boundaries around television scholarship has been voiced by Willard D. Rowland and Bruce Watkins in their introduction to *Interpreting Television*. They discuss 'this old and contentious issue', largely with reference to a myth of American 'dependence' on European thought, and show that, although that dependence is mythical, the consequences of reiterating the myth have been real enough. They argue that, although it is tempting, it is inadequate to categorize current research by means of a 'bi-polar, European/critical versus American/liberal dichotomy'. They conclude that 'it is becoming increasingly difficult to speak about any pure national or even regional tradition of thought, especially in communication and cultural studies'.[4] If it is indeed difficult to speak of pure national traditions of thought in this context, it may be easier, certainly more productive, to speak of impurity. It may even be possible to see in impurities not a problem but a fundamental criterion for cultural studies.

The productivity of impurity, of transgressing national boundaries unawares, has been amply illustrated, paradoxically enough, by John Ellis. Having erected pure – insuperable – boundaries between British and American television, and between British and American writing on television, he then subverts this line of thinking completely:

Sudden exposure to the often bizarre practices of broadcast TV in

> another country can stimulate fresh thinking about the whole phenomenon of TV. This is the case with Raymond Williams's concept of 'flow' which resulted from his culture shock on seeing US TV. Seeing another country's broadcast TV has the effect of 'making strange' something we normally take for granted: TV, normally habitual and bound into the life of the nation, suddenly becomes an alien and inexplicable series of events.[5]

Thus, transgressing the frontiers of the familiar, the national, produces culture shock, the bizarre, the alien, the inexplicable, which turns out to be the very condition for understanding, stimulating fresh thinking by breaking habitual bonds. Even so, it has to be noted that some bonds remain taken for granted: Ellis is still presuming that there is such a thing as 'the whole phenomenon' of television, in the teeth of his own evidence to the contrary.

TELEVISION: ANOTHER COUNTRY?

Since the concept of the nation seems to play such an important role in specifying both television and TV scholarship, it would seem to be a good idea to look at what the concept of the nation might mean. However, it wouldn't be such a good idea to substitute for the essentialism of 'television' another kind of essentialism, for instance, the notion of an essential 'America', or 'Britain', or 'Australia', or even 'the nation'. Nations cannot be understood 'purely', that is, from their own supposed intrinsic or essential features. Neither television nor nations can be understood at all, in fact, except in relational terms. They have no pure, intrinsic properties but only differences from other, related domains. Benedict Anderson has argued that they are by definition limited or impure, because each nation is defined by *other* nations:

> Even the largest of them, encompassing perhaps a billion living human beings, has finite, if elastic boundaries, beyond which lie other nations. No nation imagines itself coterminous with mankind [*sic*]. The most messianic nationalists do not dream of the day when all the members of the human race will join their nation in the way that it was possible, in certain epochs, for, say, Christians to dream of a wholly Christian planet.[6]

It follows that nations can only be defined by what they are not; their individual identity consists in the recognition and establishment of finite boundaries that are simultaneously elastic. This formula generates a well-known definition not only of nations but also of signs; like signs, nations are constructs. But, like signs, nations are constructs not of any external, referential world but of *discourses*; Anderson calls nations 'imagined communities'. They are communities because everyone has confidence in the existence of others within their nation; they are imagined because there is absolutely no external warrant for this confidence:

> An American will never meet, or even know the names of more than a handful of his 240,000,000-odd fellow Americans. He has no idea of what they are up to at any one time. But he has complete confidence in their steady, anonymous, simultaneous activity.[7]

Where does this confidence come from? Among other sources, Anderson mentions the newspaper as a mechanism for providing imaginary links between members of a nation. Newspapers are at one and the same time the ultimate fiction, since they construct the imagined community, and the basis of a mass ritual or ceremony that millions engage in every day: 'What more vivid figure for the secular, historically clocked, imagined community can be envisioned?' asks Anderson.[8] Of course, a more vivid metaphorical figure for the imagined communities of nations can indeed be envisioned. It's called television. Indeed, like newspapers, television may be more than merely a metaphor for imagined communities; it is one of the prime sites upon which a given nation is constructed for its members. And, as we have seen, the nation is, concomitantly, one of the sites upon which television has been constructed as a concept.

Like nations, television as an institution is limited, impure, with no essence but only difference from other television, other forms, other institutions. Nevertheless, television does frequently transgress national boundaries – the idea of its essential nation-ality is as imagined, or fictional, as the idea of the nation itself. Certain programme types, especially sporting championships, Olympic Games, news pictures, beauty and other contests, award ceremonies within the general showbiz domain, together with the more recent genre of 'aid' shows, may be seen more or less simultaneously by hundreds of millions of people, sometimes making it possible for producers to dream, as it were, of a wholly tuned-in planet. As well, television transgresses national frontiers in more routine ways, notably at the level of transnational ownership and control of both production and distribution, and at the level of international sales of individual shows and series. It follows that if television can be imagined as an 'essentially national activity', as Ellis puts it, it can only be so imagined on behalf of the experience of audiences: the audience is constructed as comprising those for whom television is indeed the 'private life of the nation-state'. In short, one unwarranted, invisible fiction – the imagined community of the nation – is used to invent and explain another: the television audience.

INVISIBLE FICTIONS

Television is, like nations, a construct of specific institutions; what it 'means' turns on how those institutional discourses construct it for their own specific purposes. Among the institutions that construct television discursively, three stand out: the television industry (networks, stations, producers, etc.); political/legal institutions (usually formalized as regulatory bodies, and intermittently as government-sponsored inquiries and reports); and critical institutions (academic, journalistic and – surprisingly rarely – self-constituted audience organizations or pressure groups). Each of these institutions is, of course, marked by internal contradictions, hierarchies and historical shifts, and by manifold differences from each of the others. However, despite the fact that they don't speak with one voice, all three tend to legitimate their actions and interventions in the name of the same imagined community. All claim to speak, albeit with quite different voices, on behalf of the audience.

It follows that audiences are not just constructs; they are the invisible fictions that are produced institutionally in order for various institutions to take charge of the mechanisms of their own survival. Audiences may be imagined empirically, theoretically or politically, but in all cases the product is a fiction that serves the need of the imagining institution. In no case is the audience 'real', or external to its discursive construction. There is no 'actual' audience that lies beyond its production as a category, which is merely to say that audiences are only ever encountered *per se* as *representations*. Furthermore, they are so rarely *self*-represented that they are almost always absent, making TV audiences perhaps the largest 'community' in the world that is subject to what Edward Said has dubbed the discourse of 'orientalism',[9] whereby disorganized communities which have never developed or won adequate means of self-representation, and which exist almost wholly within the imagination or rhetoric of those who speak on their behalf, become the 'other' of powerful, imperial discourses.[10]

What kind of fiction is the orientalized audience imagined to be? In the critical domain, two influential recent developments in the theoretical conceptualization of audiences seem noteworthy. The first, elaborated in relation to cinema and associated largely with the journal *Screen* in the 1970s, is applied by John Ellis to television. Here the audience is imagined as 'the subject', positioned or constructed as a textual/institutional effect of television. However, Ellis's 'viewer' is far from being an effect of television; Ellis's viewer is an effect of Ellis's stated project, which is to produce an argument about the general aesthetics of broadcast television in comparison with those of cinema. Ellis is preoccupied with the idea that television has, or might have, a 'specific signifying practice', and that such a thing is what unifies television. Hence the argument is driven, ineluctably it seems, to imagining a unified viewer to go with this unified signifying practice:

> The viewer is constituted as a normal citizen. This is the position constructed for the TV viewer by the processes of broadcast TV; many

viewers occupy the very position which TV addresses, even if they would never consider themselves to be such a strange being as a normal citizen.[11]

A strange being indeed, and one produced by that totally unwarranted confidence in the existence of the nation noted above. Indeed, Ellis's viewer is imagined as coterminous with the ideal bearer of the concept of the nation: the 'normal citizen'. Not content with imagining the 'normal citizen' as a fictional construct or textual position produced by television's signifying practice, however, Ellis then asserts (on their behalf, without consultation) that 'many viewers occupy [this] very position'. Thus Ellis's viewer is an invisible fiction, a construct that is a figment of the argument's imagination.

The second influential recent approach to audiences is that of David Morley in and following his study *The 'Nationwide' Audience*. Morley's work was ground-breaking when it appeared, offering the hope of integrating theoretical approaches such as those of *Screen* and the Centre for Contemporary Cultural Studies in Birmingham, in their different ways, with the more traditional concerns of empirical audience research. Thus, although Morley is astute and convincing in his account of theoretical issues, his work retains a commitment to an 'actual' audience that – the research paradigm *requires* it – is an independent entity. Empirical research is based on the presumption that audiences are not merely the product of research into them but exist prior to, apart from and beyond the activities of both television and television research. Unlike Ellis, but like traditional audience researchers, Morley sets off in search of the audience. Unlike traditional researchers, however, he tramps the country seeking not preferences, attitudes, opinions and tastes but the relation between television and class. Thus he seeks his audience among already-constituted groups which he feels able to identify in class terms – groups of students taking courses in various kinds of educational establishment. The shop stewards, trade-union officials, bank managers, apprentices and students of various other kinds are described in terms of their class 'background', though no warrant is ever offered for the very precise labels Morley uses. He never explains how he distinguishes between, for instance, 'skilled working class', 'skilled upper working class', 'upper working class' and 'working class'.[12] The fact that some of his chosen groups were unfamiliar with the chosen show (*Nationwide*), because he showed them a different regional version or because they habitually watched the commercial channel, is not deemed significant. And the fact that the show was screened to them in a setting that is itself discursively productive in ways that necessarily affect what the 'social subjects' said about it was, says Morley, merely 'situational'.[13]

Clearly then, for Morley, an audience is an audience, whether it is 'responding' in an educational/work setting or 'decoding' in a family/home context. For Morley, the 'cultural and linguistic codes a person has available to them' is a matter not affected by the 'situation' in which those persons are watching a programme dealing with financial and union issues during courses in banking or trade union studies. And an audience's cultural competence to 'decode' is not significantly affected by the fact that they might never have seen the show before. An audience is an audience at home or at work, despite the fact that Morley's groups are carefully chosen and sorted into class 'background' rather than being interviewed at home. Clearly, Morley's audience too is an invisible fiction, produced by his project, which was itself a product of academic/critical institutional discourses. His audience is no more real than Ellis's, and no more independent of the research than any other experimental subject. It is Morley's *method* that is empirical, not the audience he constructs for his research.

In Morley's more recent *Family Television* the method is more sensitive to audience situation and the project more interested in gender than in class. But I would still be cautious about accepting the families Morley interviews as 'the TV audience', not only because twenty or so families in the south-east of England aren't readily generalizable, but also because the whole point of the project is to test *Morley's* imaginings (against 'real' or 'natural' audiences), which means the audience as we know it in the book is called into being by the project, and is not self-constituted in ways it would recognize, let alone choose for itself. For instance, the preoccupation with gender is Morley's, not that of the families, and it derives from Morley's institutional/theoretical situation. Of course families are engaged in gender politics, but the choice to foreground them was Morley's, not theirs, as can be demonstrated by his relative neglect of gender, in favour of class, in *The 'Nationwide' Audience*. In short, *Family Television* makes sense in relation to Morley's intellectual commitments, not in relation to those of the audience.[14]

A PAEDOCRATIC REGIME

Even innovatory and critical work such as Ellis's and Morley's, whether theoretical or empirical in mode, is not exempt from a tendency to essentialize the audience. Ellis makes it essentially a 'normal citizen'. Morley's 'social subject' is more complex, being inflected by class differences in particular, but even so his project assumes that audiences have intrinsic (observable) properties, and his very title implies that they are to be found with essentially the same properties 'nationwide'. If audiences can be understood in this way in critical, academic discourses, then the tendency to imagine them as independently existing, essential entities that are also nations is abundantly amplified in the practical discourses of the TV industry and of its regulatory bodies. This is no doubt partly because both the industry and its regulatory bodies are obliged not only to speak *about* an audience but – crucially, for them – to talk *to* one as well: they need not only to *represent* audiences but to enter into *relations* with them (see chapter 5).

The way in which corporate executives and professional producers imagine audiences is particularly important, since it determines to some extent what goes on air, and it may help to explain why the industry acts as it does. Conversely, the way in which regulatory bodies imagine the audience may help to account for some of the things that don't get on the air. Turning, first, to the industry, it is clear that as far as private opinions of producers are concerned there may be as many views of the audience as there are personnel, and certainly such views will display contradictory aspects. However, in so far as audiences can be understood as imagined communities that are also nations, then it is relevant to ask what system or manner of rule or government – what *regime* – characterizes such communities. In other words, it isn't the personal opinions of individuals which are at issue here but an institutional system – a construction of the audience that organizes the industry's practices and serves its institutional needs and purposes. The institutional needs and purposes of the television industry are survival and profitability, to be achieved (hopefully) by audience maximization and by minimizing risks and uncertainties.

Audiences are *paedocratized* to serve these needs. For the industry, television is a *paedocratic regime*. The audience is imagined as having childlike qualities and attributes. Television discourse addresses its viewers as children. This regime does not govern all television everywhere all the time, of course. But there may be a 'law' which states: the bigger the target audience, the more it will be paedocratized. Thus US network television is the most paedocratic regime of all. However, smaller networks and stations are by no means exempt from the tendency to paedocratize audiences, if only because they buy network product and operate according to models of popular television generated by network. Indeed, it isn't the absolute size of a target audience that determines whether or not it will be paedocratized but rather the proportion of the population (local, state or national) that might conceivably be attracted: the higher the proportion, the more paedocratic the regime.

What do those who work at the centre of US network television imagine about the audience? How do they fill out their invisible fictions with plausible attributes? Often the fiction is invested with those attributes that best explain or justify the professionals' own practices. Many examples can be found in Todd Gitlin's *Inside Prime Time*. In fact, Gitlin saves one of these comments for the last paragraph of the book, where it refers not just to audiences but to the whole television industry, and it serves as an epigraph not only for the industry's view of its practices but for Gitlin's too. Gitlin cites Michael Kozoll, co-creator of *Hill Street Blues*:

> Which truth to conclude with . . .? Let the last word go to Michael Kozoll. . . . Halfway through the second season [of *Hill Street Blues*], Kozoll said he had finally found the metaphor for television he had long been seeking. Doing episodic television, he said, is like raising a retarded child. By which he meant that there are only so many things it will ever learn to do, no matter how much you love the child, no matter how much effort and care and intelligence you lavish upon it. It will never shine. One could add: Its little accomplishments are also miraculous.[15]

So says Todd Gitlin, whose pessimism about television seems matched only by his pessimistic and very conservative view of 'retarded' children. Elsewhere, however, Gitlin cites Marvin J. Chomsky, director of *Attica*, *Holocaust* and *Inside the Third Reich*, who justifies network paedocracy by reference to its need to win ratings:

> Our audience is the guy who's used to walking around and getting a beer. We've got to reach him. He's a guy who hasn't made much of a commitment to give his rapt attention to what we're offering, right? We're going for the eighty million who will watch something. An infant in a cradle likes to watch things that move. So there you are. We go in for close-ups and we try to find the conflicts.[16]

This 'conventional wisdom'[17] is perhaps best exemplified in the work of Aaron Spelling ('in a class by himself', says Gitlin, for network successes), producer of *The Rookies*, *S.W.A.T.*, *Starsky and Hutch*, *Charlie's Angels*, *The Love Boat*, *Fantasy Island*, *Vega$*, *Hart to Hart*, *T.J. Hooker* and *Dynasty*, among other top-rated shows. Spelling has called his products 'mind candy' and 'fast-food entertainment'. His shows have 'tennis-match dialogue' and 'show and tell' plots – 'on a Spelling show any plot point important enough to be signalled once is signalled twice'.[18] Gitlin cites a lengthy insider's anecdote which is designed to show that even the smallest details of scripting, representation and semiosis are determined by the concept of a childlike audience. In particular, narrative suspense is constructed according to the conventions of children's theatre. The insider explains Spelling's methods:

> The villain walks out onstage and says 'Heh-heh-heh! I have the secret matchbook, and I am going to hide it. I am going to put it behind this basket, and the heroine will never find it. Heh-heh-heh!' And he walks off. Now the heroine comes on and says, 'Where oh where is the secret matchbook?' And all the kids in the audience say, 'It's behind the basket! It's behind the basket!' That's what Aaron does. He believes that's what the American audience is you see.[19]

And Gitlin comments: 'by any Network standard, it all works.' Indeed according to Gitlin, 'Spelling embraced the form's simplifications so fervently he left his personal impress on the medium', in the shape of 'two-generation pairings' of a father-like 'sage and authoritative elder' overseeing a team of youthful, sibling-like peers who in turn oversee the rest of the diegetic world, 'patrolling the street nasties and keeping recalcitrant, childish reality under control'.[20] In short, the mechanisms of representation, together with the diegetic world that they produce, are paedocratically organized to communicate with an audience which is itself believed to relate to television paedocratically.

CHILD'S PLAY

Why do industry professionals invent the audience in the image of a retarded child, or of an infant in the cradle – with or without a beer – who is just about sharp enough to spot the movement of moustache-twirling villainy? One reason is that audiences are, literally, unknowable. Gitlin quotes Scott Siegler, the then CBS vice-president for drama development: 'Because it's a mass audience – it's an unimaginably large audience – the audience tastes are so diffused and so general that you've got to be guessing.'[21] But guess they must, since communication depends on what Valentin Volosinov has identified as dialogic orientation towards an addressee. For Volosinov, this fundamental characteristic of communication applies to books (and, we may add, allowing for technological developments, to television and the electronic media) just as much as it does to interpersonal speech. He calls such public performances 'ideological colloquy of large scale',[22] and producers can't escape it: not only must their programmes talk about something, they must also talk to someone. Since that someone is unimaginable, with attributes that are diffused and general, it is perhaps not surprising to find the image of a child, or an infant, being used to humanize the unknown interlocutor with 80 million or more heads.

There are, in fact, other options open to broadcasters, but for historical and political reasons these options have narrowed. In the past, and in other discursive regimes, audiences have been hailed variously as 'Workers!', 'Citizens!', 'The People!', etc., but such appellations have been abandoned for most purposes in western mainstream media, probably because of the leftist rhetorical connotations that such terms have been invested with since at least the Second World War. Similarly, there are unacceptable rightist connotations in some mobilizations of national identity, so care has to be exercised in this area; patriotism and commitment to what even Superman calls the American way may be understood as an automatic, natural reflex – but the knee-jerk must not be mistaken for the goose-step.

Thus broadcasters have to maintain an uneasy equilibrium; without being too populist or too nationalistic, they must strive to be popular, and speak to, for and about the nation. In addition, their popularity is organized not around citizenship or jingoism, but primarily around pleasure; the chosen path to survival and profitability is entertainment, understood as universally intelligible narrative fiction and spectacle. What this means in practice is that broadcasters tend not to insist on allegiances and identities that might be constructed on other sites but, on the contrary, to persuade audiences to abandon any such allegiances and identities, especially those of class (rendered as 'demographics' in television, of course), ethnicity and gender. Other 'variables', like region, age, education, family structure, even nation itself, may be significant, but the whole point of popular television is to cut across such divisions and to reconstitute the people involved into one unified constituency: the audience. The mechanism broadcasters have hit upon to do this impossible job is that of paedocracy. This isn't to say that television is merely infantile, childish or dedicated to the lowest common denominator – those would be certain mechanisms for losing the audience. On the contrary, broadcasters paedocratize audiences in the name of pleasure. They appeal to the playful, imaginative, fantasy, irresponsible aspects of adult behaviour. They seek the common personal ground that unites diverse and often directly antagonistic groupings in a given population. What better, then, than a fictional version of everyone's supposed childlike tendencies which might be understood as predating such social groupings? In short, a fictional image of the positive attributes of childlike pleasures is invented. The desired audience is encouraged to look up, expectant, open, willing to be guided and gratified, whenever television as an institution exclaims: 'Hi, kids!'

FAMILY-CIRCULAR ARGUMENTS

The paedocratic regime is not confined to the imagination of broadcasters, nor to the American networks. Broadcasters are encouraged in this view of audiences and the television medium itself by regulatory bodies that lay down broadcasting policy and programme standards. Such bodies tend to express little uncertainty about the audience and its attributes; indeed, so strong and obvious is this knowledge that it is used to account for the 'nature' of television, presumably on the principle that you grow like the people you live with. Here, for instance, is the Annan Committee, a Royal Commission whose report on the future of broadcasting was the biggest ever government-sponsored inquiry into television in Britain. The report is prefaced with this definition of television:

> We ourselves agree that it is in [television's] nature to communicate personalities more successfully than ideas, emotional reflexes better than intellectual analysis, specific detail better than universal principles, simplicity better than complexity, change, movement and disorder better than permanence, tranquillity and order, consequences better than

> causes. The broadcast audience does not require education or even literacy to understand and enjoy programmes.[23]

This is another version of the 'retarded child' model of television, and once again it is fictional imagining. Television doesn't have an essential 'nature', so – like 'the nation' – it is explained anthropomorphically (paedomorphically) by investing it with the very attributes that the Annan Committee imagines belong to preliterate children: personality, emotional reflexes, specific detail, simplicity, change, movement, disorder, consequences, non-literacy, lack of education.

Reserving to itself the opposing (parental) attributes – ideas, intellectual analysis, universal principles, complexity, permanence, tranquillity, order, causes, literacy, education – the Annan Committee goes on to speak on behalf of the audience which, like a preliterate child, may not need education but does require protection:

> The audience for a programme may total millions: but people watch and listen in the family circle, in their homes, so that violations of the taboos of language and behaviour, which exist in every society, are witnessed by the whole family – parents, children and grandparents – in each other's presence. These violations are more deeply embarrassing and upsetting than if they had occurred in the privacy of a book, or in a club, cinema or theatre.[24]

The television family is not just orientalized; it is tribalized. The image of a three-generation family sitting in a circle round a television set under the spell of taboos is a complete fiction. Three-generation families are statistically quite rare; where they exist, there's no evidence that they watch television together (quite the reverse, in many cases); television cannot be watched in a 'circle'; there are no universal 'taboos'. Even so, this strange, tribal family is imagined as paedocratic: all its members are defined in terms of their relationship with children; they are not people, or even adults, but 'parents', 'grandparents'.

The child-oriented sensibilities of this family circle are not its own private affair; on the contrary, for Annan they are matters of the highest public policy. This is because 'whatever is published is presumed to be in some way approved, or at least condoned, by the society which permits its publication'.[25] The Annan Committee doesn't say exactly who does the presuming, approving, condoning or – more importantly – the permitting, nor does it extend its notion of privacy ('the privacy of a book') to watching television in the privacy of the home. It simply equates television with 'the society', and then closes the circle by equating 'society' with the 'whole family', which, as we've seen, is governed by children.

Along the way, a potentially useful model of the relationship between television and TV audiences is invoked and then ignored in favour of protective paedocracy. This is the model of broadcasting as *publication*.

But the model of book and magazine publishing is not followed through. Instead, the 'privacy of a book' is imagined as essentially a solitary affair, while television, as a social phenomenon, is understood to require a 'permit' from 'society'. Of course, publishing is just as social as broadcasting, but printed publications can cater for a much wider range of political, personal, sexual, aesthetic, generic and other tastes – with or without 'violations' of taboos – than broadcasting ever has, without each item ('whatever is published') being seen as approved of by the whole 'society'. Publishing has had its own long history of regulation and censorship, but never in modern times has *everything* been subject to permit. If broadcasting is a form of publication, the question arises: why is it treated so differently? But the question does not occur to the Annan Committee, so strong is the image of the 'embarrassment' that would ensue if children were to be seen by their parents and grandparents witnessing 'violations' of language and behaviour (another interesting question they do not address is exactly who is imagined to be 'upset' – the parents or the children). Such is the power of paedocracy.

Turning from policy recommendations to the regulations that enforce them, and turning from Britain to Australia, it is clear that the 'publication' of television is governed by children down to the most surprising details. The Australian Broadcasting Tribunal issues a manual to commercial broadcasters ('licensees'). Having equated the 'Australian community' and the 'general public' with 'adults and children', the writers of the *Manual* go on to warn licensees of their 'overriding obligation' to 'avoid televising program material which can give offence to sections of the public or can be harmful to the young people who make up a large part of the audience at certain times of the day'.[26] Once again, it turns out that 'the Australian community' as a whole is governed by that 'large part' of the audience comprising 'young people' – the tail wags the dog. This is especially evident in the standards laid down for 'family programs', whose 'special provisions' are:

1 The selection of subject matter and treatment of themes should be wholesome and fresh in outlook. The more sordid aspects of life must not be emphasized.
2 The following in particular should be avoided –
   (a) torture or suggestion of torture;
   (b) horror or undue suspense;
   (c) the use of the supernatural or superstition so as to arouse anxiety or fear;
   (d) any matter likely to lead to hysteria, nightmares or other undesirable emotional disturbances in children;
   (e) excessive violence.
3 Morbid sound effects intended to anticipate or simulate death or

injury should not be used.

4 Particular attention should be paid to the treatment of child or animal characters, as a child's imagination can be readily overstimulated by suggestions of ill-treatment of such characters.
5 Particular attention should be paid to the use of correct speech and pronunciation; slang and incorrect English should be avoided, except when necessary for characterization.[27]

Like their British counterparts, the writers of the ABT *Manual* are confident they speak on behalf of 'a child's imagination', and they are equally certain that they know what goes on in that imaginary, tribal 'family circle'. Here is one of the regulations covering advertising (now under review):

> Because some products (especially those of a personal nature) are considered unsuitable as topics for conversation in the family circle, licensees should exercise discretion in accepting advertisements for them; if such advertisements are accepted, great care should be taken in selecting times appropriate for their transmission. Products of a particularly intimate nature which are not freely mentioned or discussed in mixed company should not be advertised through television. Illustrated advertisements for brassieres, girdles, briefs or similar items of underwear making use of live models should not be televised between 6.00 a.m. and 8.30 a.m. or between 4.00 p.m. and 7.30 p.m. on weekdays or at any time before 7.30 p.m. on Saturday, Sunday or weekdays which are not schooldays.[28]

REGIMES OF PLEASURE

Broadcasters are required to conform to a fictional image of the family circle and to an extraordinarily outdated notion of 'mixed company' on pain of losing their licence to broadcast. However, a more constant threat for television networks is losing not their licence but their market share. Does it follow, then, that audiences do in fact exert a powerful influence on broadcasters in the form of demand? Television as an industry is subject to certain market forces, but the institutional organization of the industry seems designed not to enter into active relations with audiences as already constituted trading partners, but on the contrary to *produce* audiences – to invent them in its own image for its own purposes. Certainly the relationship of the television industry to its audience is not the classic market relation of supply and demand. This is because television, as one of the culture or consciousness industries, is not like the traditional producer of goods or services which are then sold to a market. Television shows are not commodities in the usual sense – they are 'non-material' commodities –

and audiences don't buy them. The exchange is not goods for money, but symbols for time. If, as Nicholas Garnham has put it, culture is 'above all the sphere for the expansion of difference',[29] then it follows that the use value of cultural commodities like television shows is very hard to pin down or to predict. Television executives do their best. Todd Gitlin cites a list of 'mysteries' that executives offered to him as explanations for a show's success: 'whether a concept was "special", "different", "unique", even (wonder of wonders) "very unique"; whether a show had "chemistry"; whether it "clicked", whether "it all came together"'.[30] But clearly the demand for novelty or difference, for the 'very unique', is so unspecific that it barely counts as demand at all. The only discipline such demand imposes on the industry is that of variety: television, like other culture industries, cannot standardize its product but must offer a repertoire. Further, such demand cannot be stabilized. Despite the tendency to minimize uncertainty and risk by the use of repeats, long-running series (in both drama and news), recombinations of successful formulae and spin-offs, uncertainty remains: out of around 3,000 new ideas put up to each of the three American networks each year about one hundred will be commissioned to the script stage; of these, twenty-five will go to pilot stage; after testing the pilots, perhaps five or ten new series will go on the air; of these, perhaps only one will go to a second season.[31] In the face of such uncertainties, television networks are driven to ever higher production costs per item in order to maintain novelty and difference, which in turn means that they are driven to seek ever larger audiences to justify the unit costs.

But for their part, audiences treat television shows not as scarce commodities but as public utilities for which they are not prepared to pay. Like other cultural goods, such as radio shows, advertising and free newspapers, television shows are not purchased. Furthermore, they are not consumed; they are not used up in the act of reading or viewing. This means both that the products of the past are available for reconsumption, and that audiences are apt to use television when and how they like, and (despite piracy laws) to save what they like for consumption later on – an increasing tendency since the introduction of videocassette recorders. This means it is hard for the industry to maintain scarcity (and thus price), especially given the need for audience maximization.

In this context – where the industry's product cannot be standardized, where demand cannot be predicted or stabilized, where the commodity is 'non-material' and neither purchased nor consumed, and where vast capital investment is required to manufacture goods that are then virtually as free as the airwaves that carry them – in this context audiences are not television's real market. There is one sense, of course, in which audiences are literally the product of the television industry: in the commercial sector, networks sell access to their audiences to advertisers; in the public sector, the corporations must convince their funding agencies that an agreed proportion of the public is tuned in often enough to justify the enterprise. Thus audiences – or, more accurately, *ratings* – are the key to profitability and survival in the television industry, and access to them is the key to power. It follows, as Garnham has argued, that in line with other cultural industries, but unlike traditional manufacturing industries, distributors (networks) are more powerful and profitable than producers (authors). However, it does not follow that audiences have power over networks: they are created, organized and maintained *by* networks, and not vice versa. Indeed, the real relations of broadcasters are not with audiences as such but with other professionals in the industry: with advertisers, funding agencies, suppliers and – it's about as close as they get – with audience research organizations. In this context, the 'power' of the audience is contained within the networks themselves, taking the fictionalized form of ratings and of those imaginary, paedocratized representations of the audience that the networks promote throughout the industry. Networks minimize their risks by stabilizing not demand but supply, but neither networks nor producers know what will 'sell'; they don't know who they're talking to and they don't 'give the public what it wants' because they don't know what the public is. This structural uncertainty at the heart of the television industry means that networks and producers alike are afraid of the audience: afraid of offending it, of inciting it, of inflaming it – above all, of losing it.

At the level of programming, in the 'ideological colloquy of large scale', this structural uncertainty is reproduced as a constant effort to reconcile an irreconcilable contradiction. On the one hand, audiences must be appealed to and won; they must voluntarily forgo other activities and choose not only to watch television but to watch this channel, during this time slot, today. On the other hand, audiences must be disciplined and controlled; they must learn to recognize that what's on offer is, despite its requisite novelty or difference, just that kind of pleasure for the enjoyment of which they have both forgone other activities and invested scarce time resources. A further contradiction facing broadcasters is that between the audience as an unimaginably large mass and the audience as an individual viewer. Without having the slightest notion of each or any viewer's identity, the ideological colloquy has to address each in order to amass all.

In practice, such contradictions produce what can be called television's regimes of pleasure. Like other publishing forms, television channels provide a montage or repertoire of different kinds of elements in order to convert as wide a spectrum of the public as possible into the audience. Far from seeking to fix just one 'subject position', least of all that of Ellis's 'normal citizen', television, as Ien Ang has argued, has developed its cultural form as a heterogeneity of modes of address, points of view, programme genres, styles of presentation, codes of recognition.[32] Television is characterized, in effect, by excess, providing audiences with an excess of options which can nevertheless be easily recognized, and offering an excess of pleasures (one of which is to choose between those on offer) which can nevertheless be disciplined into familiar, predictable forms. Thus in order to produce an audience, television must first produce excess. But, like the audience whose demand it is supposed to represent, pleasure is a diffuse and irrecoverable concept; it must be regimented in various ways in order for the television industry to be able to supply it, and so to survive, profitably. Thus television is a pleasurable institution, but one offering a complex of channelled, disciplined pleasures which are driven towards corporately achievable forms; television operates *regimes* of pleasure.

ILLEGAL IMMIGRANTS?

But all the time the efforts of television networks and producers to regiment the audience are subverted by the audience's own excess – its tendency always to exceed the discipline, control and channelling of television's regimes, and its tendency always to exceed the imagination of television's corporate executives. Thus the interests of the audiences and television are in principle opposed. Television as an industry needs regimented, docile, eager audiences, willing to recognize what they like in what they get; and audiences, for their part, need a relationship with television in order to exist at all as audiences, but that relationship is not organized, not even represented very directly, in the institution. Their interests are discernible only as random: childish, unfocused desires for excess, transgression, novelty, difference; for play, escape from categorization, and occasionally for that characteristic childish demand – 'Do it again!'

The politics of television, then, consist in a very unequal struggle between different interests within a wholly fictional (that is, discursively/rhetorically/textually imagined) community. Since audiences don't exist prior to or outside television, they need constant hailing and guidance in how-to-be-an-audience – hailing and guidance that are unstintingly given within, and especially between, shows, and in the meta-discourses that surround television, the most prominent among which, of course, are those publications aptly called television guides. Thus television is not just a regime, or complex of regimes, of pleasure; it is a pedagogic regime too. What this means, in effect, is that television producers don't have the courage of their convictions. For, if television audiences are subject to a *pedagogic* regime of pleasure, then it follows that they do not live, while acting as audiences, in a democracy. But nor do they live in a paedocracy either, since a pedagogic regime cannot be governed *by* childlike qualities but on the contrary constitutes government *over* them. In fact, the paedocratic regime of television discourse is itself, in the end, an invisible fiction, because audiences have no voice of their own to speak within the institution. Like the discourse of orientalism, paedocracy too often functions within the industry not to explain audiences but to explain them away, to contain their potential threat, to render obvious their need for protection, regulation, rule. The paedocratized image of television audiences that circulates within the industry and around its academic and regulatory observers as an obvious truth is not necessarily devoid of force for those who actually watch television – but its primary function as a discourse is to serve the purposes of the professionals engaged in professional survival. For them, any irruption of actual audiences would spoil their routine assumption of the power to speak on behalf of a disorganized community which hitherto has existed almost wholly within their own imagination and rhetoric. Thus it is true that television networks act, as Todd Gitlin has put it, *in loco parentis* for the audience, but it is not the childishness of the audience that produces this situation; nor is it, as Gitlin is tempted to conclude, 'a projection of their [the networks'] own childishness'.[33] On the contrary, it is a system for imagining the unimaginable; for controlling the uncontrollable. Luckily for the networks, few among the audience seem to have bothered much about it, at least until now.

Chapter 7

The real world of audiences*

Sir Karl Popper is not a name one often encounters in travels through textual theory. But I'm tempted to use it after an article by Martin Allor on the conceptualization of the television audience in current critical debate.[1] Allor's article, in the American journal *Critical Studies in Mass Communication*, sparked off a series of responses, including this one, which appeared in the same issue (the debate rumbled on in later issues too). I was struck by an apparent struggle going on between polarized textualism and realism throughout Allor's article, culminating in his conclusion that 'audience exists nowhere; it inhabits no real space, only positions within . . . discourses'.[2] What struck me about this was not the conceptualization of the audience as existing only in discourse, a position with which I agree (see chapter 6), but the presumption that *discourse* is 'nowhere', 'no real space'; that is, not real at all, or opposed to 'the' real. I am an avowed textualist, and one moreover who has tried to avoid the 'naïve epistemological realism' that Allor recognizes in some writings about audiences. But instead of turning to familiar French luminaries to speak about the *reality* of *textual* positions, I invoke Karl Popper. A realist philosopher, Popper has plenty to say about science, knowledge and the real. He even has a name for the 'nowhere' of discourse. He calls it (without a hint of irony) 'the third world'.

Both the audience, and those who analyse or address it, live not in Popper's first world of 'physical objects or of physical states', nor in his second world of 'states of consciousness or of mental states', but in his third world of '*objective contents of thought*, especially of scientific and poetic thoughts and of works of art'. Among the inmates of Popper's 'objective third world' are theoretical systems, problems, problem situations, critical arguments (the 'most important inhabitants'), together with '*the state of a discussion* or *the state of a critical argument*; and, of course, the contents of journals, books, and libraries'.[3]

* Originally published as John Hartley (1988) 'The real world of audiences', *Critical Studies in Mass Communication*, 5(3), 234–8. Reprinted by permission of the Speech Communication Association.

A property of this third world is that it is real. It is the material world of knowledge, but it's not just a static world of things (like this book). On the contrary, like this book, it is a changing world, full of contradictions and disputations, and its mode of existence is, in principle, dialogic, like Volosinov's 'ideological colloquy of large scale'.[4] In Popper's terms, it's a world of 'language, of conjectures, theories, and arguments – in brief, the universe of objective knowledge'. There are no human 'inhabitants' as such in this third world (neither audiences nor analysts as subjective individual bodily persons); for Popper, world 3 is autonomous, 'exosomatic'; that is, discourse that develops outside the body (in writing), and therefore, it follows, a discourse that produces knowledge which is literally objective (as a spider produces an exosomatic web). For Popper, 'knowledge in the objective sense is *knowledge without a knower*: it is *knowledge without a knowing subject*'. In this third world, knowledge exists independently of its human author, and it exists whether or not it is communicated to a reader.[5]

Audiences, and those who analyse them within the disciplinary discourses of media studies, are denizens of Popper's third world. Both audiences and their analysts are real, and they both exist in 'real space', but only as representations, and only in *texts*. An analytical position is a discursive position, not a personal (subjective or world 2) one, and audiences are objects of knowledge, not people.

Of course, there are relations between the third world of objective knowledge, the second world of consciousness and the first world of physical states. Audiences as objective knowledge feed back into the second and first worlds. But that feedback needs to be understood not in terms of the contrast that suffuses Allor's article between the 'abstract theoreticism' of 'ideal readers', 'the reader' and similar 'textual questions' and the 'naïve realism' of 'real individuals', 'respondents' or 'real women' who pre-exist their analysis. Nor can the relation be assumed as a simple correspondence, as it appears to be by Ann Kaplan when she equates the 'decentered, a-historical model spectator' with those who 'appear to live'.[6] Such conceptions merely perpetuate the idea that critical writing is either parasitic upon a pre-given object, and not creative of that object, or, alternatively, that criticism creates a fascinating but imaginary theoretical object (like the ideal reader), whose relationship with lumpen reality in the form of, say, teenagers, is a matter of faith (not proof).

Against this line of thinking, I would argue that the intellectual work conducted in Popper's third world has a rather more powerful effect on the other two worlds of conscious and physical states: it has the effect of shaping their contents. Further, I would not confine the idea of intellectual work to what 'we as a discipline'[7] might do or say. Intellectual work also includes the constructions of audiences that are imagined and circulated within the broadcasting industry, the public opinion industry, and in regulatory discourses sponsored by governments, for instance (see chapter 6).

It is clear that broadcasters imagine audiences differently from the way that (for instance) feminist reader-response criticism does. But equally, if the concept 'audience' is a 'chaotic conception', too unified and abstract to be of any critical use,[8] then the same goes for the concept 'we'. 'We as a discipline' is an abstract unity that serves to separate academic critics from other intellectuals (producers, legislators, pollsters), and to create an imagined community which reduces structural functionalists, social psychologists, political economists, post-structuralist film theorists, feminist reader-response critics, cultural studies critics and postmodernists (to mention only those named by Allor) to 'we'.

Such a procedure has a double effect: it diverts attention away from what other communities are up to, and it depoliticizes intellectual work within the critical domain. Some attention needs to be devoted to the different ways that the relation between intellectuals and audiences has been imagined, since it is a changing, historical one. Umberto Eco, writing from the position of an intellectual addressing other intellectuals (in a book that nevertheless aspires to mass sales), suggests for instance that the relation is *Medieval*:

> We find a fairly perfect correspondence between the two ages that, in different ways but with identical educational utopias and with equal ideological camouflage of their paternalistic aim to control minds, try to bridge the gap between learned culture and popular culture through visual communication. In both periods the select élite debates written texts with alphabetic mentality, but then translates into images the essential data or knowledge and the fundamental structure of the ruling ideology. The Middle Ages are the civilization of vision, where the cathedral is the great book in stone, and is indeed the advertisement, the TV screen, the mystic comic strip that must narrate and explain everything.[9]

If there is a gap between literate culture and popular culture, it's a gap that is clearly rather productive; if cathedrals are the TV screens of the Middle Ages, then equally TV screens are the cathedrals of this age, and both these works of wonder are produced out of – even because of – that gap, the gap (the relation) between intellectuals and masses.

But Eco writes of educational utopias, ideological camouflage, paternalistic aims, controlling minds, ruling ideologies. Another gap opens: a *political* gap between intellectuals as producers of ideology (cathedrals, TV), and intellectuals as critics of those products. Once again, the site of the gap is also the site of the audience, a site of struggle. And Eco is explicit about who should conduct the fight:

> The idea that we must ask the scholars and educators of tomorrow to abandon the TV studios or the offices of the newspapers, to fight a door-to-door guerrilla battle like provos of Critical Reception can be

> frightening, and can also seem utopian. But if the Communications Era proceeds in the direction that today seems to us the most probable, this will be the only salvation for free people.[10]

Actually, since 1967 Eco himself has retreated from this utopian position, and relocated himself within the domain of the third world of knowledge-production. He explicitly abandons his own 'provo' call-to-arms – to 'teach the addressees to "read" the messages, to criticise them' – as 'another dream of '68'. Eco goes no further now than to say: 'Well, it's all over. We have to start again from the beginning, asking one another what's going on.'[11]

But the means he uses to ask his question, to discharge his 'political duty . . . as a scholar and a citizen', are no longer (if they ever were) the means of door-to-door semiological guerrilla warfare. On the contrary, Eco returns to the traditional intellectual, pedagogic means of 'learned culture,' conducted wholly within the discursive media of Popper's third world. His duty and pleasure is to research and write academic books, 'to teach, to expound still-imperfect ideas and hear the students' reaction. . . . To write for the newspapers, to reread myself the next day, and to read the reactions of others.'[12]

Intellectual production, then, is conducted discursively, and the product is objective but textual. Both the audience and the position from which it is imagined and/or addressed (the position of 'we') are sites of struggle, and the struggles are political.

To make clear the implications of this argument, it might be an idea to turn from fully fanfared theoretical expositions on audiences to some less rigorous but much more pervasive positions. In the mainstream media themselves, especially the press, there is a standard view of media audiences. Critics from the academic domain are accessed to 'source' this view (conversely, critics who don't endorse it are rarely accessed). What is this common-sense conception of the audience? It is, of course, the psychologistic one, trotted out on the occasion of serial killings, rape-murders and other negative events. Mass murders are explained by reference to the habit of watching television and videos. The audience is conceptualized as an object, pushed around by powerful media influences. It is made of individual, subjective people, who can be caused to behave badly (never well) by acting passively (an absurd but commonplace notion of what audiences *do*). Of course, this notion of audience is contradictory, discredited and self-serving (the press never accuses itself of crimes committed by 'the media', and psychologists are always curiously exempt from the influences they discern in their long-suffering subjects). But irritating and demeaning though it is, this notion of audience is, as it were, the industry standard. It remains in place partly because 'we as a discipline' – who put it there in the first place – haven't mobilized our considerable collective resources to contest or replace it. Instead, we worry whether what we imagine is real or not.

In the real world of critical discourse, the audience is literally a creation of criticism. The monster who watches TV and then goes on the rampage is a *metaphor* – a creation of criticism. So too are other fictional characters of our times – the woman who watches soap opera and then becomes a distracted, decentred housewife (men watch soap operas too, but are rarely accused of catching domesticity as a result); the child who watches TV and becomes a zombie (politicians spend most of their waking hours with one eye on the screen, but perhaps we'd better not pursue that contrast).

Much less common is the construction of the audience that has as its object the creation of a critical reader in the image not of some silly nightmare vision, but in the image of the critical process itself. 'We' need the courage of our convictions and a little more self-assurance. Since the inhabitants of critical discourse cannot avoid the intellectual work of audience-creation, let it be explicitly creative, and not hidden behind the fiction of a 'real' audience that's always located somewhere beyond the critical activity itself.

At this point, it becomes a question not of what kind of audience we have, but of what kind we want; not a question of what 'we' as a discipline must do to 'move forward',[13] but of what 'we' are moving forward towards.

Critical discourse is pedagogic, instructive and expansive. But it's not always communicative. There remains that gap between the intellectuals and popular culture. Rather than looking ruefully at the width of the gap, perhaps it is time 'we' as a discipline shouldered our social, political and intellectual responsibilities (which we cannot avoid), and, secure in the knowledge that audiences are made not given, proceed towards an active intervention in the process.

Such intervention certainly includes disciplinary colloquy, disputation, theorizing – such as the dialogue to which this is a contribution. It also includes criticizing the popular hegemony of psychologism. In other words, intra-disciplinary criticism is the foundation of objective knowledge about the audience, which is why it's important not to conceptualize a unitary discipline any more than a unitary audience.

But active intervention in the process of audience construction goes further than this. Umberto Eco's work has itself bridged the gap between elite and popular culture, and perhaps Todd Gitlin's critique of prime-time does too, in the American context. At least Gitlin is concerned as much about a critical and creative citizenry as he is about disciplinary procedures; while he is scrupulous and explicit about his methods, he uses them to mount an argument about an imagined America in a book designed to mobilize its American audience.[14]

But even these heroic efforts are not enough. An astonishing aspect of media studies, especially television criticism, is the extent to which it ignores what's on television. Neither film nor literary studies are quite as emancipated from the quotidian products of their media as is TV criticism. And both literary and cinematic critics sometimes intervene directly in their media to make contributions in the form of fiction and films, even occasionally using the medium to criticize or analyse itself. Television studies, in comparison, is still waiting for Godard.

This is partly, perhaps, a matter of history. Writing in 1920, Frances Taylor Patterson ('instructor of photoplay composition' at Columbia University), bemoaned the lack of an informed, specialist and instructive cinema criticism. She is, like Eco, unashamedly pedagogic:

> Cinema critics must be trained in order that they may educate the public up to what is best in photoplays, which knowledge will in turn lead them to demand the best from exhibitors and producers.[15]

And, like Eco, she is quite sure where this education should take place:

> The work of the good critics stands out from the mass of mediocrity like beacon lights on a dark sea. . . . The papers are content to publish this inadequate and often misleading criticism because the general impression is that the photoplays which are being put on are not worth much more. . . . The vast majority of people are in need of guidance in the matter of photoplays. It is no longer a question of giving them what they want. It is a question of so directing their tastes that they will want what is best. And they can come to know what is best only through that organ of universal enlightenment, the public press.[16]

In case such a project should (unlike Eco's canny rhetoric) now seem naïve and quaint, it's worth noting that Patterson is not arguing for 'the best' from the position of a know-all outsider who comes in to tell the fledgling medium (and its audience) what's good for it. Quite the reverse:

> Granted that most of the photoplays shown upon the screen are not worthy of much consideration, there is yet some good in the worst of them as well as some bad spots in the best of them, which ought to be held up to public attention, if the people at large are ever going to appreciate and demand the best in photoplays.[17]

Therefore, concludes Patterson, 'the cinematic critic ought to take his [*sic*] mission in life seriously':

> He ought to learn all there is to be learned about his profession, cultivating a knowledge of all the other arts from which the photoplay borrows . . . . Sometimes the inadequate criticism of current plays is due to the more or less antagonistic attitude the critic adopts toward the motion picture. . . . Often his criticism is not analysis, but vituperation and abuse.[18]

Such terms as 'best', 'worst', 'taste', 'enlightenment', 'appreciation' – not to mention 'vituperation and abuse' – belong, of course, to the ideologically unsound branches of evaluative literary criticism that 'we' as a discipline have learnt not to touch with a barge-pole in these postmodernist days. But perhaps we've gone much too far in the opposite direction, covering evaluative judgements in the cloak of disciplinary truths, scientific methods, philosophical niceties. And perhaps we dodge the issue of what *we* mean by quality by wandering off into aimless discussion of reality. Maybe some naïve, evaluative guidance is just what 'we' as a discipline could do with just now, never mind the public at large. In short, as Patterson says, 'the person who cannot see the possibilities of the photoplay as an art form, who cannot recognize its beauties and powers even in its present undeveloped state, is not abreast of progress'.[19] With hindsight, it's easy to see that she had a point in respect of cinema as art. It's perhaps less easy to agree that 'progress' has occurred, since there's an uncanny degree of fit between her analysis of cinema in 1920 and the situation that now exists in relation to television.

But if we are going, as Allor puts it (with equal commitment to progress), 'to move forward on this issue, the central problematic of the field', we do indeed need 'a different model of the relation between analysis and intervention within the human sciences'. But Allor goes on to say that that analytical reconstruction 'will fail however if it doesn't then return to a reconstructive engagement with the individuals in the quotidian'.[20] Not so. It will fail as long as it is in thrall to the idea that there *are* individuals in the quotidian, or at least that such individuals constitute the audience for media. Being an audience is an act among others for individuals; a learnt, specialist, critical, discursive practice. The location of the subjective site of that practice is an analytical red herring. More to the point than deciding the issue of what a 'social subject' might look like if we fell over one is this question: how can we *persuade* audiences to take up those positions that our critical analysis suggests are *better* than others? If we don't start asking this question in relation to the popular media, the third world is undoubtedly where, as a discipline, we shall stay.

Chapter 8

Out of bounds*

MARGINAL POLITICS

Television and parliamentary politics have a lot in common. To begin with, both are founded on the concept and practice of representation. Members of parliament are our elected representatives, the government represents the will of the people in action, and various groups make representations to parliament. Television makes representations, too, though of a slightly different kind. It represents events, people, places, ideas.

Like parliament, the institutional organization of television is the adversarial, two-party system. The BBC and the ITV companies slug it out, getting progressively more like each other as they chase the same floating viewers. But occasionally there are crisis periods in both politics and broadcasting in which the marginal, grey area between the two mighty opposites takes on an apparently disproportionate significance. The two-party duopoly itself seems threatened by the minor parties that occupy the ambiguous terrain around its edges: there is much talk of mould-breaking. In the event, the mould turns out to be surprisingly resistant to challenge, and the threat is contained in an institutional form that blunts its cutting edge.

In the 1960s, the ambiguous terrain between the two mighty opposites, Conservative and Labour, proved fertile ground for the 'Orpington Liberals' (a group of middle-ground politicians who won a series of by-elections including the seat of Orpington), the Welsh and Scottish Nationalists, who also won parliamentary representation, and BBC2, the first British minority TV channel. In the 1980s, the same ambiguity was represented in the form of the SDP (the Social Democratic Party), a schismatic group of former Labour MPs and peers, Sianel Pedwar Cymru (S4C), which is a Welsh-language TV service for Wales, and Channel 4, the second minority TV channel. Oddly enough, Channel 4's inaugural

* Originally published as John Hartley (1984) 'Out of bounds: the myth of marginality', in Len Masterman (ed.) *Television Mythologies: Stars, Shows, Signs*, London: Comedia.

board was a hotbed of SDP activists, and its political ideology, at board level at least, was the same as the SDP's commitment to pluralism and mould-breaking, not to mention the proportional representation of minority groups (see chapter 4).

In parliamentary elections, as every television viewer knows, the focus of election specials on TV is not so much on the opposing parties themselves as on a different kind of opposition, namely that between safe and marginal seats. This is hardly surprising, since the difference between a Tory and a Labour government can turn on the distribution of a few hundred votes in key marginals. These seats also provide clues about the shape of things to come – they are the signs that stand for the future. Here the boundary between parliament and television becomes truly ambiguous, since in an election there is no parliament, and the transition from old to new is ritualized by television. At the very moment when politics moves from normal executive and legislative safety to its risky, democratic margins, television takes over and distends the marginality of the occasion into a late-night orgy of suspense. In true soap-opera style, the outcome is endlessly deferred, and people's actions and decisions are endlessly discussed by the familiar cast of commentators and politicians. Throughout, the marginal seats are a constant focus of fascination for these representatives of TV and politics, because such seats magically prove the rhetoric of democracy. They provide empirical evidence of the possibility of change within an overall structure that is not disrupted but vindicated by such change. In elections, then, the marginal is the site of change and development; the ritualized boundary between one state and another; and the opposite of safe.

Margins can thus appear, contradictorily, both as peripheries (the site of outsiders who don't count) and as zones of danger, where the security of safe territory is threatened by what's going on at the edges. Once again, a parliamentary analogy will serve to clarify the implications of this. Both the major parties occasionally have to deal with groups which occupy their left margins. In the case of the Tories these are the so-called 'wets'. During Thatcherism the wets were understood (in popular/media mythology) as irrelevant and peripheral – they didn't count. For the Labour Party, however, there is the Militant Tendency, which has been understood (again in popular/media mythology) as both threatening to the party as a whole, and even made up of outsiders who have infiltrated the party for their own purposes. Thus, from the centre of each party, things that are going on at the edge can be seen as either irrelevant and peripheral (undervalued), or disruptive and threatening (overvalued).

It is obvious from this illustration that margins aren't naturally one thing or the other, wet or militant. They have to be made sense of as either irrelevant or as disruptive, and the way they are represented makes a lot of difference to our understanding. Think how we would view British politics if we were used to hearing about Edward Heath in terms of the rhetoric of militant tendencies, and about Tony Benn in terms of wetness. But here a further problem arises, and it is one which applies to television. That is, the rhetoric which makes sense of a margin in terms of irrelevance may itself be the product of a struggle. In other words, if you can convince yourself and others that a potentially disruptive margin is, in fact, an irrelevant periphery, then any threat it poses to your security is thereby reduced. However, the more successful this strategy is, the more dangerous it becomes, since the sense of security it encourages is false.

THE POLITICS OF MARGINALITY

Applying this idea to television, the most important lesson it teaches is that television *as a whole* has been subject to such undervaluing representations in this way ever since it became the dominant popular medium. Even among radical critics, television has tended to be seen as less important, less worthy of serious attention, than other media (such as literature, cinema and the press). It has attracted few major theorists, either academic or political, and it is often dismissed as a bastard medium, whose only interest lies in the way it debases both purer forms and people's consciousness. Such attention as it does receive frequently looks at TV in terms of values and assumptions that come not from its own practices and regimes, but from more prestigious areas of knowledge. Its genres are understood in terms of film, its politics in terms of the press, its values in terms of literature, and so on.

In short, television has been made sense of in terms that emphasize its wetness, as opposed to its militant tendencies, so much so, in fact, that it is sometimes hard even to imagine that it has any radical or disruptive potential at all, apart from negative behavioural or moral effects on vulnerable individuals; not so much militant as malevolent. Many radical critics of television, both within the organized left (the labour and trade union movement) and in progressive intellectual circles, tend to dismiss television as marginal to the main business of political endeavour. Thus, apart from ritual condemnation at annual conferences, the organized left has no policy at all concerning the representation of its own self-image on television. It hasn't got beyond the nineteenth-century notion of a newspaper to represent its alternative point of view. And although there are many studies of how television misrepresents certain groups, ideologies and points of view more or less systematically, the disorganized (academic) left hasn't succeeded at this point (1984) in showing how interventions may be made in mainstream practices to change these things.

Television producers are preoccupied with issues that the critics have hardly begun to address – issues of populism, appeal and pleasure in a fragmented and disunited society. There is little hope of influencing them to change their ways while the criticisms come from a standpoint which simply doesn't take television seriously on its own terms. Far too much effort is expended on exposing TV's (inevitable) capitalist tendencies, on showing how it mythologizes or naturalizes the values of a capitalist system that it is both a product and representative of. But not enough effort is expended on exposing just how much the habit of mythologizing belongs to critical thinking too. Thus, critical thinking that represents television as irrelevant or marginal to the central issues of modern politics is not critical at all, but mythical. It provides a false sense of security for the critics who can point to TV's inadequacies without inspecting their own. But it is dangerous thinking, because it encourages ignorance – it encourages us to undervalue television's potential for disrupting and threatening the very system it seems so naturally to represent.

This, then, is what I mean by the 'myth of marginality'. It is that kind of thinking which makes sense of margins as irrelevant and peripheral when they can equally be understood as disruptive and threatening. It is mythical thinking because it magically resolves the ambiguity of margins. It simply understands that what happens at the edges either doesn't count or, worse, isn't there. So the antidote to the myth of marginality is to look carefully at marginal, irrelevant areas for evidence of change and transition. Taking my critical cue from TV itself, I now want to look at its own practices to see how different kinds of boundaries are erected and transgressed, and how different marginalities act as disruptive agents of change, even whilst TV itself encourages us not to notice them. I have divided what follows into two classes of marginality: the *structural* and the *representational*. I shall look at each in turn.

STRUCTURAL MARGINS

The myth of marginality is doubtless given credence by the literate origin of the term itself. On paper, the margin is the edge of the page. Go past the edge, and you come to the brink. Go over the brink, and you fall off. This Flat Earth metaphor discourages a sense of margins as relational, occupying the ground between two zones. Broadcast television has no edges, only discontinuities between programmes. We are constantly being reminded by continuity announcers and Raymond Williams alike to see television as a flow; in this regard, the contents of whatever is broadcast between programmes, i.e. trailers, time-checks, announcements, advertisements (continuity itself), must constitute the principal structural marginality of television. Thus the myth comes into operation right away. We are encouraged to watch these marginal broadcasts (they have contents), but to treat them as if they weren't there (they are structured as gaps). They're not mentioned in the TV guides *TV Times* or *Radio Times*, or in audience research, and they occupy a timeless, not-television slot in the schedules. However, they are far from insignificant (see also chapter 11). The broadcasting corporations have recognized their inherent danger, which for them is loss of viewers, by turning continuity and trailers into a genre, with its own specialized production departments, its own conventions, and its own appeal and pleasure for the viewers. This genre, together with the nationalized margin of the closedown (in Wales they put out *two* national anthems), is strongly marked and specific to television. It accounts for a significant proportion of annual broadcast hours. In 1982/3 the BBC broadcast 404 hours of continuity, or 4 per cent of total output. This is comparable to minority programming, like news (4.5 per cent), schools (4.2 per cent), drama (4.2 per cent), etc.[1]

Continuity is often technically innovative. Quantel, for instance, was first extensively exploited in Britain in trailers. More importantly, continuity and trailers establish channel identity, along with the most direct address to the viewer, and real time. In these ways they perform the ideological function of naturalizing and giving concrete expression to the pleasure of watching television: the announcer's familiar face tells us what enjoyment actually looks like. And trailers encourage the knitting together of our personal plans and those of the broadcasting corporation. We are positioned into relations of warm anticipation in the marginal non-space and non-time of in-between-programmes. And, sometimes, trailers are more pleasurable than the programmes they trail, since they can dispense with boring exposition and simply show the good (telegenic) bits, with the magic (how *do* they do it?) of computer graphics thrown in.

This margin-genre is actually distending into programmes themselves. The title/credit sequences of regular studio programmes are quite capable of costing as much as one whole episode of the show itself, and titles increasingly partake of the generic features of trailers. They also display other attributes of advertisements, namely frequent repetition and the promise of pleasures to come. But unlike trailers and ads, of course, these boundary sequences are structured not to take us through, but to take us in.

Beyond the marginal broadcasts produced by the corporations themselves, we come to commercials; the ultimate TV show, where you can see just how much power can be packed into a gap in the schedules. Yet in the myth of marginality advertisements aren't there. Even though they finance it, they are presented as *supplementary* (to borrow a suggestive term from Derrida, who uses it to describe the relation between speech and writing) to the mainstream fare of broadcasting. Despite, or because of, their *populism*, ads somehow don't count in serious discussions of television's programmes, whilst their producers and the agencies that make them are normally neglected in critical studies of the history and practices of television production.

But advertisements are pacemakers for the consciousness industry. They are one of the most developed forms of capitalist production, since they promote consumption in general and in particular, whilst themselves producing a non-material commodity, individual consciousness. Along the way, they put safe television to shame. They can be breathtakingly costly (a reputed £350,000 at 1983 prices for a Levi jeans advertisement, using fourteen hours of footage, enough to make a feature film); they are formally and technically innovative; responsive to changes in cultural consciousness (audience taste); and, sometimes, outrageously honest about the relations of production. They tell us the blatant truth about capitalism.

A good example of this is an advertisement for Del Monte orange juice that was carried for two or three seasons in the mid-1980s on Channel 4, made by the SJIP/BBDO Agency. In a western/Mexican (or, to make the point, an El Salvadorian) setting, the 'Juice-Man' travels in a black sedan to a village, where he decides whether or not to select the local oranges for Del Monte. When he nods approval, not only the Mexican growers, but even the oranges themselves, jump for joy. The landscape, music, faces, action and characters make up a world that is independent of any that we might inhabit, but it is nevertheless instantly recognizable. The stranger, a Man with No Name, has a marginal status in the village. He is an outsider. But he has the power over what happens next, since the outcome of his intervention will decide whether the village is saved or destroyed. And his black sedan signifies a different kind of marginal disruption, that of the gangsters of Chicago. So, although this independent world is fictional, and not one you could ever visit, it is real enough.

The social relationships established in the strange landscape are real enough too. Another western world – that of corporate power – meets the insecure, dependent (but loyal) third world, and decides its fate with a nod of the head. The power of the corporation over the people who produce the goods is the device used to sell those goods. And the power of television to produce knowledge and consciousness, to make sense of the world, is used to represent that least marginal, most dangerous relation – between capital and labour – in the fictional guise of the western, which is historically one of the most efficient vehicles for presenting actuality in mythic form. We don't need tuition in how to read what's going on under the dusty surface of the fictional forms. It's a familiar language. All it takes is thirty seconds in the gap between programmes.

REPRESENTATIONAL MARGINALITY

So much for the television that isn't there. But if we pursue the notion of marginality, and move from the so-called periphery into the safe, substantive areas of mainstream programming, we find that marginality persists. Here, however, it is not so much a structural gap between discontinuities, as a representational marginality. In both fictional and factual output, marginality seems to be a paradoxical by-product of television's commitment to realism. In soap operas, for instance, there's a commitment to representing family and community life realistically. But if you look at any long-running serial, it transpires that this very commitment drives the families and communities in question progressively towards the margin of what viewers might recognize as realistic. In both *Dallas* and *Coronation Street*, for example, first marriages are very rare. The shows are peopled by widows, divorcees, remarriages and relationships that border on the incestuous (Lucy and Ray in *Dallas*). Children are uncommon, and where they occur their status is usually uncertain – marginal. Thus, the *Coronation Street* family of Len and Rita Fairclough and Sharon looked like a real family on screen, but the biography of each of these characters would make scandalous reading in the Sunday papers, as indeed it did in the case of Deirdre, Ken and Mike.

As for the communities of the serials, they are, despite the lack of real children, *symbolic paedocracies*: that is, they are ruled by childlike qualities, childlike preoccupations and actions. The adult characters rarely engage in adult practices: work, sex, politics, household management, watching TV. Instead, they are decentred into adolescence: endless talk of self-discovery and personal relationships, endless looking for affection, love or esteem from others. Relationships are eroticized and gossiped about, but rarely sexualized. They are oral, communal and leavened by play, banter, humorous put-downs and endless impending crises. Everyone is easily distracted from occupational tasks in order to talk. While talk of public affairs and politics is rare and embarrassing, there's little sense of individual or even family privacy, either. And all these paedocratic self-indulgencies are just what inspire and sustain our desire to watch. The appeal of the serials is not their realism as such (by itself realism would bore us to death) but the ever-more marginal aspects of family, community and personal life that are used to represent or symbolize it. Although they are committed to realism, serials are driven by representational marginality.

Similarly, in actuality and news coverage, TV's commitment to realism drives it towards marginality. News seems often to represent important issues by means of one of their marginal aspects and simultaneously to marginalize the important aspect of those issues. An example (taken from

ITN *News at Ten*, 25 October 1982, and dealt with in more detail in chapter 2) is where the politico-military troubles in Northern Ireland are made sense of by translating them into a human interest story about families. In this context, the politico-military events are literally senseless, and this is how they are described in the news. Meanwhile, the story also marginalizes the significance of the overall politico-military situation. Using a discourse of domesticity to make sense of that situation does not help to explain it to the family audience; it only promotes understanding of the concept of the family. In this case at least, the family is marginal to the event, so that from its point of view the situation in Northern Ireland is senseless. QED, ITN-style.

This illustrates a general attribute of the myth of marginality. The myth proclaims that whatever is on the news is important (when it is often marginal), whereas, conversely, it suggests that actuality coverage outside the news and outside prime-time – for example, late-night documentaries on Channel 4 or early-afternoon discussions on such 'women's interest' shows as *Afternoon Plus* – is marginal (when it can often be important).

Marginal areas can, in fact, be so important that they attract extra special attention, and this takes us on to another dimension of the concept. Instead of being undervalued as peripheral, some marginalities are overvalued as dangerous, ambiguous, even scandalous, and they become the locus of actual or metaphorical border patrols, frontier posts, barbed wire. Just as national boundaries are policed by vigilant troops, so are social and ideological boundaries policed by vigilante groups. Television is not exempt from this militant tendency. Placing itself on the safe, commanding heights of consensual common sense, TV semiosis makes sense of the surrounding terrain by seeking to construct clear, unambiguous boundaries between us and them, between acceptable and unacceptable actions, beliefs and groups. But in order to sort out what should be inside from what should be beyond the pale, television over-represents the marginal, ambiguous, scandalous areas of society. Action series, drama, news and movies alike are founded on violence, murder and criminality; on deviance, dissidence and pathological behaviour; on illicit, over-displayed or abnormal sexuality; on break-downs, break-ups and break-ins. These kinds of marginality, exploring the grey areas between black and white, serve both to define the norms that they are shown to be transgressing, and to drive television's productivity as a system for the production and circulation of knowledge and pleasure, or sense and consciousness.

Thus marginality can be both peripheral and dangerous, and television cannot do without it. But equally, it cannot control the meanings that are produced in the process. For, in order to limit meanings, it must first produce excess. Television's signifying practices are necessarily contradictory. They are driven by marginalities whilst proclaiming their centrality, they are developed and changed in the peripheral gaps that they encourage us not to notice, and they produce more meaning than they can police. It follows that no matter how strongly certain readings are preferred, television's signifying practices are more open to challenge than is sometimes thought. Even if television, like formal education, tends to work in the interests of the efficient development of capitalism, and despite its undoubted success in popularizing hegemonic consciousness, the fact remains that, like schooling, it produces more knowledge than such functions require. And that knowledge is not under its control, either at the points of production, or at the points of consumption. Watching TV is relatively autonomous from producers' and controllers' intentions and even from textual determinants.

To make matters even worse for those who like to think of TV as a closed system of dominant ideology, another potentially risky margin has begun to threaten the security and discipline of the system in recent years. This is the margin between television and not-television, namely video and other forms of non-broadcast TV. For TV audiences can now break up the carefully constructed schedule by time-shifting, they can play around with naturalized images by using the freeze, creep and search facilities, they can even re-edit and dub recorded images into scratch-videos. This isn't exactly the mass appropriation of the means of production (neither are two more organized uses of non-broadcast TV – pop music and community video). But all of these are further evidence of how television practices escape the intentions of controllers and the notice of critics. Such practices mark a further moment both in the fragmentation of television and in the growing confidence and power of its viewers. Critics who bewail TV's ideological closure can only sustain their argument by ignoring or dismissing these marginal developments, when they should be using them as the basis for challenge, change and development in the social means of sense-making.

ACCOUNTABILITY

This brings us back to the connections between TV and parliament. Even radical critics of television seem to have been taken in by the myth of marginality, for their policy is often no more than a pale reflection of the parliamentary model. In other words, their response to television's disproportionate representation of marginal characters is to demand proportional representation for everyone else, as if the over-representation of law-enforcement agents on TV as compared with so-called real life can be countered by ignoring the symbolic status and narrative function of such characters and replacing them with a demographically accurate sample of the workforce, which would mean spending our evenings watching the next memo drop into the in-tray of the local civil servant, rather than seeing how civil society itself is created and sustained in symbolic cohesion by our real representatives from Angie Dickenson to Dixon of Dock Green.

Silly as they are, the demands for demographic proportionality are directed only at the safe, mainstream areas of news and entertainment, whilst the margins I have discussed are largely left to their own devices. In short, radical criticism of TV hasn't got far beyond a policy of parliamentarianism to solve the problems of minority representation. The result to date has been a kind of television version of the SDP. Adversarial opposition is rendered into a harmless and not very appealing alternative fragment (so-called minority programming) which is dangerous only to the viewing figures.

But the final irony is that even such interventions as these are rare, and are initiated more often by innovative professionals than by the organized left, or by cultural progressives who think a lot about the politics of signification. The latter groups, who claim to be in the vanguard of organizing counter-hegemonic consciousness, have swallowed the myth of marginality to such an extent that collectively (though with notable individual exceptions) they treat television as a whole as a marginal supplement to modern society – dangerous but peripheral. Their political energies and creative efforts are directed elsewhere, to the nostalgic safety of print, cinema, performance or live (but socially dead) media.

Meanwhile, because there's not enough organized critical discourse to account *for* them, and because there's not enough organized policy to bring them *to* account, both capitalism and popular consciousness continue to develop and change *unaccountably* in the margins of television.

Chapter 9

Regimes of pleasure: a fragment*

Q: Are you interested in young people?

A: I'm interested in people, I don't categorize. I think the division is more television and non-television. Those of us who grew up before television existed, our minds work in totally different ways. I don't really understand how the mind of a television person works. It seems they're much more bitty, much more in scraps, a much shorter attention span. They have a large, general, superficial knowledge of a number of things, but that's it.

(Gore Vidal; interviewed in *The Face* [London], August 1984)

One of the things that distinguishes the independent sector from mainstream cultural production in any medium is the existence of a critical debate about what such production should be for, and how it should differ from what is on offer commercially. Whether such debates are engaged in explicitly, with full theoretical fanfare, or implicitly, with working assumptions and practices, they have a strong bearing on how those who work in the sector judge their aims and objectives, their successes and failures.

But, just like the media themselves, these debates come from somewhere – they have a history. And whether their emphasis is on the aesthetic, formal aspect of independence or on its political, social aspect, the history of these debates often seems to be completely emancipated from developments in the practical production work itself. The ideologically sound flavour of the month can appear to be very remote from 'films that I like' – or make. In short, critical assumptions and frameworks of explanation are relatively autonomous from the practices they make assumptions about.

The result of this can be that productions that are ideologically sound get funding and critical acclaim (until you actually see them), whilst all sorts of innovative goings-on at the margins of critical attention are neglected.

* Originally published as John Hartley (1984) 'Regimes of pleasure', *One-Eye* (magazine of Chapter Film Workshop, Cardiff), 2, 6–17.

Perhaps this is one reason why the independent film sector has had such a hard time gaining recognition – it has not yet found a way to make sense of the things its members actually produce in terms that the current critical debate understands.

Frequently there's a very strong impulse to resolve this dilemma by trying to modify what's done so that it fits the demands of the critical consensus (which is of course often encountered as the funding body). However, in this article, I would like to pursue the opposite line. Instead of being at the mercy of radical orthodoxy, it might be interesting to think about where some of our critical assumptions have come from, and whether they are adequate for contemporary independent production. In other words, maybe the critical debates need to be modified in the light of developments in the media (both mainstream and independent), and not just the other way around. In the end, the reason for doing such an exercise is not so much theoretical as practical – it may offer a way of both making and making sense of what's done in the independent production context that is less dependent on outmoded judgements, and more confident about justifying itself in its own terms.

One of the things that started me thinking about this issue has to do with the way critical debates about television have developed over recent years. At first sight, it might seem that TV has little to do with what goes on in independent filmmaking. But it isn't so. In the first place, TV will increasingly form the frame of reference for independent productions (will they get a TV sale?), and for independent producers (will I get work?). Second, TV is by far the most important site of cultural production in the west generally – no attempt to carve out an independent form of cultural production will get far without paying due attention to TV, even if the chosen form is film. Third, the people who are now coming through as producers, in whatever medium, are the first generation whose own personal/social formation has been inside television – unlike those who have produced films and TV so far, we were raised on it, and by it.

But in spite of television's pervasive presence in our personal and public lives, critical debates about it are still to some extent locked into pre-television consciousness. We have inherited the ways we talk and think about TV from those, like Gore Vidal in his essentializing comment at the head of this chapter, for whom it was new, strange, threatening or silly. Even radical or avant-garde critiques of TV share a common-sense suspicion of it that can lead to quite disastrous policies of intervention, and to terrible films, too.

It is hard to intervene in critical debates about television without falling prey to already established preoccupations, policies and frameworks of explanation, even when these produce neither adequate understanding of TV as a cultural phenomenon, nor adequate policies that would change it without making everyone switch off. One of the impediments to progress in this context is the new left orthodoxy which is so convinced of TV's ideological and hegemonic role as an agency of class power that anyone who likes television cannot, *ipso facto*, be on the left.

I like television, and I always have; along with films, radio, print, photographs. The media have been among the shaping influences on me, though it doesn't feel like the sinister kind of influence that you often read about in critiques of the media (from both left and right). On the contrary, I have felt that my morals, my sense of self, my critical powers, etc., were under far more insidious attack in such contexts as school, church, family, theatre, etc., than in front of the media. Somewhere between the small screen that I've been watching and the big wide world of untrammelled capitalist exploitation that the critics have been watching, there is a missing link.

Critical debate about TV is still missing the link too often. Television is, at one and the same time, both what they say it is (a profit-making industry that is also a means of social control), and a popular source of pleasure, information, sense-making and self-building. Television is both of these things, and that's the link; the hegemonic is popular, the dominant regime is a regime of pleasure. But so far radical criticism has concentrated on the negative aspects to such an extent that it has become intellectually disabled and politically marginal: it tends to be neglected by both the professionals and the public at large.

This is not a satisfactory situation. Unless there is an organized critical discourse, and an organized collectivity of some kind (the organized left, intellectual culture, call it what you will) to produce, develop and popularize that discourse, then television will simply continue to transform its own and its audience's consciousness unaccountably. But any organized understanding of TV will have to get back in touch with whatever it is that makes television appealing: its regimes of pleasure.

À LA RECHERCHE DU TEMPS *PERDIO*

Just for the sake of argument, I thought it might be interesting to send critical theory on its summer holidays; to forget what it knows about television (and the other constituent media of the consciousness industry). Instead, I've been thinking about the place TV occupied in my own personal (social) formation. How does my own history fit in with that of TV? As it happens, I am among the first generation of TV viewers – just as I was getting established in the world, so was TV. So where does my television consciousness come from, and what did it feel like or connect with at the time?

I was sent to an orphanage boarding school at the age of seven or eight in 1957. Soon afterwards, I had my first encounter with television. This is how I remember it. The men stood in a row across the front of the school assembly hall. We, the assembled object of their collective gaze, did as we had been drilled to do. We danced the sword-dance, producing the magical star of six interlocking wooden staves at the end. We thought it was very clever. The men didn't say very much. One of them was the prime minister, Harold Macmillan. All of them had baggy trousers, and looked very old and big. Two of them held beige-coloured, streamlined, whirring objects to their eyes. I think they were clockwork, but it was hard to tell, since you didn't stare at strangers, not even when they were filming you. I had seen my first movie camera.

Later, other men came and set up a screen to show us what had happened. We saw a boy from our class, called Larkin, propped up in bed in the school sanatorium, being looked at by the prime minister. There was no sign of the sword-dance. So my first brush with the tube was atypical, since it was in an institutional, not domestic, context, and to do with production, not consumption. But, more typically, I was disappointed by the amount of coverage they gave to this prime minister person, not to mention Larkin, and by the fact that I had been edited out. I wished I'd been ill too.

Actually, the place where the prime minister had stood was already magical. It was normally occupied by the Scottish headmistress, whose accent, skin, hair-colour and power were the customary focus of attention in morning assembly. Later it was the place where I had my first experience of watching television.

Again, it was an untypical first encounter, since the school had been given a TV-projector. This stood in the middle of the hall, a big wooden box with a big round lens at the front. It had a spring-loaded tape-measure just under the lens, and you had to put the screen exactly at the distance of the extended tape. Then, everyone sat cross-legged in the darkened hall, all around the silhouetted box, gazing raptly at an image that magically appeared. You couldn't see the picture at all if you looked into the lens (a forbidden practice), so much of the viewing time was spent on speculations about how the pictures got on to the screen. What they were actually about I do not remember, except that they were puzzling or meaningless; intimidating evidences of a world we did not yet know. I do recollect the intrigued discovery of a place called Hartlepool in the otherwise baffling football table. I knew you were supposed to support one of the names, so I thought this one might have something to do with me.

Soon afterwards I learnt that there were real people involved in making television, and that such people were much to be admired. The occasion was a school prize day, when we juniors, the senior girls and the senior boys came together for the only time apart from church on Sundays (they were on three separate sites although part of the same school). The visiting speaker was a famous and honoured man, of whom I had not until then heard, who was not only successful and famous, but more importantly an

Old Royal – a former pupil of the school. He talked impressively, though I don't remember what he said. But he wasn't cowed (as I was) by our numbers and the governors, dignitaries and formidably hatted benefactors. It was a death-defying performance, and I felt personal loss when, not long afterwards, Gilbert Harding (for it was he) actually died.

When I graduated into the senior school in 1960 aged eleven, my strongest impression was of the overwhelming authority of everyone and everything. The school was run like a Victorian public school and much was made of duty and discipline, of power and punishment. In this context, I was introduced to the pleasures of cinema. I had been to films before – I wet the seat of our local picture house when I was taken to see *A Night to Remember* – but this was a regular treat in the school itself. Films were shown in the Victoria Hall, and the marble bust of the late Queen gazed imperiously at us whilst we got used to the idea of being in that authoritarian place (the daily site of prefects and put-downs, of hymns and the head) for pleasure without obligation, for purposeful enjoyment.

They took a lot of trouble getting us into the hall, and discipline was maintained until you sat down. But after that no-one extolled the virtues of lofty thought. You just watched the film. Even peer group pressure was relaxed. I remember pointing out on one occasion to my friend Matthews, who was from Wolverhampton and had decided views on the subject, that the people we were looking at were coloured (as we said then). But it was alright, he said, because they were in their own country. It was a great relief to me, since I had supposed that – since I was in thrall to Matthews – I should think what he thought, even in the privacy of my own head, and even though I had no idea why he was so vehement. But in front of the films it was different. You could be amused and amazed without having to impress or appease anyone in authority, from Matthews to Queen Victoria. And this uncontrolled regime of pleasure was constructed for me in the very same place that you sat in to reaffirm your allegiance to the authoritarian regime itself. Pleasure, in such a place, was akin to the sin of Saint Peter. Cinema has had something of that stolen selfish feeling about it for me ever since. I still find the opulence of both film production values and cinema buildings a bit subversive of authority – all that money for *fun*?

After leaving that school at the age of fourteen to return to a day school, I got used to being in a domestic environment again, and started watching TV regularly. My sister and I caused a serious fire in the kitchen when, in a hurry not to miss *Emergency! Ward 10*, we left the chip pan on the Creda. On another occasion we turned on the set to watch it, only to find a still picture and solemn music. I was at a loss. 'President Kennedy is dead', she said. It turned out she was right; such is the unfathomable wisdom of elder sisters. We had arguments too, of course. I hated *Jane Eyre*, or was it *Little Women*, on a weekend afternoon. But I found it hard to carry on glueing fiddly bits of rigging on to the USS *Constitution*, all the same. It had something to do with Ann Bell's jawline. I was fascinated by the personal style of speech, and by the household arrangements, of Herbert Lom and his 'daughter' (Sally Smith?) in *The Human Jungle*. It was a great treat to be old enough to stay up and watch it, just as it had been earlier to get further than the opening music and bell-ringing Wolseleys of Inspector Lockhart's *No Hiding Place*. I liked *The Plane Makers* (afterwards *The Power Game*), *Criss Cross Quiz, Rawhide, The Beverly Hillbillies, Bonanza, The Outer Limits, The Great War*, and, because others at home watched it, wrestling (our kitten was named after a wrestler called Togo). I don't remember the sitcoms (I didn't start taking them seriously until *Whatever Happened to the Likely Lads?*), but I do remember being bet ten shillings that I couldn't sit still and silent for the whole of one episode. I moved, but I got the money anyway.

Television was one of the ways I explored my early sexuality. I certainly looked out for bodily shapes and movements in variety shows like *Sunday Night at the London Palladium*, and I can remember getting a dreadful crush on one of Fred McMurray's 'sons' in *My Three Sons*. Then there was Cilla Black, Susan Maugham, Herman's Hermits (Peter Noone?), Dusty Springfield – I fancied them all. I took to other familiar faces in different ways, being particularly prone to admiring serious men with kind eyes – often journalists like Julian Pettifer and Derek somebody (Hart?). I couldn't imagine how you learnt to talk like they did, though sometimes I was deeply shocked and embarrassed when they caused some mysterious potentate to lose his temper.

All these unselfconscious and indiscriminate responses to TV were uncritical and non-political by any standard that I'd recognize now (though I suppose it was a paedocratic regime of viewing). And not all of the responses were positive ones. I don't actually remember what I disliked, but I often used to watch TV as a way of deferring other household tasks, or filling in time till the others came home. I watched a lot of horse racing that way, without ever getting to like (or understand) it. But, overall, by the time I finished school, TV was a central but unremarkable part both of my own sense of self and of our home routines. It even became an arbitrator between us, so that the domestic hierarchy was reproduced and modified in the choices about what to watch, and of course it was a source of things to talk, argue and enthuse about.

But meanwhile, untrammelled capitalism was doing its stuff, and we were mere unwitting subjects of its onward march. Somewhere along the line, our personal and its social formation made contact. After the Second World War there was a reorganization of the British economy, accompanied by the establishment of the Welfare State and a baby boom; I was one of those babies, being born two months after the National Health Service was opened in 1948. This period was followed by a consumer boom, presided over by that long, uninterrupted 'thirteen years of Tory misrule'. At the time, one of the highest priorities of the government was *house-building* – the annual figures seem impossible now, and were a source of both propaganda and amazement then. In such a conjunction of forces – babies, homes, welfare, a laid-back political climate ('Butskellite' consensus) – capitalism didn't seem all that bad, and capitalism wasn't slow to make the most of it.

Having built the houses, there was a progressive drive, with women as its primary target to begin with, to get people to *live* in them – not just to use them as dwellings, but actually to organize their lives around the domestic unit. And to achieve that, you have to have more than just an ideology of domesticity; you have to deliver the goods too. You have to fill the houses up with interesting things to do, useful things to have, and pleasant things to live among. Things like sofas, carpets, linoleum, vacuum-cleaners, washing machines, fridges, cookers, radios, TVs, freezers, stereos, washing-up machines, videos and computers. These goodies didn't all arrive at once, of course, and some are second-generation – stereos and video replacing the radiograms and TVs we'd got used to. Slowly, we chucked out all the Utility furniture and bedlinen, and the war was finally forgotten when everyone started eating muesli and sleeping under duvets.

But long before that, television had become established as a central object in every living room. It was no respecter of class (or gender), except that the working classes favoured big, grand 26-inch tellies with lamps, photos and embroidered runners on (our lamp was a kneeling black female nude figure holding up a shade made of scarlet plastic pretending to be pleated taffeta); whilst the middle classes went for smaller screens, and eventually broke into two camps. Either they pretended the TV was a Chippendale cabinet, and not a TV at all, or they sported the Perdio portable, with its 8-inch screen and grab-handle ready for the next upwardly mobile move.

As the 1960s progressed, capitalism (or someone) made all the TVs obsolescent, and they started spilling out of the houses, to be found mangled at every street corner. We had to go for 625 lines, and BBC2, and colour. But by this time, it made no difference. Television had gone beyond the stage of being an object to be wondered at in the home, a consumer-desirable (my only recollection of the first TV we had at home is of its shape and position in the room – I can't remember watching it, except to wonder why radio *Children's Hour* wasn't on). But by this time, television was not so much a product to be sold or rented as a handy means for the sellers to tell us about all sorts of other products we might like to have as well. By this time, we'd all forgotten how, or why, it had got there in the first place, and what we had thought of it at the time.

Along the way, we'd also forgotten how it felt in the early days when half the nation (not just half the TV audience) might be watching the same programme. Television had been, for a while, like a national church, a force for common popular symbolic unity. But not any more. The middle-class paterfamilias had to start letting his daughters watch ITV, and although it took years to get round to it, even the BBC regionalized its output. Then there was talk of new channels. Unity gave way to pluralism; the national culture to consumer demand, consensus to fragmentation. And although our elders and betters fretted endlessly about what it was doing to us, they gave us what we wanted – *more*.

AFTERWORDS

One of the things that did not fragment so quickly when television began to offer more was the barrier between popular entertainment and critical discourse. There remained a brick wall between those who watched television and those who went to art college and university to be trained in cultural production and critique (even when the two sides were located in the same body). Here it transpired that many productions and practices were seen as critical largely because of their self-conscious distance from popular media. Television justified the very existence of the independent sector by being the 'other' it was reputedly independent from.

Moreover, watching television remained insulated from theory, which had no influence on my early viewing formation because I'd never heard of it. Furthermore, my own case history didn't support the then dominant 'effects' theory. Television didn't make me violent or passive, or affect my standards of language, behaviour or morals; in that department it was no match for other disciplinary institutions, which took such matters seriously. Nor did TV liberate me in any self-conscious way; it was not a site of resistive pleasure, because the pleasures it offered always seemed to be its own, not specifically prohibited ones. It didn't brainwash me into acceptance of capitalism, nor did it soften me up for recruitment to the other side. It had about as much effect on me as did speaking English, which may well have been considerable, but which is invisible to effects theories.

I think the major 'effect' of television in my own early days was waste. Programmes came and went, taking their knowledges and emotions with them. Perhaps official policy-makers were so fearful of TV's potential effects that everyone in a position to know worked hard to make sure it didn't have any. Despite its political content, TV was not a site of citizenship. Although I liked to look at it, it was not a medium for aesthetic appreciation. Nor was it an authoritative source of knowledge about such subjects as history, nature, music and America, in all of which it nevertheless excelled. It wasn't even a vehicle for placing and understanding the drift of everyday life, of which it was so effortlessly an integral part. In short, its regimes of pleasure were neither self-reflexive nor organized around viewer participation. If you wanted to make anything of it, that was up to you, but you got no encouragement. The ambitions of the audience in relation to television as such were not stimulated beyond the immediate horizons of piecemeal sensation.

Without a public discourse to encourage it (but with plenty to discourage it), television failed for a long time to attract the attention of many from among its own first audience who might have had something to contribute to it, as part of a 'television culture' of producers and viewers bound together by dialogue around its growing body of work. Meanwhile that audience went to art school and university to learn how to participate in cultural politics and in the arts, where the traditional literary and visual cultures were nurtured well out of sight of popular TV. Given that television is far from communicative when it comes to telling the public about itself in any but promotional terms, and given that cultural politics does not as yet include the *right* to participate in any artistic medium, TV included, it was not perhaps surprising that few among its first audience noticed its potential for their own sense-making productivity.

In effect, what eventually sparked my interest in television as an object of study was not its own internal or immanent properties as such, but the gap between these and its public reputation. What was television *for*? Despite its familiarity, popularity and pleasure, there was no positive answer to that question for its first audience. In the traditional discourses of criticism, appreciation and social theory, TV was reputed to be *against* various established standards, but it wasn't *for* any. It just snuck into the living room, and was supposed to attract about as much critical and creative interest among those who lived there as the design of the sofa on which they flopped to watch it. That is, if the work of design, creativity and criticism was noticed at all, it was supposed to be seen as finished, for good or ill. The gap between production and use, between critical culture and popular understanding, couldn't have been wider.

Perhaps things are different now. The forces of production in the economy of sense-making are more developed than ever. Production, use and critical culture may yet come together. By the time they do, however, television, in its classic form of broadcast services to whole populations, may no longer be popular. It is not inevitable, but it is likely, based on the history of such forms as the novel, cinema, even comics, that just as critical culture catches up with popular culture, the latter will have decamped. Then the artists will have elbow room and the critics will be able to sift and assess in peace, but a new generation of semio-consumers will be disappearing over the horizon, wondering what's going on.

Part IV

Photopoetics

Chapter 10

The politics of photopoetry*

ON PHOTOPOETRY

The debate about 'culture' has, historically, been conducted around literature; since Arnold, Eliot, Leavis and the instatement of English as the 'Queen of the Humanities' in education, the question of the relationship between aesthetics and culture has been debated via (and reduced to) largely graphical matters: the domain of alphabetically printed literary writing. In short, poetry is print.

However, I begin instead with the concept of vision. Vision, the faculty of sight, has long been used as a metaphor for its opposite, for seeing that which is not here. The seer, the visionary, is the traditional bearer of truths, or at least knowledges, which serve to inspire, discipline or even countermand the truths and knowledges of the material world. In the twentieth century, such vision has escaped the confines of mere metaphor; we have the technology for seeing that which is not here. Television and video, and their popular predecessor, cinema, are the means by which matter can be taken and turned into an image.

'Far sight' = *television*; 'I see' = *video*; 'movement' = *cinema*; these are the 'making or creation' (Gk = *poem*) of imagination. The matter that they take is of course light; 'light-writing' = *photography*.

These things – light-writing, vision, poetry, imagination, image – are the stuff of what? Not necessarily of 'learning', nor of 'judgement, decisiveness', even though those concepts came into English from the classical languages, respectively, as 'literature' and 'criticism' – the stuff of literary culture. The contemporary visual media are literally 'I-see-far-movement', and they produce what I'll call *photopoetry* (making or creation with light). The imaginative poetics of visionary far movement is the domain of popular culture.

MEANS OF PRODUCTION, MEANS OF VISION

I want to start with a distinction that Humphrey Jennings made between

* Originally published as John Hartley (1990) 'Culture and popular culture: the politics of photopoetry', in Martin Coyle, Peter Gardside, Malcolm Kelsall and John Peck (eds) *Encyclopedia of Literature and Criticism*, London and New York: Routledge.

the 'means of production' and the 'means of vision' in *Pandaemonium* (a book he was working on in the 1940s but which wasn't published until 1987).[1] Jennings is best remembered as the wartime filmmaker (and co-founder of Mass Observation) whose propaganda films – *London Can Take It* (1940), *Listen to Britain* (1941), *The Silent Village* (1943), *Fires Were Started* (1943) and *Diary for Timothy* (1944) – mark a high point of British cinema poetics. His book, *Pandaemonium*, is 'the imaginative history of the Industrial Revolution'. It comprises several hundred short quotations ('images') from writings dated between 1660 and 1886, from John Milton to William Morris, on the coming of the machine.

In his introduction Jennings argues that the function of the poet has, historically, been subjected to a division of labour, such that poetry becomes more specialized, until at last it has no subject but itself. Meanwhile, the function originally performed by poet-sages like Homer, Hesiod, Moses, Lao-Tze, namely to deal with '*all* problems of life – religious, scientific, social and personal', did survive, but outside poetry. Furthermore, the Industrial Revolution wrenched the means of production and the means of vision apart from one another. In what Jennings calls 'Magical systems' there was no distinction between ploughing and praying, eating and blessing, hunting and magic, building and glory.

For him the Industrial Revolution (capital, free trade, invention, machines, materialism, science) raises a question that is urgent:

> In what sense have the Means of Vision kept pace with these alterations? I am referring not to the Arts as a commodity for Bond Street, or as a piece of snobbery in Mayfair, or as a means of propaganda in Bloomsbury, or as a method of escapism in Hampstead . . . but to the Means of Vision by which the 'emotional side of our nature' (Darwin's phrase) is kept alive and satisfied and fed – our nature as Human Beings in the anthracite drifts of South Wales, in the cotton belt of Lancashire, in the forges of Motherwell.[2]

The distinction Jennings makes between the means of production and the means of vision is interesting, not only because it is crucial to an understanding of the life of the imagination in industrialized countries (which it is), but also because Jennings doesn't take sides; he argues for imagination and for industry, not for the primacy of one over the other. His own work as a filmmaker, in both its means of production and its imaginative vision, is photopoetry; our nature as human beings, if you like, in the drifts, belts and forges of industrial culture.

Unlike the cultural criticism whose hegemony is being forged in Bond Street, Mayfair, Bloomsbury and Hampstead even as he writes, Jennings does not seek to rubbish civilization in the name of culture. He assumes that 'the poet's vision does exist, that the imagination is part of life, that the exercise of the imagination is an indispensable function' of humanity, 'like work, eating, sleeping, loving'. In the intellectual climate of mid-century England, this integrated theory of poetry and industry is nothing less than counter-hegemonic; subversive of the dominant cultural regime, and deliberately so, in the name of quite different interests which Jennings sought to represent.

ON MELANESIANS (AND PUNKS)

T.S. Eliot will serve to illustrate what Jennings was up against. Regretting the death in 1923 of the popular music-hall artist Marie Lloyd, 'the expressive figure of the lower classes', Eliot proceeds to regret also the technological successor to music hall, and the future promised by the industrial means of production. 'With the encroachment of the cheap and rapidly breeding cinema', he writes, 'the lower classes will tend to drop into the same state of protoplasm as the bourgeoisie.' And this tendency, for Eliot, is lethal. He invokes the Melanesians, whose 'natives . . . are dying out principally for the reason that the "Civilization" forced on them has deprived them of all interest in life. They are dying from pure boredom.'[3] Eliot's vision of the future is this:

> When every theatre has been replaced by 100 cinemas, when every musical instrument has been replaced by 100 gramophones, when every horse has been replaced by 100 cheap motor cars, when electrical ingenuity has made it possible for every child to hear its bedtime stories from a loud-speaker, when applied science has done everything possible with the materials on this earth to make life as interesting as possible, it will not be surprising if the population of the entire civilized world rapidly follows the fate of the Melanesians.

I suppose this must be the 1932 equivalent of the Sex Pistols' 'No future'. It's tempting to re-read Eliot's rhetoric as a fastidious version of punk graffiti, just as Matthew Arnold's Victorian vision of culture might be read as no more than an early version of 'Anarchy in the UK'. It's hard to resist the image of Eliot as culture-punk, pogoing furiously in his own *Wasteland* and gobbing contemptuously on his own audience. It's tempting to make fun of an adversarial ideology that lines up theatres, musical instruments, the horse and bedtime stories (presumably because they're all 'live', including the horse) against the 'entire civilized world'.

But I refrain, because what's important, to Eliot and to this discussion, is not the content of the ideology but its adversarial structure. For Eliot, Arnold and their loyal fans, the hope of poetry lies in pitting it against civilization; distancing the means of vision still further from the means of production. Culture is anti-technological, anti-modern, anti-popular. Popular culture is thus *structurally* the opposite of 'live' culture; that is, it is death. Its content doesn't matter.

THE HOPE OF POETRY

For Jennings, on the other hand, the hope of poetry lies in 'the "emotional side of our nature" (Darwin's phrase)'. However, on looking up Darwin's phrase near the end of *Pandaemonium*, it's clear that the hope of poetry *qua* poetry is not what it used to be. Charles Darwin is actually quoted as finding no solace in it. Quite the reverse:

> But now for many years I cannot endure to read a line of poetry: I have tried lately to read Shakespeare, and found it so intolerably dull that it nauseated me. . . . The loss of these tastes is a loss of happiness, and may possibly be injurious to the intellect, and more probably to the moral character, by enfeebling the emotional part of our nature.[5]

The hope of poetry, it would seem, lies outside poetry; even Shakespeare is inadequate. Darwin himself makes much of the interest he retains in any writing other than poetry: history, biography, travel, essays and novels.

> Novels which are works of the imagination, though not of a very high order, have been for years a wonderful relief and pleasure to me, and I often bless all novelists. . . . I like all if moderately good, and if they do not end unhappily – against which a law ought to be passed. A novel according to my taste, does not come into the first class unless it contains some person whom one can thoroughly love, and if a pretty woman all the better.[6]

The solace of popular culture is ever thus, but there's more at stake here than the origin of speciousness. The debate I have tracked through *Pandaemonium* is on the evolution of the politics of culture.

THE POLITICS OF POPULAR CULTURE

Pandaemonium is engaged in a politics of memory. Jennings's book is *anamnesic*, bringing to mind a history that is in touch with, but radically different from, the history of F.R. Leavis's 'great tradition' or the 'selective tradition' of Raymond Williams. It is a constructed history whose politics are post-Marxist, and this in the 1940s, long before such a term was current in cultural theory.

Jennings's history is Marxist in two fundamental ways. It is based on an acceptance of the determining force of the means of production, the form of ownership and the division of labour; and it is committed to a political socialism corresponding to the interests of the industrial productive classes (South Wales, Lancashire, Motherwell). But it is *post*-Marxist because its central focus is on images, imagination, the poetic function of humanity and the politics of culture ('animism' vs. 'materialism'). That is, Jennings does not make culture superstructural but basic. His book is an attempt to trace the archaeology of a discourse. It brings to the reader's attention not just a reminder of thoughts expressed in the past, but also, in its principles of selection and in the specific items selected, an implicit theory of ideology.

More importantly, this theory and this archaeology are not designed for the community of professional intellectuals to whom Eliot and other theorists of culture normally address their remarks. It's not *intra*-class communication, but *inter*-class alliance-building. Jennings wanted *Pandaemonium* to appear in popular form (i.e. as a mass circulation paperback). To find out why, it's useful to turn to a film.

ON PROPAGANDA

Picture this eye-riveting scene. A South Wales miner, face blacked like a coal-commando, eyes shining with the intention to kill, crawls towards his oppressor with a rifle. In answer to Lenin's famous question 'What is to be done?' a voice intones instructions from the communist newspaper *Lais y Werin* ('Voice of the people'): 'Work slow. Sabotage your machines. Put water in the oil.' Meanwhile, the Welsh hymn 'Ar hyd y nos' ('All through the night') renders this revolutionary programme at once nostalgic and patriotic. All through the night, Welsh miners deal out death.

Is this a scene from a nightmare vision dreamed by the home secretary of the day, Winston Churchill, during the Tonypandy riots early in the century, when soviets were formed by the miners, and, on Churchill's order, troops were sent into the streets of mining villages to pacify the insurrectionist Welsh? No. It's a scene from a film made by the Crown Film Unit; propaganda for the wartime government led by Winston Churchill. It's a scene from Humphrey Jennings's *The Silent Village*.

For those who have eyes to see, the film's closing speech, delivered by a representative of 'the Fed' (the miners' union), about the 'power, the knowledge and the understanding' of miners to oppose oppression wherever it occurs, is as much a statement of counter-hegemonic class consciousness as it is an idealization of popular British war aims. Such is the power, the knowledge, the understanding of Humphrey Jennings's film that it can posit the war as a people's conflict against fascism, conducted by those who had less reason than most to support British governments; in Jennings's hands it's a socialist war, and a war for socialism.

Jennings was committed to a class alliance between intellectuals and workers, between – if you like – poetry and industry. He took the opportunity to lecture to the miners themselves on this topic while in Wales to make *The Silent Village* (and these lectures were one of the main spurs to get on with *Pandaemonium*). But more than this, his filmmaking practice, and his films, represent and promote an alliance between the photopoet and the people. The alliance is not merely metaphorical; the community filmed in *The Silent Village* is in fact a mining community, and the characters play themselves – schoolteacher, collier, union official, mother, shopkeeper and so on. During his stay Jennings wrote:

> I feel we have really begun to get close to the men – not just as individuals – but also as a class – with an understanding between us: so they don't feel we are just photographing them as curios or wild animals or 'just for propaganda'.[7]

Or as Melanesians, we might be tempted to add.

PHOTOPOETIC POPULAR CULTURE

The relationship between filmmaker (or any other textmaker) and audience is always founded on actual or potential alliance. The possibility of a radical result requires not only radical intentions and practice on the part of the producer, but radical potential among the audience constituency; an 'understanding', as Jennings puts it, between the two parties, via the textual apparatus. Jennings's films are radical in the sense that they depend for their success on that understanding.

There's always a disconnection between the imaginative domain and the productive domain, as well as a connection. Jennings's vision of the people is precisely that, a vision, not a mere reflection of some pre-existing lumpenreality. If, as a result of seeing such photopoems as *The Silent Village* and *Listen to Britain*, or of reading *Pandaemonium*, certain ways of making sense of the domain of production begin to circulate among members of the productive classes as a means whereby they can grow in 'power, knowledge and understanding' of their situation, then the credit for that belongs to them, not to Jennings. The power of a text to mobilize specific responses, whether of action or imagination, is not in the gift of the text.

However, what makes Jennings unusual is that he recognizes the possibility or potential of a relationship between the aesthetic and the industrial domains, between colliers and himself – a 'thoroughly intelligent tough aesthete . . . way above the ordinary run' as one of his collaborator-subjects called him.[8] That's why he wanted his work in popular editions and in popular media.

The Silent Village is ostensibly about a Nazi atrocity in the Czech mining village of Lidice, dramatized for greater impact as if it takes place in Cwmgeidd, South Wales. So it's a true story, but a visionary drama. It's a documentary, but poetic. The figures on screen play fictionalized roles, but they play themselves. It is government propaganda, but it celebrates the power of those whose interests oppose the government; patriotic but socialist. It is a celebration of a popular culture that's not based on entertainment at all; popular without being populist.

And it's not alone. Down the years, there has been a great tradition of popular films and television productions committed to the politics of the popular imagination. By itself such a commitment doesn't convert its holder into an intellectual, much less a political, heir of Humphrey Jennings, but it is worth mentioning that in the decades when television was taking its own hold of the popular imagination, there were radical innovators right at the centre of it.[9] They include some obvious names, but also others whose work is less obviously politicized.

From the 1960s there is director Ken Loach and producer Tony Garnett's *Cathy Come Home*; Loach and James McTaggart's *Up the Junction*; director Peter Watkins's *Culloden* and *The War Game*; writer Johnny Speight's *Till Death Us Do Part*; writers Dick Clement and Ian La Frenais's *The Likely Lads*; the early *Coronation Street* (from December 1960); *Z Cars* and *Monty Python's Flying Circus*. From the 1970s there is writer Trevor Griffith's work including the series *Bill Brand*; Loach, Garnett and writer Jim Allen's *The Big Flame* and *Days of Hope*;[10] Colin Welland's *Roll on Four O'Clock* and *Leeds United!*; Philip Martin's *Gangsters*; Ian Kennedy Martin's *The Sweeney;* Clement and La Frenais's *Whatever Happened to the Likely Lads?* and *Porridge*. From the 1980s there is Alan Bleasdale's *Boys from the Blackstuff*, produced by Michael Wearing, who also produced Troy Kennedy Martin's *Edge of Darkness* (which I'll come back to later) and *Blind Justice*; the BBC's serial *EastEnders*, and a whole swag of imaginative output from the minority commercial Channel 4, perhaps even – given its highly successful interpretation of its statutory mandate for innovation and experimentation in form and content – Channel 4 as a whole, at least under its founding Chief Executive, Jeremy Isaacs.

I invoke these names – and there are plenty of others, including all those from America, where the context of network TV makes cultural radicalism look quite different[11] – in order to show that popular culture has an intellectual and aesthetic history that's all too often lost in the perennial arguments about high and low culture. The 'money, snobbery, propaganda or escapism' of high culture has resulted in a general view that there's not much in common between them. But the two domains are in much closer touch than Eliotic rhetoric would suggest.

MEDIA + EDUCATION = MEDICATION?

There is indeed something in common between high and popular culture. High culture is a product of popular culture. High culture as a concept, as a discourse and as a body of texts, is a product of two social institutions (institutions of memory): education and the media. Its imaginative hold upon the public, if any, is created and sustained by teaching, and by constant reminder.

Education was established in the nineteenth century as universal and free – that is, mass communicated and compulsory – but that doesn't mean it was democratic. On the contrary, one of its original purposes was to innoculate the people against their own unhealthy tendencies: to infect them with a controlled dose of culture in order to forestall the outbreak of more dangerous contagions like moral decline and civil commotion: culture vs. anarchy. In the twentieth century, the arts are still seen by their propagandists as a shot in the arm;[12] while for the people at large the injection of culture into the curriculum produces only antibodies – the natural responses of rejection and development of resistance.

The scholasticization of Shakespeare means among other things that a division of labour has occurred between the pedagogic professionals who profess his art, and the public at large, for whom Shakespeare means nothing other than Schooling – compulsion, tedium, arbitrary power, capricious morals and a collective wearing of the dunce's cap. Shakespeare's art is lost on generations of groaning students (including Darwin), for whom it is as universal and liberating as a well-swung sock full of sand.

A ROSE-TINTED SPECTACLE

The media comprise the second of the social institutions of the art of memory in contemporary culture. They're the 'bardic' remembrancers[13] who spin into narrative and spectacular stories the doings and sayings of cultural heroes and villains.

On 12 March 1989 a news story appeared in the largest circulation newspaper in Western Australia, the Perth *Sunday Times*. Here's part of it:

> LONDON: Actor Ian McKellan climbed down into a large muddy hole and cried out: 'To think that the voice of William Shakespeare echoed from these stones.'
>
> Around him, archeologists scraped at the foundations of the newly discovered Rose Theatre on Bankside, where the Bard made his London debut as an actor in 1592. . . .
>
> Traffic crossing the Thames River thunders along Southwark Bridge, where passers-by idle to stare at the diggers below.
>
> McKellan was joined by 17 other Shakespearean actors and actresses supporting efforts to preserve the remains of the Rose.
>
> . . . The dig has found thousands of hazelnut shells – the Elizabethans' popcorn – and clay pipes, one with a bowl as small as an acorn.
>
> . . . Museum of London experts who uncovered the remains after an office building was torn down two months ago, originally had only until this weekend to dig before quitting the site to allow a new office building to go up.

> But after meeting with developers Imry Merchant Securities, Harvey Sheldon, the museum's archeological officer for Greater London, said time had been gained . . .

The image of an actor ten thousand miles away crying out in a hole in the ground, trampling over 400-year-old hazelnut husks and upmarket dog-ends, surrounded by collapsed walls and building sites, voice muffled by thundering traffic, playing to an audience of journalists, attracting the idle gaze of the accidentally passing public, to marvel at London's 'first commercial theatre', is perhaps a suitably complex and perplexing metaphor for the relations between high culture and popular culture in the twentieth century.

On the other side of the planet someone thinks this is newsworthy, albeit only on page 52, squashed up against a display advertisement for another kind of culture, requiring another kind of muddy hole in the ground – ready-to-install prefabricated swimming pools. It is in this unlikely context that the contours of culture are drawn.

The story is one of celebrity conflated with culture. It narrates some contemporary oppositions: heritage vs. development, art vs. commerce, performers vs. spectators, even echoes vs. hazelnuts. Meanwhile, the story meditates on death and immortality – preserving the remains of the Rose. These are not unimportant matters but they're not innocent either. The Manichaean oppositions characteristic of journalistic discourse (see chapter 5) serve to separate and oppose the means of production (development, commerce, spectators, hazelnuts) from the means of vision (heritage, art, performers, echoes), or, civilization from culture. In this version, the opposition makes heroes out of Shakespeare (and McKellan), so it tends also to make villains out of the rest, which includes the world that both the news media and their audiences actually inhabit.

Shakespeare is invoked to represent values that reproach the contemporary world. That's pretty much the only role left to him nowadays. His name supplies the necessary element of conflict around which the latter-day bards can weave anamnesic fictions, barely conscious of the contempt they show to themselves and their readers.

INVESTIGATIVE DRAMA

Troy Kennedy Martin's first television success was the long-running BBC-TV police series *Z Cars* (1962 to the mid-1970s). Acclaimed at the time for its realism, its apparently honest depiction of the bureaucratic and routine side of police work,[14] it was nevertheless as much about television as about policing, with strongly identifiable characters, action, location and genre, in stories written for prime-time popular entertainment. *Z Cars* did what good television can do, using the police series as a vehicle for pursuing investigative drama into the symbolic side-streets of its own times and culture. It provided the popular audience with a shock, not of the new, but of recognition.

Much later in his career, Troy Kennedy Martin wrote the best police drama series ever made for television. *Edge of Darkness* (BBC, 1985) tests its genre to destruction. Its photopoetic vision sheds not light but darkness on the familiar landmarks of the generic and social landscape.

Its structure, the investigation of a murder by a policeman working on the edge of the law, is familiar. As he discovers just how wrong his initial assumptions are, Inspector Craven's investigation disrupts and exceeds its conventions. Generically, the drama moves from the centre of a popular entertainment form to the edges of experimental innovation. Diegetically, it moves from the concerns of an ordinary man to a heart of darkness. It's a dangerous journey to the rotten core of global power games, from the familiarity of home to an undiscovered country where understanding and death are coterminous.

TO HAVE GREAT POETS

What sets *Edge of Darkness* apart is the relationship between the text, its makers and its audience; a relationship of trust, both textual and social. Textually, it relies on the viewer to enter its imaginative space without constantly labelling the landmarks, without doing the work of understanding on behalf of the audience; both parties are on the edge of darkness (though not that of a muddy hole rendered sacred by history and shouting). Socially, it trusts its audience to desire understanding; the shock of recognition triggered by the device of defamiliarization. The rewards are tangible; *Edge of Darkness* can get away with visions that under other circumstances (e.g. documentary or current affairs) wouldn't make it to the screen, and its method of investigative drama can unravel some of the complexities of public life more truthfully than investigative journalism.

Unlike Humphrey Jennings, Troy Kennedy Martin displays nothing more than a dramatic vision in this work; his photopoetry is not founded on an explicit theory of ideology, but, like Jennings's films, it does build alliances with a popular audience it knows and trusts. The means of vision do keep pace with the means of production; *Edge of Darkness* offers the contemporary viewer an image of – and a sense of personal responsibility for – 'our nature as Human Beings' (Jennings's phrase) in the era of nuclear power and environmental destruction.

The result is not just good drama, but good politics. Todd Gitlin closes his definitive study of American television, *Inside Prime Time*, with these words of Walt Whitman: 'To have great poets there must be great audiences, too'.[15] Like Shakespeare and Humphrey Jennings, Troy Kennedy Martin is a great poet, and his greatness is founded upon that of his audience – the *culture* of popular culture.

THE POLITICS OF MEMORY

But to have great audiences, critics must take photopoetry seriously, too. Gitlin's invocation of Whitman is actually a pessimistic response to his conclusion that American network TV is fawning and condescending. The networks 'are not *trying* to stimulate us to thought, or inspire us to belief, or remind us of what it is to be human and live on the earth late in the twentieth century; what they are trying to do is "hook" us'.[16] If the commercial entertainment of consumerist popular culture has no other purpose than to act as a hooker, it may be because the alternative (respectable high culture) is too awful to contemplate. It's a long time since the BBC used the brute force of its monopoly to broadcast Bach cantatas at prime-time, believing it could cultivate the people against their will and better judgement, but the cold war that has been waged between popular and high culture in the domain of criticism and cultural policy throughout this century is just as responsible for the perceived inadequacies of popular culture as it is for the preservation of the perceived qualities of high culture. The contribution of cultural criticism to popular culture cannot successfully take the form of tarting up Shakespeare for popular consumption while despising the people and what they consume. It doesn't work.

Criticism – the stuff of literary culture – is historically a failure in its attempt to preserve in literate memory a vision of culture divorced from production and opposed to it. The vision is there, right enough, but it hasn't succeeded in disciplining popular culture.

However, within that domain there is another history, some memories of which I have tried to jog in this essay. In other words, popular culture is not and never was as banal as high culture's wilfully ignorant and disdainful view of it. Instead of cold-shouldering popular entertainment, a strategy that lets it off the hook of critical self-reflexivity, cultural criticism needs to remind popular culture of its past and its potential.

Fortunately the cultural cold war is giving way slowly to a period of detente and even Gorbachevian goodwill in recent times. This is just as well, because discourses organize practices, and the practices of popular culture can only be organized through discourses that are widely circulated and themselves part of cultural memory. The means of vision in the late twentieth century are too important to be squandered in forgetfulness, while the function of criticism is too important to be squandered on Shakespeare.

Chapter 11

Continuous pleasures in marginal places*

TELEOLOGY

Some time ago, in wooden de-mountables on the wrong side of the campus, or on the other side of town across the binary divide of the tertiary sector, television studies was taking corporeal form. What a peculiar thing it was. Traditionally, people who take up textual studies of a given medium – literature and cinema for instance – are drawn to it because they think it's important or they like it. Television studies, perversely, was peopled by those who thought television trivial or despised it: a ratbag collection of tired ex-professionals seeking serenity in early retirement and vanity publishing; psychologists relentlessly pursuing the victim in order to justify their own brutal methods and personal nightmares; Marxist sociologists schooled in false-consciousness berating the media in the afternoons and watching telly at night (and never noticing the connection); renegade literary critics desperately looking for a way to grab the attention of card-playing hulks who earned more than they did but who were forced to attend liberal studies before they qualified as mechanics and mining engineers.

People who actually did like TV and knew a bit about it were also despised. But then the general public never do get much of a look-in when professional intellectuals gather in any number. Not that the general public was all that interested in despised academics from despised institutions looking at a despised medium, academics who couldn't even explain what they did for a living to the grocer or hairdresser.

Academic discourse, like knowledge of all kinds, grows out of institutional sites. But in the disciplined departments of the ivy league, television was not so much a branch as a *twiglet* of knowledge. Even now it isn't corporeal enough to have its own name – there are no departments or professors of, or degree programmes in *television*. So television studies appeared merely as marginal activities conducted by the undisciplined younger element within traditional departments, or, in down-market institutions, as a block, unit, module or stream in communication, cultural, or media studies – anything but television.

* Originally published as John Hartley (1989) 'Continuous pleasures in marginal places: televison, continuity and the construction of communities', in John Tulloch and Graeme Turner (eds) *Australian Television: Programs, Pleasures and Politics*, Sydney: Allen & Unwin.

The first thing needful, in such unpromising circumstances, was *theory*. What better than to follow the fashions of respectable radicals, to borrow the cast-offs of cinema and literary theorists, especially as the labels were all in French, so who knows what part of the body they were actually designed for? This was fun. After a while all the theorists were dressed up (they even went through a strutting-in-front-of-the-mirror phase), putting on *New* French *Accents* and asking 'Does it suture?' 'I'm doing Lacan-can!' chortled one. 'Look at my Lyotard!' retorted another. 'Après moi, le Deleuze!' moaned a third. 'Rhizomes, simulacra, what's the *différance*?' agonized one more. 'Cherchez la femme!' warned the only woman present. Then everyone joined in the chorus: 'Hey-down, ho-down, derry-Derrida! Among the LeaviStrauss-O!'[1]

It was a foregone conclusion. Tele-ology was born.

REARVIEWMIRRORISM

When printing was first invented in the west, it was made to look as much as possible like the medium it was destined to supplant. The so-called *incunabula* didn't look like books at all, they looked like manuscript writing. Likewise, when concrete was first used to build a house (called Gregynog Hall, in Wales) it didn't look like concrete at all. It looked like Tudor half-timbering.

This phenomenon is called 'rearviewmirrorism', or so says Marshall McLuhan.[2] In the early days television's own mainstream genres were developed on the rearviewmirrorist principle.

> This wonderful age
> Goes to show that all the world's a stage.
> First you heard,
> Now you see,
> And you wonder what the next thing on the list will be!

That song, called 'Here's looking at you', was composed for the first-ever public television broadcast by the BBC at the Radio Olympia Exhibition in August 1936. Referring back to both theatre and radio, not to mention Shakespeare and technological progress, its incunabular rearviewmirrorism was confirmed in the items chosen for the show – current variety acts from the London stage and Pogo the pantomime horse.

Right from the start television displayed many of its later characteristics at the level of repertoire, scheduling, genre and style (not to mention the levels of corporate organization and financing, regulation and control). But its diet was gathered almost indiscriminately from existing media – the legitimate and variety theatre, the press, cinema, radio, pantomime and popular music.

Broadcast television was officially launched by the BBC on 2 November

1936. After the opening speeches the continuity announcer, Leslie Mitchell, introduced an edition of *British Movietone News* (made for cinema), which was followed by the popular singer Adèle Dixon. A magazine show called *Picture Page* hosted by Joan Miller had already been piloted and went on to become a twice-weekly regular. Drama was produced from the BBC's studio at the Alexandra Palace (the Ally Pally) from the outset, and within a year the BBC Television Service was doing outside broadcast specials of civic and sporting events like King George VI's coronation, the boat race and the Derby. Walt Disney soon rang up from Hollywood to offer the fledgling medium one of the cinema's great successes, and indeed viewers were in the middle of watching a Mickey Mouse cartoon when the BBC unceremoniously pulled the plugs on television in September 1939 at the outset of the war.[3]

However, one ingredient was missing from this rearviewmirrorist recipe, perhaps the most important one – the audience. To begin with, television was transmitted for only two hours a day (3–4 p.m. and 9–10 p.m.), to a potential audience restricted to the reach of the single transmitter at the Ally Pally in North London, and restricted further by the prohibitive cost of a receiver. So careless of their audience were the radio-minded BBC management that to begin with they even failed to put out test transmissions during the hours when dealers could demonstrate TV sets to prospective customers. Television was a side-show foisted on them by government decision, and they saw no need for a campaign of audience building. The BBC's top brass didn't see television as a mass medium at all.

It was precisely at this point that rearviewmirrorism failed. It was a mark of television's coming of age as a medium when it broke free and developed beyond mere invention and form to become a cultural force in its own right. Despite the fact that the BBC was then and still is the biggest single broadcasting organization in the western world, it played no part in the *emancipation* of television as *popular* culture; it was off the air in the crucial period until 1946.

Appropriately television's successful bid for freedom occurred in the democratic vistas of America, after the launch of commercial TV in the mid-1940s. It was this that mobilized the beginnings of a mass audience, recruited to TV as part of the post-war wave of optimism and consumerism, a consumerism which included an unparalleled concentration on the home and domestic, private life. For the first time the home began to be defined as a space for leisure pursuits and life-style, as well as being seen as both a secure refuge and an efficient machine for sustaining and motivating the workforce. New post-war priorities, after the demobilization of women from active participation in the war effort, centred on the family, leisure, welfare, modernization, hygiene and gadgetry. Television was a product and promoter of these forces (see chapter 14).

Theorists of culture were uniform in their response. They were horrified.

The unselfconscious invention of television's own specific genres and forms went unnoticed, unaccounted for because the only respectable attitude towards television – for conservative and progressive radicals alike – was not even as forward-looking as rearviewmirrorism. Television's first critics simply turned their backs on it.

Since then, masked and gowned against contamination, one or two of them have turned round. But even now their purpose is often not so much to account for television as to demonstrate their own theoretical razor-sharpness. Eventually they think they've got it all stitched up, get bored and wander back to the leafier surroundings of high culture. But, however deft they may be, surgical skills that have been honed for another purpose cannot anatomize television without making a bloody mess of it.[4]

What's TV all about? 'Suture self', they reply, munching a Twiglet.[5]

Left to its own devices at last, television theory can only take the advice of a departing well-wisher, whose words still echo down the corridor: 'Well, it's all over. We have to start again from the beginning, asking one another: what's going on?'[6]

MARGINAL PLACES

Some time earlier, in wooden de-mountables on the wrong side of the continent, or on the other side of the world, Western Australia was taking corporeal form. What a peculiar thing it was. King George III had entrusted Captain Arthur Phillip with a fair bit of land in 1787, but its western margin was defined as longitude 135 degrees east (not quite as far west as modern Alice Springs). The present state-line, 129 degrees east, shares with that original border the distinction of marking, from the top of the continent to the bottom, *nothing*. But in 1787 the nothingness extended westwards. There simply was no Western Australia. Nor did the New South Walians expand westwards, American-style.

The colony was implanted, directly from Britain, from the sea, twice (first at Albany, then at Fremantle/Perth), mainly to keep the French out. More than twice it failed, but teetered into the twentieth century on the back of convict transportation, Kalgoorlie gold and Aboriginal enslavement.[7] It was never confident of its corporeal integrity; there was once a plan to sub-divide it into Northern and Southern States, and its (white) citizens voted for secession from Australia in 1933. Even now it isn't unified into a community – its regions and its citizens still have less in common with each other than with their sources of immigration from over east or overseas.

Western Australia is an experiment, one of the last deliberately experimental societies on earth. Among the experiments is community building, done in a self-conscious developmentalist style reminiscent not of the old country but of, say, Singapore. Indeed, the creation of a public, of an image for the state and its capital city, an 'imagined community'[8] of Western Australians, is, as in Singapore, semi-official policy.

To newcomers from old-established countries, where communal selfhood is taken for granted, and where nationalist rhetoric combined with capitalist money and provincialist self-aggrandizement smacks of fascism, such policies are often dismissed as dangerous and naïve, all the more so given that the main vehicle for the promulgation of positive, euphoric images of Western Australia is commercial television. Occasionally everyone does come to the party together (though not all to celebrate), most spectacularly during the 1986–7 America's Cup at Fremantle. On this occasion, however, the tides of people who flowed through WA for the event ebbed away all too rapidly afterwards (see chapter 12).

Western Australia, like television itself, remains a marginal place, regarded by rearviewmirrorist observers as hardly worth bothering about.

But to dismiss self-conscious community building as quasi-fascism (*manqué*) would be a mistake. First, because it's often just a symptom of the effortless superiority of those who think they know where the centre of the world is. This usually turns out to be their home-capital for Europeans, a bad habit they've passed on not only to New Yorkers but even to the so-called t'othersiders of Australia for whom it's Sydney (or Melbourne). Secure in their own self-centred metropolitanism, such observers may not notice the lesson of the America's Cup episode for Western Australia. This effort, led by the media, failed to raise the temperature of a sufficiently critical mass of citizens to produce fusion into a self-renewing community. Everyone just went home. But that only demonstrates the need for investment in community building, not the failure of it. Second, community building is a continuing struggle even in old countries, as anyone from *old* South Wales can testify. Wales, a neglected western margin, reduced to an economy of primary, extractive industries, with an indigenous population whose language, culture and land is under tremendous pressure from Angloid settlers, and where unity is impeded by the isolation of small communities connected not by roads but by sheep, is a 'nearly-nation' having more in common with Western Australia than might appear from their relative physical sizes. Both have experienced a continuing struggle to define their small, internally divided communities as different from the much stronger states to the east which control their economy and political structure, if not their culture and politics.

Where Wales differs markedly from WA, however, is in the antagonistic rhetoric and action that defines it *in opposition* to England/Britain; an opposition led by professionals, intellectuals and the public sector. WA, conversely, has tended to consign self-promotion to the private, commercial sector, where it more often takes the form of glossy publicity than that of adversarial politics. Wales might learn about euphoric self-constructing imagery from WA ('Love you Cardiff' seems ludicrous, probably because no-one's tried it). And WA might learn something from Wales, where a ten-year campaign co-ordinated by Cymdeithas yr Iaith Gymraeg (the Welsh Language Society) culminated in the only U-turn of the first Thatcher government with the establishment in 1982 of Sianel Pedwar Cymru (S4C, i.e. Channel 4 Wales), dedicated to broadcasting Welsh-language programmes at peak viewing hours, despite the fact that Welsh-speakers are a relatively small minority in their own land.

If we're to believe myths of typicality, prime-time TV coincides with those times when people cast off the cares of economic survival and indulge in a little self-building and family-bonding – creating micro-communities for which they can take personal responsibility. Television's intellectual and artistic achievement is to have found a way of contributing to this process. Although it turns millions of individuals into its audience, it's watched inside those micro-communities, each of which constitutes itself as audience in its own evolving way, and uses television for its own idiosyncratic purposes.

In modern societies there are a few communities which cut across demographic boundaries like class, nation, region, age-group, gender, race; prominent among them are intellectuals and artists. But by far the biggest such community is that of *popular culture*. Corporate television is impelled by its own institutional imperatives towards populism (or, if it's lucky, true popularity once in a while). It produces non-material commodities that no-one buys, bartering symbolic unity and diversity, novelty and familiarity, conflict and consensus, to a community it has itself produced, in exchange not for people's money, but for their valuable time.

Among the products of that exchange are knowledge and art; not formal, professional intellection or 'fine' art to be sure, but popular knowledge and accessible art. In marginal places like Western Australia, the imagery that binds the micro-communities of dispersed families to their environment and to the wider community is supplied free, gratis and for nothing, by marginal television. Cute, euphoric and partial it may be (like so many successful pedagogic tactics), but it's just about all there is on permanent public display to differentiate *here* and *us* from all the other locations and characters in the global scenario.

AMNESIA (LEST WE FORGET)

Globally, television is one of the culture industries (like religion, pop music, tourism, education) – industries where the commanding heights of power and profit are not at the point of production at all, but at the point of distribution.[9]

In fact, TV never went through an individualist, entrepreneurial mode of production (as cinema did), and producers never had power over their products or over the industry. Now, traditional basic industries like food are in the same boat – owning the means of production is neither here nor there, as farmers from Illinois to Bangladesh can tell you. Even in food, it's transnational agribusiness, controlling distribution, which has cornered not just the market but the whole vertically integrated industry from top to bottom.[10] But television started that way.

Just as Burbage's theatre and Shakespeare's Globe were among the very first fully capitalist enterprises (joint-stock companies of capitalists, managers and actors selling popular drama on an entrepreneurial basis, outside the regulation of the city or the patronage of the court, to the public for profit),[11] so television is the model for twentieth-century economies. Contrary to habitual thinking, which dismisses the cultural industries as mere Mickey Mice in comparison with the macho sectors of primary industry and manufacturing, culture is the cutting edge of advanced monopoly capitalism. There's more in common between the Swan of Avon and the Swan Brewery than you might think.[12]

The distinctive features of television are produced not out of any intrinsic or essential form but by an irresolvable contradiction right at its corporate heart. On the one hand, networks (controlling distribution) must maximize audiences in order to survive, and they must do it every day since the invention of overnight ratings and people-meters. On the other hand, people watch TV in the hope of seeing something new, or at least novel versions of the familiar. And this means that no-one can tell in advance what will prove popular. So the problem is to get viewers into the habit of re-consuming non-material commodities they've never seen before, a trick broadcasters must perform without having an accurate idea in advance of what sufficient numbers of the viewing public will find appealing or who that public is.

Economic imperative coupled with institutional insecurity – this rather than aesthetics is the foundation of the form of television as a creative medium. It explains why TV offers a repertoire rather than one standardized product – hedging of bets raised to cultural policy. It explains scheduling, the art of capturing particular categories of bums on seats (or, since this is TV, potatoes on couches) at different times of day – mums, kids, families, dads, in that order. It explains why networks are more powerful than creative personnel, since no one producer can bear the costs of the number of failures it takes to sustain each success in the game of predicting the unpredictable. And it explains TV's cultural forms – the genres most likely to offer novelty within a habit of reconsumption – drama serials and news, sport and mini-series, and not least the weather (see also chapter 6).

Fifty years after its first broadcast, few writers bother with television *as television* – neither journalistic nor academic writing has noticed the potential of the medium poking out between the programmes, like concrete glimpsed through the illusion of Tudor timber. Indeed, like concrete glimpsed when you think you're looking at 400-year-old wood, television's own genres look tacky, duplicitous, kitsch and cheap compared with the supposed authenticity of former forms.

It's only when you start looking at them concretely, in their own terms, that their illusory veneer becomes interesting.

ANAMNESIA

Continuity is the television that isn't there. You cannot find reference to it in TV guides, and unlike news, drama, the weather and sport, it doesn't occupy an established place in peoples' conversation about television. No other medium has anything quite like it, not even radio, which has found other ways of being continuous. Interestingly the two media seem to be heading in opposite directions in this respect. Radio appears to be minimizing the boundaries between programmes and segments, and many shows have dispensed with their own theme music, so the listener is carried over the threshold in the least bumpy manner. Television continuity takes thresholds much more seriously, with full fanfare, confetti everywhere.

Continuity is the gap between programmes, between whatever you're watching. You may not notice that you're watching it even while you are watching it. It's filled with familiar emblems, oft-repeated slogans, jingles, images and ideas. It's used to promote the channel that you're watching, the programmes you might watch on that channel, and to promote the country in which all this is happening (see also chapter 8).

Its use value for the channel is strictly pedagogic: it teaches you what and when to watch; it teaches you how to watch, how to feel, what to look for, how to look. It's the yardstick against which all the other TV genres can be measured, because it assumes no prior commitment from you – not only does it have to work, or not, entirely on its own merits (no-one promos promos, though there have been ads for ads), but also it is vital to the interests of the broadcasters; they use continuity to keep you. It occupies the dangerous time when channel and viewer can go out of sync. with each other; when repertoire, scheduling, capital investment and fat executive salaries can be countermanded by a squirt of infra-red from the disaffected couch potato: remote-control democracy.

Its use value for viewers is more pragmatic: it lets you make a cup of tea. That is, it reinstates real time, and it restores to the viewer a sense of agency, a gesture of self-recollection. Viewers, multi-conscious,[13] can do more than one thing at once; as well as clearing your throat, your bowel, your mind, you can plan, desire, reject. You use continuity to position yourself in relation to television, to *sidle up* to it.

Continuity performs the rhetorical function of *anamnesis* – the opposite of forgetting – the function of *bringing to mind.*

FROTTAGE

Nowadays, on commercial television, it could be argued that continuity is the norm, programmes are the deviation. There are whole channels devoted to programming what is, formally, nothing but continuity – MTV and its clones, for instance, or the two cable weather channels in America.[14]

Even more remarkable is the propensity for continuity to distend; to become bloated, tumescent. This usually happens at times of self-induced national euphoria, brought on by either a sporting or a civic occasion – the America's Cup, the Bicentennial. On such occasions, there are shows lasting perhaps half a day, consisting entirely of continuity. They are the most costly, most complex, most technically sophisticated shows that TV can do, and only TV can do them (see also chapter 15, part II).

Here postmodernist self-reflexivity is raised to the status of referentiality – it's what such programmes are about. Here's the plot of *Australia Live* (1 January 1988): not 'Happy 200th Birthday, Australia', but 'This is how many people at how many locations, using so many gew-gaws for such an amount, on so many channels in this many countries, that it will take, is taking, has taken to say "Happy 200th Birthday, Australia." ' That's entertainment – literally the *big time*, in this case four straight hours simulcast on one commercial and two public channels.

Such shows, together with ordinary continuity and commercials, are the interface between television as an institution and its public. For the viewer, they are the moments when, in the privacy of the home, secure from public gaze behind decently draped suburban windows, we can take pleasure in *being* the public.

This pleasure is akin to frottage – traditionally defined as sexual excitement associated with rubbing up against another's clothed body in public. In the case of television continuity, the pleasure is not directly tactile but it is the pleasure of getting *in touch*, kind of furtive brushing, a glimpse, a frisson of excitement provoked by taking private pleasures from public contact. Like frottage, this pleasure can lead to ennui if carried on for too long – a sixty-second, unselfconscious stimulation can be surprisingly

---

Looking: 'Launch 85' opens by introducing us to the simulated audience; dancers whose performance is to look; we look at them-as-us, and learn how to look with warm anticipation. We see the set; a musical stage cum election studio. The props celebrate the euphoria of looking: stage-lights; clairvoyance; sports T-shirt on pretty body. A smiling couple look at a source of light symbolizing anything from a drive-in cinema to a street-cafe, faces shining in the reflected light of heterosexual consumption. The action begins with a contractual handshake between the dancers, simulating the relation between Channel 9 and its audience, and as a dancer's leg swishes past the camera, acting as a curtain opener, it reveals the early evening celebrity and game shows whose hosts are electronically marched up to claim our instant recognition, before the promo marks time by teaching us how to recognize both television scheduling and family ritual, via the nightly community service announcement (in line with the Australian Broadcasting Tribunal's definition of 'C' time), that sends the toddlers to bed with Humphrey Bear and his kiss-blowing minder before adult programming begins at 7.30 p.m.

Channel 9 Perth launches 1985: *'There's never been a year like this before!'* – Part 1
A sixty-second promo, intensive training in how to watch TV.
(For the lyrics sung over this promo see note 24)

agreeable, but if the same type of stimulation is prolonged for hours, as in the *Australia Live* show, it can irritate more bodily organs than just the skin.

The private/public, clothed and furtive pleasure of frottage is ambiguous – if it is to be a pleasure at all, there must be some question about who is furtively brushing up against whom; a question not only of seduction but also of reciprocation. Does TV continuity caress us with its seductive surfaces, or do we perve on the symbolic contact it offers us with attractive others?

The contact of continuity, positioned at the interface of public and private, is the place of modern citizenship. Television, the modern forum,[15] is the place where we can jostle pleasurably, keeping in touch, to see, hear and participate in the otherwise imaginary community to which we belong – our nation. And it's the place where we can identify ourselves as the public, as citizens and as consumers, the source and destination of *publicity*.

WINDSCREENWIPERISM

Television's stratagem for differentiating sameness is a special part of continuity: the *trailer*. Trailers are the art form of time, locking the viewer's future into the here and now, erasing distinctions between fact and fiction, between the past and the news.

Trailers are quite unlike the genres that surround them; they're not the rearviewmirror but the windscreenwiper of television, the neglected but vital component for seeing into the future. Trailers are dialogic, participatory, explicit about who's talking to whom, ephemeral, conversational, focusing our attention on our personal future (will I, won't I?). Trailers do much of their work using the very stuff of their opposite; that is, observatory, third-person narration and drama. The trailer promotes time-based consumption while simultaneously subverting it – it can compress the longest mini-series or special to half a minute. The sophisticated viewer takes as much pleasure or more from trailers as from the programmes themselves, which often feel like coercive and tedious filler in comparison with trailers' fragmented, postmodern aesthetics of excess. From the

---

Prime-time drama: Now we see our simulacra performing the act of drawing closer to the source of visual pleasure as a multicultural but not Aboriginal community, teaching us how to look at (American) television by looking at us looking at them-as-us. Prime-time teaches gender-choice, with shows for men: *Hill Street Blues*, *Knight Rider*, *Remington Steele*, *The Fall Guy*; and for women: *Love Boat*, *Dynasty*. Two shots from each show dissolve into the next on an action or character cue, before the dancers' bodies whirl in as curtains to end Act 1 of the evening, performing the euphoria of frottage as the men hold the women and the women, electronically joined by the Quantel magic of Channel 9, hold each other.

Channel 9 Perth launches 1985: *'There's never been a year like this before!'* – Part 2

viewer's point of view trailers are the *originals*, seen first and determining the *authenticity* (promise) of the narrative whose image they are.

And so the tail comes to wag the dog, or at least the trailer wags the drama. On US network TV, one-off telemovies and documentary specials (the leading edge of mainstream experimentation) are not commissioned unless their genre, plot, characters, stars, action, mood and topic can be conveyed, euphorically, in a twenty-second grab repeated during the couple of days before TX (transmission) time.[16]

i-DEAS FOR i-DEAL PEOPLE

Time is relative on television. A TV-hour is fifty-two minutes, whereas a TV-minute is sixty-two seconds. The former leaves room for continuity and commercials, the latter leaves a margin to make sure continuity is continuous.

An ID (or ident) is anything from a fifteen-second logo to a two-minute promo. A station or network uses its ID and logo, as well as graphics, movie openers, news openers, news bumpers, personality launch campaigns, nightly line-ups, seasonal promos and other presentation material, as the foundation of its public image:

> The 'front man' for a TV station, the ident has to project that station's values and personality while appealing to a mass audience over a long period of time.[17]

i-D is a magazine, the self-styled 'worldwide manual of style, the indispensable document of fashion, style and ideas', launched in London in 1980. Maria Del Sapio describes *i-D* thus:

> It announces a new art politics, an art of living, 'art as informational combat'. It is a politics that recognizes the role of the mass media in continually rewriting the past in the name of the present and turns this into a zone ripe for the individual art of adaptation and exploration: clogging the system, overloading the lines, scrambling the codes, generating new possible senses through the kindling of a plurality of meanings. . . . It is an aesthetics that deals not only in the exhibition of the surface effect, but also in the exhibition of the process of creating,

---

Actuality: Real life gets a look-in with a ticking stop-watch; the lesson in genre classification continues with popular weathermen, personality current affairs presenters, celebrity eye-witnesses peering into reality for us in *Sixty Minutes*, and the local news anchors with 9's own news on the studio monitor. Now, ushered in by the athletic bodies of the youthful dancers, the curtain opens on sport, including a lesson in how-to-look-horrified and how to recognize world-class Australians, before the insatiable dancers gather to squat in leggy readiness for whatever's next.

Channel 9 Perth launches 1985: *'There's never been a year like this before!'* – Part 3

> recalling, juxtaposing, manipulating, deforming, imagining, and thinking with signs . . . within a technological space where the intensified circulation of signs has problematized the primacy of the subject as the origin of meaning as well as such concepts as causality and linearity.[18]

If all this is so, and if *i-D* isn't just a magazine for bone-headed bimbos and postmodern hairdressers (or even if it is), then it's easy to see where it got its name from, not to mention its i-Deas. Television IDs are stupendously costly, taking six to nine months to produce, using the very latest animatics, Quantel or Harry digital production, 3-D effects, computer software (and even, in a recent bold move by the ABC, live-action photography). According to insiders, Australian production companies are 'certainly world-class', and Australian TV-IDs are 'most definitely the best produced in the world' (although many of them are produced in Los Angeles). Each channel's ID is broadcast many times a week, and each ID is designed for a long, evolving life-span – anything from a year (the 7 network) to a decade (the ABC). Such repetition could easily become irritating and monotonous, making the audience see infra-red instead of the intended rosy glow, hardly a desirable outcome from the network's point of view – hence the investment.

Oddly enough, the insiders don't seem awfully sure if the investment pays off in terms of viewer response. One from the 7 network, admitting that the different channels do compete for the best ident, said: 'I don't know how much the viewers care. It's just important to have a very classy image and a better profile than some of the country stations.'[19]

An ABC executive, commenting on the highly praised new logo for the national broadcaster, said:

> The contemporary feel can work as a tiny psychological trigger, reinforcing the identity the network wishes to project. We don't expect an immediate response to the colour-coding but over time it will become second nature to even occasional viewers and, as a bonus, it adds an interesting diversity to on-air presentation. The test will be how the idents look as they go to air in a package (there will ultimately be 15) and whether they have a different kind of effect in the lounge room. We believe they have a definite Australian feel without us having rammed it down the viewers' throats.

Prestige drama: Movies are signified by instantly recognizable sprocketed images rolling down the screen. The lesson in 'reading televison' climaxes with specials, Australian-produced drama serials and mini-series by means of an electronically turning story-book page, superimposed over the dance stage. The dancers break in to combine nationalism with sexuality, the Aussie flag and Hogan's ANZAC heroics proposing the supremacy of the nation, which itself turns into the imagined community of 9's dancing viewers, holding cut-outs of 9's celebrities, simulacra in the hands of simulacra, until the orgasmic balloon finally goes up on the last chorus, exactly sixty seconds after the first chord.

hannel 9 Perth launches 1985: *'There's never been a year like this before!'* – Part 4

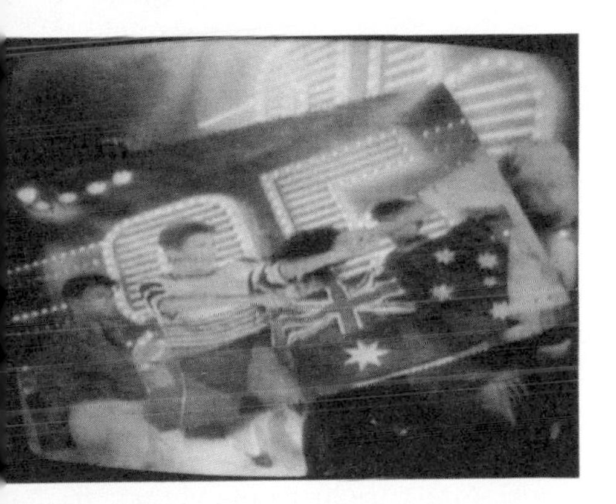

Network 10 is more self-confident about the intention of their logo, but silent on its reception: 'The new logo was developed with specific goals in mind and in the briefing it was deemed desirable for us as a network to be perceived as exciting, dynamic, professional, energetic, entertaining and sophisticated.'

The 9 network could only enthuse about the glass effect in their national 'travelling map' logo, in which each capital city can see itself reflected: 'The cities will each have their own look, which is very important to the local viewer.'[20]

LOVE YOU PERTH

And of course the local viewer is very important to the networks, for despite the global production and distribution of TV programming, the audience experience is always local (see chapter 12). Australian television stations, never more than so-so in their efforts to encourage local production (see chapter 13), have got into the habit of flattering their audiences with local images. This can be seen for what it is – a commercial imperative to maximize ratings. Commercial imperative dictates that state/city-based programme production doesn't extend much further than the quotidian news and current affairs shows that inveigle their way into the local topography by means of giant advertising hoardings around town, sporting the visages of toothsome personalities whose job it is to introduce items generated *there* to people located *here*.

But to get a picture of here and us you need also to look at the gaps between programmes. In those margins which are nevertheless the *sine qua non* of commercial television, Western Australia itself and its citizens are constructed into legibility. Television continuity and advertisements exceed their commercial purposes even while fulfilling them, for to create viewers and consumers is also to create a community, to bring the global, national and local together into the home.

Until 1988 there were two commercial channels in Perth: 7 and 9. They vied with each other to picture what it is that makes this part of the world lovable and shiny. Channel 7, with its 'Love you Perth' promo, concentrated on the city itself and some of its pretty, cute, friendly representatives, from policemen and nuns to the local band V Capri, who all signalled their community with each other by holding up seven fingers. Channel 9, made of sterner stuff, showed the country as well as the city, and work as well as leisure locations, with representatives of different ages and ethnic origins (though, like 7, no Aborigines), in their 'Shine on 9' series. Being

We love you Perth – because we invented you. Channel 7, Perth's first television station, continues to construct the community, taking the diversity of newscaster, child, city, nuns and musicians, and turning it into the symbolic unity of a hand and two fingers (in that order); Perth loves 7 too, it seems.

hannel 7 station ident 1985:
ove you Perth'
arious versions, from fifteen seconds to two minutes (at closedown).

Alan Bond's America's Cup station at the time, 9 devoted much of 1986 to an evolving promo called 'Sailing Australia' (to the tune of 'Waltzing Matilda'), which traced the history of the Cup back to the 1983 victory, and introduced us to the faces, syndicates and boats that were congregating off Fremantle. As the challengers and defenders were whittled down to the final contenders, so the promo was updated, until at last in early 1987 there was nothing left to euphoricize in that direction, and 9's promos turned their attention away from local images to concentrate on images of television itself, in a series with the rather poignant title, under the circumstances, of 'Still the One'.

For their part, commercials interact with the local community in various ways. The most telegenic ones tend to be for (inter)national brands, which consumers will then see in the local supermarket or check the price of in the local papers. Among the best of them, as I write, is an advertisement for Decoré Family Shampoo. This takes a classic rock and roll tune, puts Decoré lyrics to it, and sets it in the bathrooms of bright and shiny families. We see a pretty young woman singing in the shower while subjecting the shampoo bottle to the masturbatory gesture made familiar by raunchy rock singers. Other bathroom artistes join the fun, though not each other, until we end with a picture of a clean, healthy and thoroughly *sexualized* family. It seems to have gone down well in the suburbs, whose inhabitants are perhaps grateful to sec themselves represented on the cusp between sex and *driers* and rock'n'roll, for a change:

> We would like to congratulate the makers of the Decoré advertisement. We think it's the best advertisement we've ever seen on TV. We love the music and can only wish all advertisements could be as good as this one. If they were, it would be a pleasure to watch them.
>
> (Spitzer Family, Willetton)[21]

Here then is frottage incarnate, enacted, and located in the imagined community of ordinary family life. It's not an image of Western Australia, but of popular culture, which in Willetton at least means the same thing.

However, there are plenty of advertisements that do associate local products and places – stubbies and sunsets. But, this being WA, 'local' doesn't always mean quite what you'd expect; for instance, viewers of the statewide country station Golden West Network (GWN) might be treated to an advertisement for a local hardware store which is in fact a couple of day's drive away. Even so, you can sometimes get a glimpse of what does drive local preoccupations; another current GWN ad promotes silos for the farming community, showing semi-trailers trundling round a dirt track with the gleaming silver monsters strapped on their backs. As if this isn't curious enough for a TV commercial, a replica AC Cobra pops up at the end of the advertisement – a classic sports car of the 1960s frolicking in the wake of the semi-trailers. It turns out you can buy one of these from the same

TV commercial for Roy Weston Real Estate Ltd:
'Perth, the loneliest, most isolated capital city in the world'
McCann-Erickson Advertising, Perth, 1985.

We love you Perth – but where in the galaxy are you? A real estate commercial perplexes itself with helicopter shots over water, 'Star Wars' captions and vertiginous views of the cityscape. The cinematic language of desire and postmodernity did not transfer well to the small screen, apparently – people in Perth didn't appreciate being told they live in the television equivalent of a galaxy long ago and far away, and this ad soon disappeared, to be replaced by a series showing a homely, female, busy-bee of an agent doing things quickly for ordinary euphoric clients in the comfort of their golden-lit homes.

company. Sports cars, silos and semi-trailers – far flung, far fetched, far out.

In 1988 the third commercial channel (10) opened in Perth. Along with ownership changes and the move to national networking, this event has had its effect on both continuity and commercials. Increasingly, even these are produced in Sydney for national distribution. But there's still profit in appealing to the local viewer, it seems. Channel 7 has moved deftly into the new era by doing something I think no TV scholar has yet attempted – an *archaeology* of television promos, naturally its own. The 1988 promo shows a TV screen, on which we see, anamnesically, clips from 7's promos going back to the days when it was Perth's first and only TV station (in 1959). This TV on TV comes into bigger close-up as we come up to date, ending with the most recent and familiar images and slogans – 'Love you Perth' and 'Say Hello'. Putting itself in quotation marks, 7 proposes its relationship with the Perth community as being *precisely* one of *continuity*. It's the last word in rearviewmirrorist tele-ology.

HOW TO BE AN AUDIENCE

I came to Western Australia in January 1985. I turned on the television. It was an episode of Trevor Griffiths's first TV series, *Bill Brand*, followed by an old *Sweeney*. I was reminded of something Trevor Griffiths had said years earlier about this particular conjunction. This is what he said:

> I simply cannot understand socialist playwrights who do not devote most of their time to television. . . . It's just thunderingly exciting to be able to talk to large numbers of people in the working class, and I just can't understand why everybody doesn't want to do it. . . . If for every *Sweeney* that went out, a *Bill Brand* went out, there would be a real struggle for the popular imagination.[22]

Bill Brand is a drama serial about the career of a British left-Labour MP, whose political and personal affairs provide a vehicle that Griffiths uses to pursue topical political and moral issues. *The Sweeney* (devised by Ian Kennedy Martin) also stars a couple of working-class heroes. But between the unglamorous South London locales and the protagonists' jokey relationship, class antagonism somehow slides into defensive mateship. Political and moral issues are there right enough (I once called *The Sweeney* the television of recession[23]), but politics is rendered as the relationship between the lads and their immediate environment, in which the vehicle used for the pursuit of moral issues is a Ford Granada.

Shine on 9 – The whole State of Excitement, country and city, old and young, workers and schoolkids, America's Cup yachties and ethnic communities, is unified in diversity by 9's people and places, its smiling faces. Step up to a Ninier, Shinier Tomorrow!

Channel 9 station ident 1985:
'*Shine on 9'*
Various versions, from twenty to sixty seconds.

I must say I was glad to watch these two worthy sparring partners from long ago and far away struggling for the popular imagination in the long, hot Perth summer. But what really caught my eye was something I'd never seen before. It was Channel 9's 'Launch 85' promo, right after *Bill Brand*, and it spoke to me personally. Actually it sang: 'There's never been a year like this before!' I couldn't have agreed more, as this simple jingle prompted me, windscreenwiperistically, to peer into my own imagined future in a new country through what Channel 9 reckoned it had in store for its thunderingly excited viewers.

On closer inspection, this pedagogic promo was a lesson in *reading television*, if I can put it that way. The opening shots *performed* the act of looking, and of preparing to look with a mood of excited anticipation. It wasn't actors but dancers who played the role of the audience, and I gazed on them like some latter-day phrenologist, looking for the bumps that might tell me wherein lies Australianness.

In one television minute, I was guided in genre and scheduling, and shown how to be a young, attractive, heterosexual, energetic, euphoric, partying viewer with my smiling face lit up by the nearest source of visual pleasure. Meanwhile, more than a dozen personalities and as many shows were electronically sutured, embellished with Australian but not Aboriginal icons and presented through hi-tech effects which choreographed faces, gestures and actions into instantly recognized personalities and genres.

Now *that*, I thought, is struggling for the popular imagination in no uncertain terms: it's literally *enacting* the popular imagination, making it visible and hummable. It proposes the symbolic unity of viewer, nation and television, at one with Channel 9; it's the viewers (live, jigging up and down) who take over from the stars. They end up literally as cardboard cutouts in the simulated viewers' hands; paedocracy triumphant.

The odd thing was, no-one I spoke to about this promo seemed to have bothered much about it. It seems the popular imagination is *self-erasing*, although I did have the jingle rattling around in my head for weeks.[24] And, permanently marked for me by this augury incantation, 1985 did turn out to be quite a year. But that's another story.

Chapter 12

A state of excitement*

The familiar radical slogan is: 'Think Globally; Act Locally'. This advice was not so much subverted as inverted during the America's Cup in Western Australia (1986–7); the trick was to act globally but think locally. An event induced by media, the Cup attracted 3,000 or so visiting journalists and created a new meaning for WA in the eyes of the world's TV. But it generated more than euphoric images of Australia, sport and leisure for the tourists; it provoked, within the host community, an unwonted but sustained bout of self-reflexivity and utopianism. It became the mechanism, or rather the *practice*, through which questions of national or state identity and signification could be thought through; it was a race against time, space and structure. What follows can be read as a review of some aspects of an exotic local event; equally, however, it can be seen as an account of an increasingly international cultural–political phenomenon – the *euphoricization* of democracy and the mobilization of national unity as a commodity to sell on the open market of the consciousness industries within a global economy of commodified meaning. Within this economy, the distinctions between texts and contexts disappear – the bodies and actions of the people involved (which is everybody) are *textualized* into a cultural practice of competitive performance; to put the local on show for the global – to *act* globally.

A STATE OF EXCITEMENT

Western Australia is a sign in need of a referent. The size of Western Europe with the population of, say, greater Croydon, it is the site of mines and other holes in the ground,[1] surrounded by, well, nothing. Its metropolis, Perth – according to a 1986 advertisement broadcast on local television on behalf of the Roy Weston Real Estate company (the 'HouseSold Name in Real Estate') – is the 'loneliest, most isolated capital city in the world'.

* Originally published as John Hartley (1988) 'A state of excitement: Western Australia and the America's Cup', *Cultural Studies*, 2(1), 117–26.

After the America's Cup, Western Australia displays, in defeat, questions. It is characterized by space, emptiness, isolation, disequilibrium, enigma. Its history is of successive immigrations in the form of rushes, followed by disappointment, stagnation, regression and slow, ebbing depopulation. Founded in 1829, it still has more immigrants from overseas or over east than native-born citizens. Successively, land areas and specific means of economic exploitation are worked out; mines are abandoned, forests felled, crops are swallowed up in salt and sand.[2] People are reminded that they belong elsewhere. They go. Some go, some die.

The questions aroused by the America's Cup, by another cycle of rush, defeat, depopulation, are, like Western Australian industries, *primary* questions. They're not 'what kind of place is WA?'; not 'how do people look at it?' Those are interpretative, value-added questions, relying on the familiar manufacturing processes of realist intellection where signs and discourses are combined with referents in an expanding, self-sustaining economy of knowledge. But such questions, which concentrate on fitting suitable fictions to known facts, presuppose the prior existence of primary referents. For Western Australia, this would be incautious; here, the primary questions are 'is it?'; 'is there anything to look at?'; 'is there anyone to look?'

Of course, there's a land mass and a population. But just as the state's economy has not, as yet, achieved integration, complexity, or self-sustaining expansion, so the land mass and the population are not, as yet, integrated into a sign that self-evidently proclaims 'Western Australianness'. They have not achieved legibility within an economy of coherence. Like the slogans on the state's vehicle licence-plates which continue to proclaim, after its loss, that WA is the 'Home of the America's Cup', or that it is, in defeat, the 'State of Excitement', they are pure signs, uncontaminated by referents.

In the familiar, white, western economy of knowledge, Western Australia must be tamed, shorn of its realities and then spun and woven into realism; it must be transformed from nature to culture. As it stands, it cannot *stand for*; to white, western eyes it is a giant, fearful, unthinkable Other – the only remaining vestige, perhaps, of the old imperial *Heart of Darkness*, 'the horror, the horror'.[3] In an entirely appropriate exchange of symbols, after the America's Cup, victory is – literally – swallowed up in death. A representative of culture in the shape of a 24-year-old American part-time model, partaking of the ultimate tourist experience, has attended the Cup event, and is now cruising around the Kimberley coast in the state's far north-west, accessible only by sea. She stops for a swim (or perhaps the call of nature) under the falls on the Prince Regent River. In a latter-day version of 'The Convergence of the Twain', the 'grotesque, slimed, dumb, indifferent' representative of nature, in the shape of a large crocodile, queries 'What does this vaingloriousness down here?'[4] The weapons of culture, in the shape of a shoe hurled at the crocodile's head, do not prevail; the woman is, as the local euphemism has it, 'taken'.

But horror is not confined to the natural world in Western Australia, it suffuses the social world too, both public and private. Just as the competing crews were taking a few days off over Christmas 1986 for resting and rorting, there was another death, in Perth. A 25-year-old Murdoch University student had been imprisoned for a month for driving whilst under suspension. In prison he fell ill. As is customary in Western Australia, the prison authorities assumed he was under the influence of illicit liquor or illegal drugs. So it was only after some days that he was taken, dying, to hospital. Although he was delirious and had only five days of a sentence for a victimless, minor traffic offence to serve, he was, as is the custom in Western Australia, shackled to his hospital bed with a stainless steel leg-iron, and guarded by two warders. No-one from the prison bothered to inform his mother. Her comment, as given to the *Sydney Morning Herald* (18 April 1987), was:

> Nothing can justify the State being worse than the worst among us. It was the most barbaric thing I have ever seen – something you wouldn't inflict on the wildest, most brutal animal.

In the same *Herald* story, Tony Vinson, Professor of Social Work at the University of New South Wales and former head of that state's Corrective Services Department, said that the 'very common' custom, in WA, of chaining sick prisoners to their hospital beds, no matter what their crime or condition, was 'medieval and barbaric':

> It's something that is practised by no other country that pretends to be nearly civilised. I cannot find words to express my horror.

And horror visits the private sector too, in this State of Excitement. Two boys, aged 16 and 17, who were employed to look after two giant cattle stations in the state's north-west, disappeared just as the finalists for the America's Cup defence and challenge were sorting themselves out. Four months later, the boys' bodies were found, one with a bullet hole in the skull, on the edge of the Great Sandy Desert. Their Datsun 'ute' had become bogged down, and there was little they could do but walk, sit under trees whose shade may have reduced the daytime temperature to around 50 degrees, and then either wait for, or hasten, death. Why were they there? It seems they were running away – from reputed beatings with stockwhips, routine violence alternating with unremitting labour and long periods of complete isolation on the otherwise unmanned cattle stations. They may also have been afraid of getting into trouble for taking the Datsun for their flight. No-one saw them, and no-one imagined they would take the route they did, so the search planes, whilst covering an area the size of the State of Victoria, missed them. This was the fate of two school-leavers, one from South Australia and one from New South Wales, who had no reason to know what life as a 'jackeroo' in WA was like, and no training to deal with it. They had simply answered an ad in the paper.

Such is the potential reality of WA, the limit case of the referent. Small wonder, among this gigantism, inhumanity and horror, to find that knowledge of it, constructed into a realist coherence, is not what characterizes its discourses. On the contrary, and necessarily, Western Australia, both natural and social, must be *forgotten* by its citizens. The forgetting process is, historically, racial – as always, each type of death noted here attracted widespread media and conversational coverage precisely because, for a change, all the victims were white. Even so, forgetting white terrors by projecting them on to Aborigines is not enough. Hence, the first thing needful now is not facts but ignorance; an economy that produces ignorance of what is all-too-well-known, in favour of new knowledges, ignorances that bring the possibility of comfort, of coherence, even of survival. A part of the economy of ignorance is the America's Cup.

A RITUAL OF LOCOMOTION

Twelve-metre yachts travel at about nine miles an hour. The difference between the best in the world and the also-rans – each with its twenty-million dollar budget, computer-enhanced design and tactics, and its three-year development programme using, in Conner's case at least, facilities normally associated not with sporting but with military hardware – is about one-twentieth of a knot.

Western Australia is a laboratory of locomotion; distance, heat, time, space and isolation exert their tyrannous imperatives. To get in, to get out, to get around – these are all *hard*. It was only as the Cup's preliminary races were getting under way off Fremantle that, in September 1986, bitumen was laid from Fitzroy Crossing to Hall's Creek in the far north of WA, completing the biggest civil engineering project ever undertaken in Australia, a sealed 'ring road' right round the continent.

To make a thirty-tonne yacht travel at one-twentieth of a knot faster than others – this too is *hard*. And like a strip of bitumen just wide enough to allow two road-trains to pass, it is not by itself very spectacular. But bitumen, travel and speed are manifestations of – if it has one – the essence of modernity, namely mobility:

> In recent decades, mobility has exploded to the point of characterizing everyday life much more than the traditional image of the 'home and family'. Transport ceases to function as a metaphor of progress or at least of 'modern' life, and becomes instead the primary activity of existence.[5]

The America's Cup is a ritual of locomotion, a spectacular, euphoric, historic, nationalistic, excessive performance of the ability to transgress the laws of space/time, to dissolve the distinctions between here/now and there/then. It celebrates the achievement of the modern military–industrial democracies – to *mobilize* their citizens. Now, it's no longer travel *to*, travel *through*, or *for*; it's just travel, emancipated from destination or mere functional utility. Paradoxically: to travel, an *intransitive* verb. And mobility excites not just the bodies of the citizens, but meanings too – there is mobility of signification. Organized around the familiar fictions of sporting, corporate and political competition, the America's Cup is not just two boats and two syndicates sailing, spending and psyching their way slowly to victory. It is a ritual of locomotion, in which the Derridean supplementary aspects take precedence over the supposed primary event (which no-one can see clearly in any case, except on TV). In and around Fremantle the old-fashioned, titanic struggle of the age of realism, between the icy truth of actuality and the vainglorious falsehood of media hype, is simply superseded. The traditional course of events is inverted, actuality becomes a media production.

In a spectacular performance of photogenia, and in the service of the new media science of *global euphorics*, all possible modes of transport congregate in, off and above Fremantle, to participate in the ritual, to be there, to be photographed.[6] Many of them already enjoy celebrity status as media stars, besides their spectacularity as visual confirmation of the age of mobility. In pride of place are the liners, reminders of pioneering, epic, luxurious, dangerous transport. There's the *Achille Lauro*, star of spectacular, terrorist politics; one of P & O's *Princesses*, star of TV's *Love Boat* (which was timed to arrive for the final but missed it by a day because *Kookaburra III* went down 'four-zip' to *Stars and Stripes*, instead of forcing Conner to the best of seven races); and there are a couple of Cunarders. There's *The Bounty*, star of the eponymous film and ready for its trip to Portsmouth to become the flagship of the First Fleet re-cnactment for Australia's bicentennial celebration. The USS *Missouri* stops by, to remind everyone what real warships look like and recalling the day when the Second World War was brought formally to a close at a signing ceremony on board, inaugurating the new post-war era of mass mobility. There's the armada of private luxury boats, from Alan Bond's and the Aga Khan's to John (Foster's Lager) Elliott's historic Cardiff-registered *Welsh Falcon*, and unique wonders like the Maori war-canoe imported to enhance the 'Kiwi Magic', or the replica Viking longship built in a shed in the Perth suburb of Myaree, not to mention the giant Japanese cargo ship that sailed straight through one of the races.

Then there are the specially built, converted or imported floating television sets. Perhaps the most spectacular is the square-rigged barquentine *Leeuwin*, built for the Sail Training Association of WA with the help of a $600,000 donation from local businessman Denis Horgan (whose Island

Hopper helicopters are another prominent feature of the Cup spectacle). Horgan has chartered the *Leeuwin* for the duration of the Cup and spent a further $300,000 on fitting it out 'to world class luxury'; 'a solid, warm, clubby sort of feeling. Lots of brass with tan and burgundy upholstery' and 'beautifully detailed European ash joinery'.[7] But all these fittings are to be ripped out after the Cup, along with the many television monitors, one of which is located on deck to allow full integration of actuality and image – real sensurround. The spectator fleet also includes the big cats like the *Motive Explorer*, each fitted out with TV sets and running commentary whilst following the action. Naturally, the *Motive Explorer* has since been re-named the *Kimberley Explorer*, and sent off to tour the now-famous waters of the far north-west, along with others like the inappropriately named *That's Life!*, whose newspaper advertisement cheerfully encourages life to follow art, if not death:

> You've seen *Crocodile Dundee*, *World Safari* and *The Wonders of Western Australia*, now experience the excitement and exhilaration of our 'wild north' first hand! Sail north from Broome to mighty Prince Regent River on magnificent 'That's Life!'. From $982.

Naturally, the ad graces the TV page of the Perth *Western Mail*'s colour magazine, and features a photo of the very spot where – as everyone remembers – crocodiles lurk, waiting for unsuspecting tourists.

Not only at sea, but also on land and in the air the transportation flocks. Jumbos luxuriate at Perth's new international air terminal, helicopters throng Fremantle's new heliport, the little ones dancing over the regatta, occasionally towing the biggest Australian flag you ever saw, the big ones clattering over to Rottnest, holiday island. And lumbering over them all, the anachronistic Bond Airship, futuristic hi-tech retro throwback, flagship for and constant visual reminder of its ubiquitous, tubby, friendly owner. Naturally, it advertises Swan Premium Lager, stylishly outshining the noisy little mono- and bi-planes which hawk their way up and down the beaches, towing advertising banners until the final day when an enthusiastic but over-hasty message is unfurled: 'Congratulations Stars and Strips' (*sic*).

On the ground, transportation intensifies. The roads are signposted: 'This is a Commonwealth Funded America's Cup Project'. On them scurry white push-bikes, rented out to advertise Radio 6PR, and you can also rent mopeds (an allusion to Eileen Bond's favoured mode of transport), or Mini Mokes, last seen on TV's classic series *The Prisoner*. *The Prisoner* was filmed in the Welsh 'town' of Portmeirion, a virtually full-scale architectural folly or *trompe-l'oeil* designed to look like a Mediterranean city. Fremantle is perhaps the first example of the *Portmeirionization* of an existing city, though opinions differ on whether its pastel colours are quoting the Mediterranean or *Miami Vice*. But if you don't see yourself as Danger Man, then there's the 'tram', specially created, there's the stretched limo service, the Hotham Valley Railway on the *Spinnaker Run* through Fremantle by real coal-fired steam engine, there's the 400 extra taxis, or you can even buy a limited edition *Challenge* version of a Mitsubishi family sedan. There's a jocular hymn to free enterprise, popular culture and engineering: the longest Cadillac in the world, complete with unlikely fittings including swimming pool, cinema, helipad and bedroom. Its spectacularity is too excessive, however, for it to appear on the streets – you have to pay $2 and cram into a little marquee on the Esplanade to see it, before crossing the green for refreshments at the converted railway-carriage snack-bar. And among it all, crocodilian, lurks the biggest force of traffic cops ever assembled in WA, ready to enforce the law's dim view of spectacular behaviour and (chemically induced) euphoria.

Perth's cup floweth over when it glimpses, *en route* from kissed airport tarmac to Ascot racecourse, the vehicle that is a mode of transport by itself, the ultimate in uniqueness and spectacularity, the Popemobile.

THE CHALLENGE

From the state government's point of view, the point of view of surveillance, the population of the land mass known as Western Australia is not to be trusted; it displays a disorganized gaze, a lack of bodily integrity, a need for discipline. However, during the Cup, the authorities averted their eyes and handed the people over to the media, to be recruited, mobilized, into acting as the cast of thousands, extras in the performance of modernity. Their gaze was deregulated, privatized, their bodies let loose, their spaces, sounds, times and movements were untrammelled. Of course, this was countenanced mainly to impress the visitors from over east and overseas, to flatter them with the idea that Western Australia isn't a parochial backwater but a teeming, colourful image of their expectations of it – a flattery which also declared that Western Australians haven't really got an identity of their own, but exist only as products of the visitors' perceptions, figments of the foreign imagination.

After the Cup, in defeat, the people were required to delegate their desires back to the state and local government, to submit to the former regime of untrustworthiness in which the authorities decide where and at what they can look. Hotels were forced to ban the strip and lingerie shows that had proliferated during the Cup. Drive-in movie theatres were threatened, because pictures were spilling out of the confines of the carparks into the windows of the neighbours, and some of those pictures were sexy. The new and proposed buildings in Perth's central business district were judged to be too exuberant, and in need of regulating down to a height commensurate with the horizons of the planning minister's imagination. And constabulary boots tramped laboriously across the sands of the city's beaches, putting a stop to topless sunbaking – an illegal practice (for women) to which the authorities had turned a blind eye during the Cup.

The people's gaze was reorganized, directed, made respectable once more. But, once invoked, rights cannot be revoked with impunity. Now people displayed mobility of another kind, by voting on the new regime with their feet – they deserted not just the hotels, drive-ins and beaches, but the city and the streets as well. In an attempt to win them back, Perth City Council could think of nothing better than to regulate their hearing. It banned buskers from the city centre during peak hours, so that shoppers wouldn't be distracted from single-minded concentration on their civic duty, to enter shops and spend money. During the Cup, shopping had been promoted not as a duty but a pleasure; for the first time stores had been allowed to stay open on Saturday afternoons. Now they were forced to shut again, so there was little time to waste on pleasurable congregation, assuming people had managed to outwit the government's bizarre revenge on modernity – to build a city that absolutely requires you to get about by car and then closing virtually all the petrol stations in the evenings and over the weekend. These impediments to mobility and regulations of time were such that it didn't matter that the pubs were forced to close earlier too, since no-one was left on the streets to notice.

As if to confirm their power over people's senses, the powers-that-be celebrated the end of the Cup with a reminder to the citizens of Fremantle that their city's primary purpose and function was to serve as a conduit, removing the produce that primary industry had managed to scrape from the surface of the land. The famous Fremantle Doctor, the breeze that had so recently carried Dennis Conner to victory and the Cup to San Diego, was now the bearer of other, olfactory realities. Day and night, the otherwise empty Commonwealth Funded America's Cup streets reverberated to the sound of trucks laden with hundreds of thousands of live sheep, to be herded on to strange, Beirut-registered ships with twelve-storey superstructures to house the animals on their way to an exotic death in Libya. As the smell of shit pervades the city, the citizens are reminded just how close they are, from the point of view of the state, to sheep.

To official eyes, then, the population of Western Australia is *ovine*, not yet people. They are bits of people – eyes, ears, noses. They are bodies, to be herded into the time and space deemed fit for them. They are bodily functions, to be protected from the accidental discovery that life is sexually transmitted. In short, the people are merely one more example of the primary produce for which Western Australia is so justly famous; they are raw materials.

The challenge, however, is not just to extract this material from the hole in the ground, as is customary in Western Australia, but to transform it – from nature to culture, from bits and pieces to a complex, fully functioning product, from immobility to self-sustaining activity, from raw materials to surplus value. That is, those gazes, times, sounds, movements and functions have to be made into people. And those people have to be made into a community. This is a challenge which the state is content to leave to others – specifically, to television.

THE POLITICS OF EUPHORIA

The Challenge – is it a car? Is it a race? Is it a harbour? Well, yes, but it's also a mini-series. Broadcast on Alan Bond's Channel 9 in Perth, sponsored by Alan Bond's Swan Premium Lager, it is about Alan Bond's successful challenge for the America's Cup in 1983 and, for all we know, Alan Bond was watching it with Eileen, hoping it would psych the visiting syndicates for the 1987 challenge who were no doubt watching it too. The imagined community of Western Australia is united around the figure of Alan Bond, dissolving the distinction between reality and fiction, engaging the audience's gaze, organizing sights and sounds into an economy of coherence by means of audio-visual excitement, a pedagogic and seductive regime of pleasure within which there are multiple spectator positions, but every one of them is OK by Bondy. Look up! It's Bondy's airship, and it's his tower that pierces skywards over Perth. Now he plans another in Sydney, the tallest building in the southern hemisphere, 76 metres taller than the Centrepoint Tower. Look there! It's Bondy's coal mine, gold mine. Look here! It's Bondy's TV station, brewery, hotel, 12-metre yacht, private university. . . .

Not only has he got the local consciousness industries sewn up, but Alan Bond personifies their myths. He arrived in Fremantle on the P & O liner *Himalaya* aged 13, took his first job as a signwriter, and had a hand in painting the giant red dingo that adorns the side of the flour mill overlooking the America's Cup course off North Fremantle. An epitome of social mobility, he's the ambiguation of opposites – worker capitalist, popular rich man, 'our' Bondy whose corporation operates globally. And he's ready to supply the America's Cup 1987 with its crowning *coup de théâtre*. On losing 'his' Cup he doesn't whinge or weep, he celebrates: buying Kerry Packer's broadcasting interests, selling his yachts to the Japanese (apart from *Australia II*, which has already been acquired by the Commonwealth as a national treasure), and so turning, overnight, from Australia's biggest brewer into Australia's biggest media baron as well. Mythic magic; in Perth he's known as 'Crocodile Bondee', at least on T-shirts.

But his power isn't just purchasing power, it's the power of mobilization, and it's not Bond's personal power, but the power of what he personifies: the power of television. It converts a city into a set, people into performers, and commands the presence here in Perth of the world's finest, stars of actuality. Appropriately, in a secular equivalent of the papal visit, the presence here of the world's media is symbolized by the arrival of Walter Cronkite (and Princess Anne) – if it has any, the essence of broadcasting (and its subject). The excitement, euphoria and activity generated during the Cup were there for the taking, emancipating Perth from the horrors and barbarities that lurk so close, and plugging it in, momentarily, to the global economy of surplus meaning that induces forgetfulness of the confines of regulated routine, and reminds the people of the possibilities (as yet unrealized) of new freedoms, of movement, of choice, of pleasure.

In the end, then, the power of television is to mobilize the citizens of military–industrial democracies in ways that official authorities seem not only unable to match but actively to resent. However, the visit of Bob Hawke, the genial prime minister of Australia, strolling the sunny streets of the Fremantle set after officially unfurling yet another gigantic Australian flag over the Roundhouse, WA's oldest building and first prison, suggests that the higher levels of government, at least, understand only too well the need to unify the people into an imagined community of citizens who can be mobilized to see themselves as free to choose in the name not of ideology but of euphoria.

In the new age of signs without referents, of media-produced reality, of pedagogic seduction, the people can make sense of democracy as competition; they can understand economics, politics and social structure in terms of sport – no longer the sport of kings but of transnational corporations and their 'barons'; they can become in the end what the media hype required of them – *The People*, ultimate fiction, stars of the show, who exercise their historic right to join the party . . . by partying.

A pity for the nearly-nation of Western Australia, if not for its newly appointed 'ambassador', Dennis Conner, the party's over.[8]

Part V

The art of television

Chapter 13

Local television: from space to time*

The Australian Broadcasting Tribunal held exhaustive hearings in 1986 to decide the award of the third commercial TV licence for Perth. 'Local production' was a key issue for the licence contenders, but after the third commercial TV channel, Channel 10, was launched in mid-1988, to dismal ratings and to criticism of broken promises, the idea of local production seemed further off than ever. This article was written for the journal of the Film and Television Institute of WA, which had made strong submissions to the Tribunal in favour of local production as a requirement for commercial TV licensees; the FTI is also the umbrella organization for local producers and independent film/video-makers. In such a context, it seemed sacrilegious, but necessary, to ask what 'local' television can and should mean in the contemporary media scene. It transpires that if 'local' means decentralized production, it is doomed; but if it is applied to the deregimentation of *time*, there is not only hope for the future but an existing model of it: SBS-Television.

LOCAL TELEVISION – A CONTRADICTION IN TERMS

Perth, population one million, has more broadcast TV stations than the United Kingdom, population fifty-five million. At the end of 1988, roughly 70 per cent of the local audience was watching Channels 7 and 9, while Channel 10 had a 15 per cent share, as did the ABC and SBS combined. But the few hundred thousand people who watch television in Perth are not watching Perth television. Given the figures this is hardly surprising; the only shock is that anyone should expect otherwise. Television as a historical fact is one of the most centralized industries in the world, and even Australia, population seventeen million, is barely large enough to raise a blip on the international market screen. The two largest centres of production in the USA, and therefore the world, are Los Angeles and New York, both of which are in states whose population is bigger than that

* Originally published as John Hartley (1988/9) 'Local television – from space to time' (two-part article), *In the Picture*, 3(4) and (5).

of the whole of Australia. Precious little American TV comes from Texas, Illinois (Chicago), Pennsylvania or Ohio, despite the fact that each of these states has a population approaching that of Australia.

So what about 'local' production? In broadcast television, it's a contradiction in terms. Even Texans have to swallow their pride and go to Hollywood. But who ever heard of Maine Television, New Mexico Television, the Dakotas Television, Idaho Television or Rhode Island Television? These are all states in the USA with populations roughly equivalent to Perth or to WA. They're so small that a whole block of them – those in the Mountain Time Zone – weren't even counted by the all powerful Nielsen ratings until the mid-1960s. Hawaii and Alaska are still excluded by Nielsen, although between them they boast roughly the same number of people as WA. But they account for only 0.6 per cent of the US population – statistically negligible.[1]

Another group of people that Nielsen doesn't count in the US is anyone not living in a house or apartment. People in institutions, hotels and motels, barracks, boarding-houses, dormitories and airports certainly do watch television, but they're not part of the domestic audience and they're excluded from the ratings. There are over six million of them.

These juicy statistical titbits tell us something we already know – Perth is not very large. So why has it got three commercial TV stations and two public ones? And why should anyone expcct it to sustain a television *production* industry when it hasn't even got enough people to count as an *audience*? First, because of state pride; the honourable Australian tradition of provincial self-aggrandizement. Second, because the long-term trend towards the fragmentation and differentiation of mass markets into audience constituencies has created a demand for localism.

Unfortunately, however, the integrated circuit of global media production allows for differentiation at the consumption end of the process much more easily than it does at the production end. Impulse Body Spray is Impulse Body Spray all over the world, produced and marketed by the same corporations. But the images they use to sell it change subtly from Sweden to Malaysia, from the USA to Italy, to take account of 'local cultural traditions' – the amount of a woman's body that can be seen on TV, for example, or whether women can flirt with strange men. That's localism, television-style.

Channel 10, newest competitor in the piffling Perth market, is not a TV station at all, if by that you mean a producer of TV. It's like your local department store – a retail outlet whose local executives, powerless to choose, price or advertise their own goods, much less make them, simply mind the cash register.

Of course, the bigger the retail outlet the more loss leaders they can afford, to undercut the opposition and establish market share. So Channel 10 was launched with its daily quota of 'local' production: *Our Town* (one-hour chat show, since axed), *Airplay* (half-hour locally hosted music videos, since axed) and *Eyewitness News*. These amount to little more than local presentation-links for news and video clips made somewhere else, studio discussions and the weather, in a weekly total of nearly four hours, bearing in mind that a TV-hour is only fifty-two minutes.

Even the commercials, thankfully, are less local than they used to be in the good old days of used-car salesman Naughty Don, or, worse, the graphics and shout-over genre beloved by Cheapo-Productions (WA) Inc.

But who says anyone wants local production?

The popular audience prefers to watch *American* television, partly through habit, partly because they like to keep in touch with places where it's really happening (Los Angeles, New York, London, Sydney – in that order), and partly because it's good television. Australian drama serials rate very well too, though none is set in WA, but soapies are still 'American' television, because they're successful to the extent that they 'localize' an American form. The demand is *first* for good television, *then* for Australian content. The soap-box comes from LA, the filling from Sydney.

And television executives don't want 'local' television either; they want *television*. You'd be more likely to see your stuff being strutted on Perth TV if you get it commissioned overseas, or over east, than if you try your luck in Perth. Witness for instance the three recent documentaries made by local independents through the FTI. They were screened in Perth because a national network decided to broadcast them from Sydney. The 'local' TV stations would not have touched them with a barge-pole. What's especially poignant about this example is that the documentaries were about Fremantle after the Cup, WA's forests and Rottnest's Aboriginal history, but they were shown on 'ethnic' SBS.[2] Perhaps this is what WA means inside television – a little local colour and ethnic authenticity; not a locality but a *location*.

As yet no Australian drama serial has been screened on US prime-time network TV. *A Country Practice*, for instance, is shown there on PBS (public television). The only way to get Australian material on to network prime-time is to get the Americans to make it. Says the president of Crawfords (one of Australia's biggest programme-suppliers) Ian Bradley:

> If they are in on it from the beginning and feel they have control over the destiny of the product, the show has a much better chance of being run on prime time. To make a product and then try to sell it to America is just about impossible.[3]

So who does want local production? Why, local producers of course. Unfortunately for them, the logic of the TV industry is that there's no such thing as a local producer. Even the Perth TV stations, both commercial and public, are caught in this logic in the wake of national networking, never mind the independents. So it's not much good knocking on their doors, or their access windows, to remedy a situation over which they have little and decreasing control. Have you ever tried arguing with a check-out assistant about company policy?

History teaches us that the only way to ensure any measure of decentralization in broadcast TV is at the structural level. It can't be enforced by the 'watch-dog' ABT, nor by moral pressure on licensees to keep their promises. The biggest changes in Australian TV in the last decade have been legislative ones with the establishment of SBS and the deregulation of ownership quotas. If local production has a future – it certainly has no past – then it must look to the long-term organization of broadcast TV.

But history is also being overtaken by developments in technology and in the global organization of the media. To lobby for localism is a waste of time, unless it's tied to a more forward-looking bandwagon than the presumed needs of the tiny local audience, which is in any case beginning to use its collective television set to avoid broadcast TV altogether by watching videos, also made in the USA.

In the meantime, the only realistic direction for anyone who wants to put Perth on to prime-time is easterly – with a stopover in Sydney if you like – to Hollywood.

LOCAL TELEVISION – IT'S TIME

Solutions to problems ought to depend on the problem, but often they don't. Some ideas are offered as intrinsically left or right wing, no matter what problem they're applied to. The organization of the TV industry is a good example. If TV networks are owned by fewer and richer corporations this is seen as self-evidently a right wing tendency. Conversely, demands for decentralization, devolved control and local production are seen as self-evidently radical. But what's radical in one context may be ridiculous in another. The historic problem with British broadcasting is that it is too centralized. The historic problem with Australian television is quite the reverse. It's not centralized enough.

The British broadcasting structure was rejected in Australia when television was planned in the mid-1950s; a version of the supposedly more competitive American structure was imported by the federal legislators. The curious lesson of history is that after thirty years Australia could end up with a structure more British than American, and this solution would be produced by something that has never operated in British television, namely market forces.

British broadcasting, both public and commercial, is founded on the principle of what the BBC's founder, John Reith, called the brute force of monopoly. It is well known that the BBC resisted commercial television for two decades and commercial radio for much longer, but it's less well known that the Reithian BBC used its brute force against itself – successfully suppressing the beginnings of *local* radio in the 1920s and 1930s, and resisting *regional* TV for thirty years – BBC Wales for instance opened only in 1964. This policy was in pursuit of the Beeb's historic aim to become an unquestioned national cultural institution – as prestigious and immune from attack as Oxbridge, the church or the *OED*. In this historic mission it has been astonishingly successful.

One measure of success is flattery by imitation. Commercial TV in Britain is a monopoly too, competing with the BBC for audience share but not for advertising. The ITV network is made up of thirteen *regional* monopolies, except in London where Thames (Carlton from January 1993) and London Weekend Television (LWT) monopolize weekdays and weekends respectively. Channel 4 doesn't compete with ITV either – it's owned and paid for by it and shares advertising revenues with it (a set-up which is due to change when Channel 4 is floated off on its own). Like the BBC, ITV is an elegantly complex brute force.

ITV is committed to what's called public service broadcasting, just like the BBC; giving the public what the broadcasters want, including low-rating 'public interest' shows even when there's little public interest in them. But equally, like ITV, the BBC is committed to maintaining an overall 50 per cent share of the popular audience. The consequence of this arrangement, where monopoly, populism and 'education by stealth' are all *structurally* in play throughout the TV industry, is simply stated – it produces very good television.

But it's a very closed world. Both commercial and public TV production in Britain is centralized in London. The BBC is the biggest single broadcasting organization in the west, a 'critical mass' of talent in one big organization. That this critical mass is over-centralized along class, gender, ethnic and educational lines rather than according to its critical creativity is also well known.

In Britain, given the existing structure, demands for decentralization may be radical. Local production, access to television by neglected constituencies, and more productions bought in from independents – these are real issues in that context.

However, the same demands may not be radical – Thatcherite moves in the late 1980s to break the BBC's monopoly and plans to hive off Channel 4 are policies designed by ideologues who are not interested in television at all but in privatization at any cost; radicalism such as this is quite prepared to test television to destruction.

Australian broadcasting policy operates on the American assumption that competition between commercial TV stations will keep them lean, hungry and accountable to their audiences. Such an assumption is unwarranted, since the over-supply of TV simply drives down the revenue from advertising, it limits the budgets available for production and programme-buying, and it causes competing stations to look more and more like each other.

It is precisely for this reason that the putative national networks have been formed in the commercial sector. Channel 10 in Perth makes very little sense in the local context; it's here because eastern states suppliers need a bigger market to reduce unit costs. Hence the launch of another TV station in Perth is ironically the very opposite of competitive decentralization or of a commitment to local production and images. The more local stations you have, the more they'll be controlled from Sydney. What looks like more consumer choice is in fact another step down the road to more producer monopoly.

Australian television is structurally a failed experiment; it simply doesn't do what it was founded to do. But current government policy is still directed towards competing commercial stations in the same city. The 1987 deregulation of ownership rules was touted as a concession to market forces, but it's not. Market forces, which in practice are not competitive but monopolistic, would eliminate at least one whole commercial network and possibly two. [Since that sentence was written, two networks, 7 and 10, filed for bankruptcy and the third, 9, was sold for a breathtaking loss, all in 1990. The only thing that prevented an amalgamation of Channels 7 and 10 in this context was the refusal of the supposedly deregulationist government to allow it.]

And if ABC supremo David Hill had his way, the ABC would amalgamate with SBS, resulting in an overall TV system that would eventually look much more 'British' than 'American' in structure.

It would, in fact, bring the cities into line with the current set-up in the country; namely, a public monopoly competing with a commercial monopoly. The radical potential of this structure doesn't have to be imagined since it has already produced results, in the shape of Imparja Television: a commercial channel run by and for Aboriginal communities in central Australia.

In the meantime urban viewers watch fascinated and powerless as corporate giants and entrepreneurs play musical chairs with the ownership of TV stations. We see the federal government scurrying about, removing a chair here, sawing the legs off one there, or adding a comfy seat for its mates when no-one's looking.

And public debate about TV policy is conducted around clichéd reactions to these shenanigans: applause here, a laugh there, occasional tut-tuttings which sound good but achieve nothing. Golly-gosh journalism simply repeats received ideas about media ownership while indulging in its own version of *Lives of the Rich and Famous*.

This ambient noise is no basis for intervention into policy debates about television. From the audience's point of view, the question of whether a local, national or (the horror) an international billionaire owns Channel 7 is much less important than the question of what Channel 7 shows.

Debate about the decentralization of television should be based not on ownership but content. That means turning from *space* to *time* as the structuring principle, and from local *communities* to audience *constituencies*.

All the commercial channels are founded on the principle of sameness within geographical difference. The difference is space: Brisbane is Brisbane and Perth is Perth, and God forbid they should love each other. The sameness is time: Brisbane and Perth get the same TV structure and the same TV programmes, so although the audience is separated by space it must perforce spend its time the same way.

But the twain have met. Despite its long history of federalism and state rivalry, there is nevertheless a national, popular culture in Australia, shared by people living in Willetton or Woolloomooloo, Inglewood or Indooroopilly, Fremantle or Footscray. Private, domestic, suburban communities are not sufficiently different from each other to sustain a demand for production based on their geographical location. On the contrary, a small, dispersed nation with a history of parochialism needs local production like a fish needs a bicycle.

The commitment of suburban consumer citizens to their locality is a commitment to private freedom, including the freedom to enjoy images and symbols made elsewhere – even from as far away as Los Angeles. Having lived in Willetton I can tell you there's nothing I'd like less than Willetton Television. However, I can also tell you that behind the suburban fibro fences lurk ideas, practices and experiments in living that would astonish you. *A Country Practice*'s Wandin Valley . . . it ain't. Suburban popular culture may be the same from one side of the continent to the other, but from one side of the fence to the other is a very different matter. Within each similar housing estate culture is as varied and exotic as Australian wildlife, and somtimes just as dangerous.

This reveals the historic problem of Australian television. It has produced a diversity of commercial channels, and different stations in each major city. The sheer number of delivery outlets masks the fact that *culturally* what's being delivered is about as diverse as two potatoes on a couch.

It is time, not space, that is the site for television diversity in Australia. You can deliver the same repertoire of programmes to Willetton as to Woolloomooloo, gathering dispersed localities into the imagined community of the nation as a whole. But within that repertoire, within that nation, there's no need for sameness.

There is already one national channel on Australian television that's organized on the principle of cultural rather than geographical differentiation. It is, of course, the Special Broadcasting Service (SBS).

SBS is a time-based channel, where constituencies of viewers are recognized, and not expected to soak up the whole output all the time. Centrally produced, SBS-TV is not centrally controlled, but controlled by each and every consumer, according to their own choice.

If TV reduces freedom, it's freedom of time. To emancipate the audience, it's not necessary to localize production, but to deregiment time and to acknowledge the choices of the new cutting-edge class, the *choiceoisie*. This is what SBS does, inaugurating a supermarket-shelf model of TV consumption, where much more is on offer, from more countries, than any individual could possibly want.

But SBS does more than this. It also inaugurates the possibility of television as a publishing medium, supplied by a diversity of 'authors' and releasing a range of titles from specialist minority material to popular bestsellers. It buys in material from other markets, and it commissions significant new work from local producers.

But because it operates as a publisher it can afford to concentrate production in one place, at Milson's Point, with a staff and budget that puts the complacent pot-bellied commercial channels to shame. SBS is the lean, hungry, efficient, postmodern TV of tomorrow. It is a radical solution to the historic problem of Australian broadcasting. Perhaps this is why David Hill wants to gobble it up, since it puts his infotainment ABC to shame too.

But SBS faces structural problems of its own, which inhibit its popularity if not its programming flair.

First, it enters an economy whose performance is measured by ratings. Ratings record the expenditure of viewers' time, whose exchange value depends on its being spent on the same product no matter which channel is tuned in. This is the couch potato economy; the habit of using TV for continuous reconsumption of universally intelligible entertainment.

It may, historically, be a dying habit, with a fragmentation in the way people use their TV screens to access not only real-time broadcasting but also videos, home movies and computers as well as time-shifted broadcast material. SBS fits these new tendencies very well, but it doesn't show on the ratings.

A further problem for SBS comes from the established assumptions which organize the production, viewing and criticism of television as a whole; assumptions about what TV is *for*. In the conventional wisdom, SBS is the very opposite of TV in general, a channel which is by definition *special*, and whose programmes are perceived not as entertainment but as a *service* providing education and welfare to minorities.

The fact that these programmes include some of the cream of world TV, and are as entertaining as you like, and that *everyone* is both ethnic and multicultural, a minority sometimes, doesn't enter the debate. Such facts don't fit the commercial definition of entertainment.

In short, the problem doesn't reside in what SBS shows, but in how people watch it.

Channel 7 has recently given itself a new name; but there's only one truly 'National Australian Network,' producing and screening the same fare for the whole country all the time, and that's SBS. But it needs rescuing from discourses of do-goodery and promoting in the true colours that commercial networks are only too happy to steal from off its back when it suits them. The audience is there, but not counted, and SBS by itself can't build it up. It's a national treasure, but the nation hasn't yet been given the least encouragement to recognize its value.

What's needed is a revision of the terms of the debate about what should count as radical TV. A national network, publishing diverse television, in which local independents vie with the best international producers to provide different audience constituencies with entertainment and with images that stretch their mental horizons – this would be radical TV for Australia. The ridiculous thing is that it's already here. Just tune to the only station on UHF.

Chapter 14

Quoting not science but sideboards*
with Tom O'Regan

PERTH HATH NOT ANYTHING TO SHOW MORE FAIR

Imagine the scene, one night in spring. All over the city and suburbs groups of twenty or more people are crowding around, in homes and in public areas, and all eyes are fixed on a new blueish kind of light. Right here in Perth, that light signals the drawn of a new age. And like the mysterious bleeps of the recently launched Sputnik, new sounds travel through space to capture all ears, reminding Western Australians of their myriad links – personal, industrial, architectural and now audio-visual – with a future world that's theirs in the making.

Of course it wasn't exactly like that. The public on whom television was launched in October 1959 was not entirely unsuspecting. Plenty of planning, promotion and practice had gone into the launch. There were only 3,300 TV sets operating on opening night, but all the same an estimated 70,000 people jostled and joked their way into the picture.

Afterwards, things did change. Perth grew, its dependence on a few primary industries being both masked and reduced by its own expanding infrastructure. Its modernity may have been masked by its deference to authority from over east or overseas, but that mask only conceals the source of Perth's power – bodily comforts. The Italian designer Ettore Sottsass – founder of the 'Memphis' movement – has spoken for Perth's well-kept secret without knowing it when he says:

> World culture today is concerned with the American vision of comfort. Today and for many hundreds of years to come humanity will pursue earthly comfort. Comfort means to possess warmth, coolness, softness, light, shade, air-travel, Polynesian spaces or Alaska. To have money

* Originally published as John Hartley and Tom O'Regan (1985) 'Quoting not science but sideboards: television in a new way of life', in Tom O'Regan and Brian Shoesmith (eds) *The Moving Image: Film and Television in Western Australia 1896–1985*, Perth: History and Film Association of Australia. Published in the USA in Michael Gurevitch and Mark R. Levy (eds) (1987) *Mass Communication Review Yearbook*, vol. 6. Newbury Park: Sage.

> means to possess sensory possibilities, not power. Sensoriality destroys ideology, it is anarchical, private; it takes account of consumerism and consumption, it is not moralistic, it opens up new avenues.[1]

Perth has been living this way for decades, opening up new avenues literally and metaphorically as its suburbs, beaches and highrises express physically the sensory possibilities that are being explored within them. Occasionally there are public demonstrations of its modernist knowledges – glimpses through the mask when the city beams skywards to the future, all its lights ablaze, joined by massed Kingswood cars in King's Park flashing their headlights, just to say 'G'day mate' to the ultimate air-traveller, passing astronaut John Glenn. There's even a mild gesture of recognition when a Concorde or QE2 passes through. People get up early to have a look. But the same fervour for comfort and sensoriality turns to fury when the American vision of comfort is transformed into its opposite: the American vision of power. So the *Carl Vinson*s and their nuclear arms are greeted not with deference but offence, and Perth opposes power with the only means it has – pleasure boats against the flotillas and inflated prices for the sailors.

For the most part, however, Perth has grown privately, non-moralistically, producing its new way of life in the everyday energy of peoples' activities. Another 'Memphis' designer, Andrea Branzi, has suggested how far the public, historical world of culture and knowledge is a product of physical, bodily qualities and sensations:

> Today we know – and the experience of body art has confirmed our knowledge – that our perception of the environment is substantially a physical process carried out to a great extent by our body, which is not a brute receptacle of sensations and stimuli (on which only the 'intelligent' mind is able to impose order and meaning), but an active instrument capable of processing environmental data and transforming them into experience and culture, utilizing them independently of their allegorical or ideological meaning.[2]

What this suggests is that culture, knowledge and experience are themselves forms of communication, but communication based as much on spatial relations, tactile qualities and tensions as on sights, colours and sounds. In such a context, the arrival of television in Perth can be looked at physically, as it were, and its subsequent changes and developments can be traced in the ways that people consumed space and time; how they learnt, or were encouraged, to accommodate their bodies to the TV and the TV to their physical environment.

One thing seems certain. Television was recognized as an agent of physical changes very early on. In 1961, E.M. Bianchi was already able to claim categorically that:

> The advent of television in Western Australia has undoubtedly altered the social pattern of the lives of the people. . . . People have tended to make adjustments in their ways of living and to alter their activities to suit the viewing of their favourite Television programmes.[3]

Indeed, television appears to have become more popular, more quickly, in Perth than in the other state capitals. Among the general reasons for television's easy assimilation into people's lives was the existence of media, especially radio and cinema, that had already 'trained' people in the necessary skills for watching and enjoying TV. Radio in particular had paved the way. Some TV programmes were literally radio shows with pictures. Much of the TV that was produced through the 1960s – game shows, today shows, kids' shows – tended to use formats made familiar in radio. More fundamentally perhaps, television was the same kind of dual distribution/exhibition system as radio, which, for the cost of a set and a licence, you could enjoy free at home. And the interaction between public broadcasting (supplied by commercial or public corporations) and the routines of domestic life had been well-practised in radio. Thus, TV borrowed radio's scheduling habits, and continued the practice of carrying advertisements during shows.

However, television had the one attribute of cinema that radio lacked – vision. This had several consequences. One was the practice of scheduling movies on Fridays and weekends, during the times when people might ordinarily have gone to the cinema. But another was to produce in the early TV audience a form of watching that retained some of the public, social feel of 'going out' to the cinema. Television was watched with an intensity, concentration and lack of conversation that would be unfamiliar today. Often the lights were dimmed or turned off. It was placed in the formal (public) lounge room and frequently watched by large groups which included visiting relatives, neighbours or friends. The transformation of a person's house into the equivalent of a public place had its effect on social habits and protocols, as Eric Fisher, a local radio and TV personality of the 1960s, recalls:

> In the early days of Television in Perth, a visit to someone's place meant just walking in and saying hello. Most of the lights would be turned off. Then you would sit down and watch Television. Someone would rush out and make a cup of tea and bring in some biscuits, and when you finished viewing for the night you went home. I can recall being quite shocked by what appeared to be rude behaviour. You would be invited over – but you'd be lucky if the host or hostess noticed you when you

> arrived. It was . . . 'come over, bring a beer, come in' . . . and then back to the box.[4]

Meanwhile, Perth was continuing to grow, but it grew out, not up. Then, as now, Perth had the lowest housing density of any of the Australian state capitals; and then, as now, its public transport systems were less frequent than those of other cities. The well-known but badly-lit suburban sprawl around Perth was fertile ground for television. Watching TV at home meant you did not have to go into the city itself or to suburban centres – it cut out dead travelling time, substituting the possibility of immediate access to entertainment instead. This was something the cinemas, drive-ins, live theatres and libraries could not provide. On top of that, if you didn't like the show you weren't stuck with it – you could switch off or go into another part of the house.

DOMESTICATING CONSUMERISM

Perth may have been fertile ground for TV, and extra fertilization may have resulted from some of its citizens being familiar with it already, coming from places that already had it. But even fertile ground has to be tilled. As a consumer item, the television set itself wasn't cheap. The average price was 180 guineas (guineas made big purchases sound both classier and cheaper), or ten bob a week. The tillage was enthusiastically undertaken in the media themselves. National publications like the *Australian Women's Weekly* had been carrying TV stories from early on – and both Sydney and Melbourne had a three-year lead on Perth. Locally, there were bank advertisements in the *West Australian* a full year before television was introduced, highlighting the 'need' for Perth people to start putting away money in order to be able to get a TV set when the moment arrived. These particular ads made much of the enjoyment people in Melbourne and Sydney were getting from television.

Such blandishments were all very well, but you couldn't touch, feel, see or hear a television with them. To make it tactile reality, the opening was presaged by so-called trade transmissions. The corporate planning behind trade transmissions was to get sufficient audience, by selling a sufficient number of sets, to make the opening night a corporate success: that is, to convince advertisers of the new medium's viability. So TVW-7 (Channel 7) went on air a full month before the official opening, showing documentaries culled from film libraries such as those of Shell, BP and the State Film Library. You could see these transmissions in electrical retail shops selling TV sets, and also at night as part of home demonstrations.

These public and private demonstrations of TV were not just marketing instruments, they were cultural events in themselves. Having been primed by the massive retail effort conducted on radio and in the press, people were prone to give television their undivided attention. So much so, that when the Highway Hotel in the suburb of Claremont installed a TV just after opening night, they felt obliged to put a sign under it reminding patrons not to let their beers get warm.

As for home demonstrations, these immediately entered the realm of neighbourhood politics. Television involved a whole new distribution system, and one which required its consumers to pay for it (like radio, but unlike the press). Early TV sets were sold mainly on the basis of home demonstrations, so the TV salesman (it was always a man) and his van became important components of the process. Having the TV man come into your house was a visible way of signifying your transition into and participation in the new and marvellous world of home entertainment. This was even more important for poorer viewers – having an expensive material possession like a TV set was a means of demonstrating a degree of economic control over your environment; and as the TV cost more to such viewers, it tended to be featured more prominently in their homes. Gratifyingly, after the TV salesman had left, the mark of your transition was there for all to see in the shape of the outdoor aerial he'd erected for you. At this point, your neighbours and family would, for a period, avail themselves of your exclusive theatrette, and you'd become an unwitting agent for the salesmen. Everyone could see what the TV did for your home, and imagine it in their own. Talk would centre on how much it cost and whether it could be afforded, on who had one and who didn't, on how interesting it was (even the test pattern), on where to site the set in the house, and on the programmes and people you had seen – sometimes you might even glimpse an acquaintance in the audience of a show. By this stage, some of your neighbours would be feeling socially outpaced, and the salesman's van would be seen drawing up to another house. As ownership or rental became more widespread, and as the novelty wore off, television viewing began to lose its quasi-cinematic, social aspect, and to take on its more recently characteristic patterns – it became a private, family activity, with just one family per set.

People were already adjusting the social patterns of their lives, but they were not acting as the 'brute receptacles' of sensations and stimuli. On the contrary, TV's rapid assimilation into their experience and culture resulted from its congruence with long-term propensities and changes that can be traced across a number of quite different domains. Perhaps the most general of these changes has been the process by which public and private space has been redefined: from the city centre to suburban shopping centres and then to malls; from public swimming baths to backyard pools; from picnicking in parks to the barbeque in the backyard; from the pub to the home cocktail bar; from health clubs to home gyms, games rooms and saunas; from cinemas to TV; from football to *Wide World of Sports*; from 'live' theatre to TV drama.

Over a long period, and throughout the advanced and industrializing world, cultural consumption patterns have been decentred from public, mass activities, fragmenting into myriad, decentralized consumer rites and pleasures in and around peoples' homes. Naturally, the previously established public forms of entertainment were obliged to adjust too. Cinema attendances fell, and its audience resolved itself into precisely those who were self-propelled out of the home environment – young people and teenagers. 'Live' theatre, already cosily dying, lost more bums from its seats, resulting in public meetings that were held to deplore the situation. Public sporting fixtures, like theatres, lost patrons, and they too had to content themselves with specialized constituencies of supporters. In future, it would take very special events to draw an indiscriminate public out all together, irrespective of class, gender, age, ethnicity, income-bracket or occupation – events like Royal Shows, 12-metre yacht races, Australia Day fireworks (simulcast on television) or summer heatwaves, especially when these coincided with non-ratings periods. Otherwise, popular culture on a daily basis was organized around private consumption, and the market leader in popular entertainment was television.

SITES (AND SIGHTS) OF STRUGGLE

The redefinition of public and private spaces meant that new energies were released in people's homes: energies that began to change the way that houses were organized. But as the 'Memphis' writer Barbara Radice has pointed out, the changes attendant on consumerism are not simply the result of corporate marketing strategies. People began to alter their ways of looking and cooking for their own reasons. Radice comments:

> Consumerism, besides being a necessity induced by the production system, is also a pleasure; and a pleasure is never completely controllable or without consequences. Putting new signs on the air means circulating new energies, producing new desires, anxieties, incentives, and conditions.[5]

Perhaps the first uncontrolled consequence of television's sudden appearance on the Perth scene was, ironically, the effect on its own neighbour-medium, the radio. Television grabbed radio's night-time audience and crippled its night-time shows. Accommodating itself to television's dominance in its own erstwhile realm of the home, radio looked increasingly to daytime audiences for advertising revenues. And it found them in another echo of American consumerism: the constant rotation of records, fast-talking DJs, commercials, news, updates and frequent station ident jingles.

The lazy respectability of speech- and variety-radio was progressively speeded up to higher pitches – producing top 100 then top 40 radio, ever more cheerfully dedicated to the circulation of new energies, desires, anxieties, incentives and conditions.

But radio was not only displaced as an institutional medium, it was also displaced, literally, in people's homes. Under the existing arrangements, radios were substantial items of furniture, filled with valves and as yet showing no sign of their future transistorization, miniaturization and micro-circuitry. But because they were listened to rather than looked at, radio sets were not the focal object of living spaces. Eric Fisher remembers TV's disruptive entry:

> In the forties and fifties there was a lounge room which always had a radio set in it. If you were lucky you might have had a radio in the kitchen too – not all homes had dining rooms then – they were for some a luxury. You usually had an open fire in the lounge which tended to be grouped around. The radio was wherever it was most convenient to have it so long as the sound could be heard. But with the advent of Television all the furniture had to be rearranged so you could view it.[6]

Such rearrangements of furniture were in fact more disruptive than may at first appear – it wasn't simply a matter of reorienting the three-piece suite. The big problem was the fireplace. But even this immovable object was no match for the irresistible force of television. Architects and builders, always mindful that rooms need focal points as well as occasional warming, had tended to make fireplaces very prominent and eye-catching, often in the centre of the longer wall. Television sets, being expensive and averse to heat and sparks, were often placed in the corner, away from the fireplace. This meant that fires were immediately displaced to the edge of one's field of vision, and the rearranged seating was now unevenly exposed to the fire. It now required looking round deliberately to see if the fire needed tending, and getting up to do it meant crossing someone's line of sight to the TV. The upshot was, of course, that the open fire fell into disfavour during the 1960s and 1970s, being replaced by less obtrusive mobile heaters, whilst fireplaces themselves were often boarded up or removed altogether. Nowadays, in older renovated houses such as those in Fremantle, the feature fireplace may be retained, but as likely as not it will be the chosen place for siting the television. Unlike the open fire itself, the TV set can be looked at all year round, instead of being an object of visual interest for the short winter months alone.

Since they were designed to be looked at all year round, TV sets had to look good in themselves, especially as they were so expensive to acquire. Despite their electrical and scientific contemporaneity, TV sets were never marketed with this aspect of their design on display. On the contrary, the chassis, tubes and valves were regarded as unsightly and even dangerous, so television never went through a popular do-it-yourself, 'cat's-whisker' phase as radio had. Instead, TV sets were sold as items of lounge-room furniture, masking the apparatus in boxes of wood or wood-veneer that quoted not science but sideboards in their design. This approach made television simultaneously familiar and exciting, intimate and mysterious. Moulded housings were used too, producing a look which allowed the TV set to express an image associated with other modern domestic appliances, from certain kinds of radiogram to fridges and washing machines. But television was never one of the 'white-goods' (even though both types of appliance may have been made by the same manufacturer). The TV set was designed for the imagination, not for working areas like the kitchen. If it quoted any outside reference, it was not the world of work and science but that of the prestige entertainment media, sometimes alluding to theatre and cinema in the shape of the frame round the screen or in the drape-like material used to cover the speaker. The naming of TV sets confirmed these up-market associations: Washington, Kreisler, Motorola.

Once installed, television could come into its own. Itself the quintessential image of modernity, it was used to promote the purchase of other things that would fit into the modern TV home. It stimulated both consumption and production. E.M. Bianchi, writing in 1961, noted: 'Television in Western Australia has also called for a market for such commodities as TV lamps, TV clothes, TV suppers and TV furniture.'[7] 'Television clothes' may sound outlandish, but this is what the *West Australian* (31 August 1959) reckoned all 'Television hostesses' should know:

> Long sessions of lounging in an armchair have been found to play havoc with formal day or evening wear. And so, for extended Television viewing anyway, the accent is on informality. Women have developed a liking for tapered slacks in brilliant, solid colours, topped with over-blouses in futuristic designs. Come summer, slacks give way to shorts worn with a shortie version of the 'mumu'. . . . But for the more exotic hostess, velvet or lurex tapered slacks with a jersey knit embroidered or glitter-sprinkled top and oriental slippers, give a sophisticated air.

As for TV furniture, how about the 'smart-modern-restful "TELE-VUE" chair: makes *looking* easier', advertised in the *West Australian* (31 August 1959)? Television sets were themselves often dressed, usually with lamps, plants and photographs, in a further attempt to domesticate and customize the bulky, recalcitrant shape; TV sets not only quoted but were used as sideboards.

Television entered and altered the rhythms of household activity. The need to look as well as to hear put pressure on meal preparation and consumption; pressure upon cooking, washing up and other household activities to contract in time; and pressure upon eating to take place simultaneously with watching. Thus the familiar lounge room coffee-table became the meal-table proper, and fast convenience foods requiring little preparation and few utensils became the vogue.

Meanwhile, television commercials and programmes alike were promoting and displaying the modern life-style of domestic consumption. This may have played its part in longer-term changes that were taking place in house design. Local architect Peter Little suggests that the major change to Western Australian housing stock over the last thirty years was to the toilet and the laundry; they have migrated. Initially they were found in the backyard, often as far from the dwelling as possible. But they were moved progressively closer; first to the verandah area, then inside, and finally, in the case of the toilet, into en-suites by the 'master' bedroom. Such a migration to some extent mimics people's own migrations from outside to inside the home, where increased time (including time spent watching TV) meant increased incentive to improve, embellish and modernize.

Television itself was used to promote cleansing practices and products which went along with changing attitudes to health and the toilet; and it also encouraged spending on decorating and equipping the newly interiorized areas. Similarly, people were encouraged to spend more on a range of products that consumerized activities they'd engaged in all along – activities like washing their houses, clothes and dishes, or themselves and their hair. And once those yukky wet areas were moved out of the yard, it too was available for home-entertainment, with pool, barbie, pergola, patio and outside phone-bell or cellular phone. The outside area could even become the site for television-watching, though not often for the TV itself. In the summer months, some Perth families have solved the heat problem simply by pointing the TV out of a window and watching it from the yard – a process helped by the characteristic one-storey Perth house style, where the yard is on the same level as the house, and often partly enclosed by it in an L-shape.

SOUNDS OF TROUBLE AND STRIFE

When television first arrived, it was welcomed into the house as a guest – it was put in the formal lounge. Here it could be shown to other guests, and treated by the family with the respect it deserved. But this situation didn't last. As TV watching became more taken for granted, and as it extended into daytime and morning viewing, people got used to doing more than one thing at a time. The productivity of the home environment increased as people dropped into the lounge to iron, sew, study, play, read, argue, make love and fall asleep in front of the television. Similarly, children could be sent in there for the TV to babysit them.

Since in many homes the lounge room is the space that is most protected from mess, these activities became a source of tension. So there was strife if the children spilt food and drink in there while watching, but tension also arose because of the privileged separation of space that was the hallmark of the lounge. On the one hand, whoever was preparing the meals was excluded both from the experience of watching TV and from sharing family activities that had abandoned the kitchen for the lounge. On the other hand, any attempt to entertain guests in the lounge was in direct competition with the family members – especially children – who were ensconced there to watch TV. Double resentments, at being banished and at missing favourite TV shows, put pressure on the organization of house space. This pressure was intensified by the fact that dividing house space into public (social entertainment) spaces like the lounge and private (family activity) spaces like the kitchen went against the grain of the long-term trend in which such distinctions were being broken down. In short, TV sets in the lounge eventually inhibited the very sensorial possibilities and consumerist home culture they were designed to promote.

During the 1960s new houses were built with a new room – the family room – in addition to the lounge. In the existing housing stock, a family room was often the first thing added in the same period's mania for extensions. Appropriately, at the same time, TV cabinet design changed, introducing moulded plastic forms and less bulky sets that heralded a less formal role for the TV itself. It was time for television to migrate into the family room. In the family room, which was usually adjacent to the kitchen, might be found the sewing machine, ironing board, boxes of children's toys, piles of magazines and books, and games. The TV could be so positioned as to allow an eye to be kept on it whilst working in the kitchen, especially as walls separating the two areas tended increasingly to come down.

Whilst these new arrangements solved the earlier problems of banishment and missing shows, they brought problems of their own. One was noise. Television sound came into direct conflict with kitchen sound. Kitchens are noisy places. Not only is there the clatter of crockery and cutlery, but mixers, blenders, dishwashers, exhaust fans and other gadgets all make their presence felt. And some people like to listen to the radio whilst working in the kitchen, too. Meanwhile, over in the family room, the favourite show keeps modulating in and out of audibility as the kitchen noises compete with the TV noises. So someone turns up the sound, and squabbling ensues.

Another problem with the family room, for children at least, is surveillance. The architect Peter Little has suggested that parents are content to put up with the noise problem because having the TV in the family room allows them to walk in (or through) and pass comments on whatever is being watched. In this way parents can retain some measure of control over both their children and their children's viewing habits. If the TV were given its own room, or put in the children's bedroom, such casual policing would be impossible. Perhaps this explains why the television set has tended to stay in the family room – it has been integrated into the process whereby parents instil their values into their children.

That parents have been prepared to put up with squabbling and noise in order to keep an eye on their children's TV habits is perhaps an indicator of the disquiet that various authoritarian bodies – especially teachers – have expressed about TV's so-called effects over the years. The permeation of this disquiet into popular consciousness can perhaps be seen in the way that TV became known as the 'idiot-box'. It might also be seen in the famous 'Life: Be In It' advertisements where the big step taken by Norm is to get out of his TV chair and walk around. 'Television addiction' became something you had actively to guard against, and an obsession with it was reckoned an embarrassment.

But the term 'idiot box' was never taken at face value. Television may have been much maligned, but maligning never took the place of viewing; rather it showed people's knowledge of the pitfalls and control over the process. It indicated a certain distance from TV, and from one's own viewing habits, and it signalled a different social role for television, where TV needed to be integrated into various activities and routines, both work and leisure based. However, it was clear that there was little popular support for the more stringent measures taken by some middle-class and educationally minded parents, who sought to enforce the duties and obligations of work over and above the pleasures of leisure and entertainment. In such households, television would be strictly rationed and restricted to approved shows or even an approved channel (the ABC). In extreme cases, or where children used their intellectual skills not to do homework but to develop stratagems to outwit their parents' dictates, the punishment took the form of sensory deprivation – removal of the TV set from the house entirely.

However, for most viewers the disquiet about television may have had more to do with its difference as a bodily activity from more traditional popular entertainment. Instead of entertaining by putting the consumer's body into crisis, like fairs and shows, TV entertained by representing such bodily activity on screen; instead of causing people to dress up and move their bodies to and from the entertainment, like theatre and concerts, TV allowed them to stay undressed and immobile. Television, especially after a while, reduces its viewers not to passivity but to immobility, which can be fine, but it can also be aggravating, the equivalent of bed-sores. However, physical immobility seems to have been the price viewers were prepared to pay for the symbolic mobility offered by the new medium.

Recent developments in audio-visual technology, and in its incorporation into people's homes and activities, have stressed the contemporary virtues of mobility and interactiveness, or, as the 'Memphis' writer Barbara Radice puts it:

> Contemporaneity means computers, electronics, video-games, science-fiction comics, *Blade Runner*, Space Shuttle, biogenetics, laser bombs, a new awareness of the body, exotic diets and banquets, mass exercise and tourism. Mobility is perhaps the most macroscopic novelty of this culture. Not only physical mobility but also and above all mobility of the hierarchies and values; and mobility of interpretations. . . . What matters to us is not their substance but their appearance. . . . It is the world of TV screens . . . where, as in Zen stories, it is never clear whether you dream you are the butterfly or the butterfly dreams it is you.[8]

THE BUTTERFLY DREAMS

And then came colour television. This often resulted in two TV sets in the house; the old monochrome receiver migrating to the bedroom, kitchen or study, the new colour one displacing it in the lounge. Mobility invested the appearance of the television set itself with the introduction of portables. These could be placed in eccentric or semi-concealed positions, finding room even on the shelves of corner stores near the cash register, and in other workplaces where periods of enforced immobility and isolation gave a whole new meaning to the idea of 'nightwatchman'. Portables could be toted around and beyond the home; but they could also be used ideologically, as it were. The small screen and appearance of not being permanently installed was just the right look for those who wished to register their superiority over TV – for them, the portable TV itself said that their owners didn't *really* watch that much, and watched it selectively. But, like everyone else, such people nevertheless placed themselves within reach of contemporary communications, despite their misgivings.

The migration and fragmentation of TV sets implied a new regime of watching which henceforth characterizes television. No longer was it the fixed, solitary object of people's gaze or attention – people had already learnt to do many things at the same time. Now television, like radio before it, had to compete for small segments of people's time. Sometimes the screen would be mere visual display, holding little more interest than other home decorations; at other times it would draw, or be given, people's full intensity of looking and listening. People dipped in and out of TV, in an alternating current of concentration and distraction.

Television screens were poised not simply to migrate around and outside the home, but actively to colonize and domesticate further the spaces that had once been strictly demarcated as public. At the same time, entertainments which once had been seen as essentially public were ready to be captured for home consumption. The marker and perhaps agent of this new phase was the videocassette recorder (VCR). VCRs were launched and have remained as a way of bringing feature films into the home. Never mind the difference in screen size, which means that the image is not just smaller but is frequently attenuated because of the difference between TV and cinema screen ratios. People had already learnt to put up with such differences through broadcast movies. VCRs meant that you could choose which film to watch and when to watch it. They also recaptured several low-intensity user groups, bringing them back into touch with TV screens. Among these were teenagers, who'd go to the video hire shop in groups as they might to the usurped drive-in, and take a film or films back to watch collectively in each other's houses. Other groups were those speaking languages not catered for by broadcast TV – any language but English. Specialist video shops proliferated, offering European, Asian and Indian films imported and circulated entirely for the video market. Thus, for instance, the Italian, Yugoslav and Greek communities have achieved one of the highest per capita levels of VCR ownership in Australia, which as a whole has one of the highest levels in the world, second only, perhaps, to Saudi Arabia.

Thus the suburban shopping malls carried the mark of television in the form of specialist video shops and video stalls in newsagents, delis, petrol stations and department stores. At the same time, TV screens themselves began to colonize the malls, being used by banks, building societies and travel agents to promote their services with specially made tapes. The foyer of Cinema City, one of Perth's biggest city-centre complexes, represents physically the breakdown of the dividing line between video and cinema by offering a bank of six videos for waiting customers to enjoy. Fashion stores like Irene Whyte have introduced video monitors as an integral part of window display and shop fitting, a logical extension of their established use of pop music for an ambience of contemporaneity and fashion, while an avant garde boutique like Orphans signals its difference by displaying a painted TV set in the cut-off boot of an old Holden car. The shops that sell TVs and monitors, from Vox Adeon to Parry's, display their wares in banked rows. Usually all sets are switched on, often showing the same picture, but rarely with the sound turned up. In fact, the difference between domestic and commercial uses of TV screens is no longer a distinction between public and private spaces, but one of excess – commercial space is identified by the sheer exuberance and conspicuous redundancy of having twenty screens showing the same video clip. Meanwhile, the discerning consumer has no need to rely on chance encounters with TV screens whilst out and about. The recent release of pocket TV in Western Australia is promoted to use 'indoors or out, in bright light or at night' – you need never miss the news or your favourite show, and of course you can use it at sporting fixtures to umpire the umpire's decisions.

Back at home, it's now not just a matter of where to put the screen or how many to have, but what kind to have and what to put on them. There's a struggle for access to the monitor, between broadcast TV and video films, between video clips and time-shifted TV recordings, and between commercially and home produced tapes. The struggle is set to intensify with the development of computers that effectively exploit the screen.

Other technical changes have reduced the isolation of the TV set as an appliance. With hi-fi and stereo-television, it is now possible to design integrated systems, where the TV becomes a component function within a total hi-fi system that will also include phono, cassette player, FM/AM radio and compact disc. As a result, televisions are now being designed with their own internal functions separated: the first thing to go being the sideboardlike stand, so the set can be placed into the system it's part of. Then there's a move to separate sound from picture. In some versions the separation is physical, mimicking the hi-fi plus two speakers format already in wide use; in others the separation takes the form of disconnecting the set's internal speakers and patching it into an existing system. The migration of sound out of the TV set means that the screen is now properly a monitor, its subservience to a larger system symbolized by the latest remote control devices which govern not only the choice between broadcast and VCR input, but the audio levels of the hi-fi component as well. In fact the remote control is the visible sign of people's control over not just their own equipment but over the act of looking too. It is no longer necessary to get what you're given: the practice known as 'slaloming' is worrying to advertisers who have found that people use the remote control to slalom from channel to channel in an effort to avoid ads before returning to the next segment of a chosen show; and they are equally worried about 'zapping', where people record a programme for time-shifting to a more convenient viewing period, and then use the shuttle-search function to zap through commercial breaks. Furthermore, the remote control can be used to select away from unwanted segments of the programmes themselves, and this is a function that will gain importance as Perth moves into the era of SBS and a third commercial channel (launched in 1987 and 1988 respectively).

Using the remote control also adds a new dimension to the facilities on offer in VCRs. Without squatting by the set or getting up from the chair, it is now possible to use the pause and search facilities to stop a narrative in its tracks, not only to eliminate ads, but to go back over a shot to see how it was done or to relish it in slow-motion; or even to use the pause to hold and to fetishize an actor's body or a scene. The appropriation by viewers of a kind of authorship of the material they view can indeed be realized literally, by re-recording clips from different tapes to make a 'scrap-book' video; or by selecting images almost randomly and dubbing on music to make the latest art-form, scratch-videos. The upshot is that broadcast television's carefully constructed realism can be seen for the construction it is; and its carefully organized scheduling habits can simply be countermanded.

For the audio-visual adepts who have a mind to do more than consume ready-made material, the way is now open to consume self-made images and sound. With the help of Super Beta, compact and super VHS, or 8mm video, and with the increasingly sophisticated domestic video cameras, enthusiasts can now integrate self-shot sequences to match pre-recorded ones, whether taken from videotape, broadcast TV, radio, record or compact disc. In the offing are previously unthinkable domestic editing set-ups that may eventually be linked to computers and computer generated graphics.

Not everyone can afford to avail themselves of all this potential, and those who do may be the minority who get a thrill from sheer technical wizardry (and expense) rather than those who have an interest in audio-visual representation as such. But the fascination of these developments is just as much in their potential as in the realizations of it by any one type of user. What these developments mean is that moving images and sounds have been emancipated from their producers' intentions, and that people's relationship with television screens is fundamentally more sophisticated and interactive than it was when TV broadcasts began.

It also means that there are yet more enticements to centre leisure and entertainment in the home, and that such leisure is increasingly under the control of consumers themselves. Among those who are adept in audio-visual culture are of course the numbers of young people who count among their repertoire of skills the ability to play video-games: an ability that includes erasing the traditional distinctions between playing and looking, between consuming a product and making their own, between being subject to others' intentions (both authorial and authoritarian) and using their bodies to process environmental data into independent experience and culture. In short, those who have been brought up on and by the new audio-visual institutions of pleasure and consumption are now poised to invert the image; to dream the butterfly.

The Brechtian vision of people exploiting the resources of modern technologies seems to be developing, however, with few of the social consequences hoped for by utopian writers like Brecht. Since the period in which he lived, the redefinition of public and private space has also played a part in redefining the spaces on which political action is conducted. No longer is it possible to make easy connections between mass communication and mass action. Now that people have begun to learn how to control the means of audio-visual production, it is clear that there will be no 'big bang' social revolution in consequence. Instead, fundamental change – a social revolution perhaps – is centred on the spaces, resources and activities that occur within the broadly defined arena of domestic consumer culture. In the nineteenth century, Karl Marx despaired for the political future of the French peasantry. Noting that their conditions of existence were similar throughout the country, he also found that these similarities did not entail any unity or class consciousness – the French peasantry, he said, formed a class to the extent that potatoes in a sack form a sack of potatoes. What seems to have changed since those epic days is not that the potatoes have been mashed together by this political ideology or that, as it were, but that they have all spilled out of the sack. Now we're all couch potatoes.

Chapter 15

Two cheers for paedocracy

I THE EIGHTEENTH BRUMAIRE OF KYLIE MINOGUE*

This is the first attempt, as far as I know, to analyse the popular Australian actress and singer's career in terms of the view of history proposed by Karl Marx in his *Eighteenth Brumaire of Louis Bonaparte*. It transpires that the lessons of history are as farcical as ever.

The birth was in Bethlehem. The date was 28 May 1968.

There was a time when a birth in Bethlehem was considered newsworthy, but times have changed. The unique place and event have become clichéd, history repeating itself interminably, diffused and deferred as soap opera. So Bethlehem becomes Bethlehem Hospital, Melbourne, and the Star in the East becomes Kylie Minogue.

May 1968 was a newsworthy month. The society of the spectacle was proclaimed by the situationists. Students and car workers mobilized on the streets of Paris, daubing slogans on the walls of the establishment: 'Sous le pavé, la plage!' – Under the pavement, the beach!

The *événements* unfolded as, in a diligent search for the beach, the latter-day Communards ripped up the paving stones and stormed the Bastille of established high culture. The walls of Géricault tottered, but the establishment held up.

Down Under the pavements of Paris, if you dig far enough, there are indeed beaches – the antipodean beaches of Australia. A perfect location for the society of the spectacle, the politics of the body.

The revolutionaries of the 1960s welcomed May 1968 as a world-historical event, comparable in significance with the French Revolution and the Enlightenment; 1968 lit up the Democratic vistas of America in Chicago and US embassies in Berlin and London, and they even saw the light in Australia. Renegade intellectual tourist terrorists flocked up to join the fun. Not Lafayette and Tom Paine this time, but Richard Neville and Germaine Greer – the American Constitution rewritten as *Playpower*

* Originally published as John Hartley (1988) 'The Eighteenth Brumaire of Kylie Minogue', *Australian Left Review*, 107, 7.

and the Rights of Man exposed as *The Female Eunuch*.

But just as the French Revolution ended in Napoleon's empire and then in farcical repetition under Napoleon III, so the *événements* of 1968 were compromised. Culture and politics, fused into one critical mass during 1968, were defused. The *Politics of Ecstasy* (Timothy Leary) and *Bomb Culture* (Jeff Nuttall) parted company. Dropouts became cultural entrepreneurs (Felix Dennis – from editor of *Oz* to radical porn merchant), and political activists became professors of sociology (Stuart Hall).

Left to themselves, the people could think of nothing better to do, politically, than elect Richard Nixon, General de Gaulle and Ted Heath. In Australia they couldn't remember who they'd elected, as a succession of conservative prime ministers came and went, one of them (Harold Holt) going out from the beach in a symbolic fusion of politics and surfing, never to be seen again.

Left to itself, the people's culture maintained a lively interest in the body and spectacle, but not in politics and society. And Kylie Minogue, a child of 1968, grew, somewhat.

Did she revere Abbie Hoffman, Rudi Dutschke, Daniel Cohn-Bendit, Richard Neville, Germaine Greer?

No, but she and her Melburnian schoolchums loved Abba, and her little life was changed when mum (Welsh ex-ballerina Carol) took her to see Olivia Newton-John in *Grease*.

This was the spectacle of the body that mobilized Kylie: high energy wholesomeness, disco dancing, toothsome Australiana at large. She went on to score the part of Carla in *The Sullivans* at the age of 11, followed by that of Charlotte in *The Henderson Kids*. Finally, she pupated, or pubertied, into Charlene in *Neighbours*.

Waiting only long enough to secure that passport to international *ahdom*, a screen wedding, Kylie rips off her little pink cardi, piles her hair up through the brim of what might be the disco version of the Australian slouch hat, and appears winking winsomely in a little black dress to rip off 1960s' star Little Eva in *The Locomotion*.

The child of 1968 has come of age, and with the help of benevolent media and ruthless managers (the notoriously successful agency SAW) she's become the sign of 1988. The global villagers are all *Neighbours* now, as the culture industry's integrated circuits reproduce Kylie on screen, in music, in magazines and on the lips of the whole world's pre-teens in the sacred time between school and tea.

But already Kylie has been out-Kylied by *The Comedy Company*'s Kylie Mole; a reproduction more authentic than the original, the revenge of the simulacrum. Maryanne Fahey's 'roolly exc'llent' Kylie Mole is the role model for Minogue, who now guests on *The Comedy Company* as Mole's friend Rebecca while Mole appears on *Perfect Match* as 'herself'. And the role model for grade six primary schoolchildren isn't Minogue but Mole:

> Teacher Colin Fletcher said: 'I think the reason the show took off so well was because we have a Kylie, Amanda and Dino in the class. I use the show in formal teaching because the kids are so tuned in. I think the kids can relate to Kylie Mole because she is such a real character.'
>
> (Perth *Sunday Times*, 18 September 1988)

And the generation of 1968 looks on, aghast, muttering *mea culpa*. Is this the reality they imagined, the society of the spectacle, the politics of the body?

Well, no, it isn't. 'The Body' is another young Australian person who's electrifying the global image circuits just now. Her name is Elle Macpherson. *Cleo* readers voted Elle the No. 1 'woman they would like to look like'. She also has the No. 1 'life-style', she's the No. 3 'most glamorous woman in the world' after Princess Diana and Joan Collins, and she's the No. 2 'ultimate role model for women today' after Jana Wendt, presenter of Channel 9's *A Current Affair* (*Cleo*, October 1988).

And what about Kylie Minogue? She came top in one category. She's the No. 1 'worst role model' for women. Says *Cleo*, 'Most respondents said they wanted to be smart rather than hanker after good looks.'

Be smart. Remember what Marx wrote in *The 18th Brumaire of Louis Bonaparte*; it refers clearly to Kylie Minogue and the *turntable* revolutions of *The Locomotion*: 'An entire people, which had imagined that by means of a revolution it had imparted to itself an accelerated power of motion, suddenly finds itself set back into a defunct epoch.'

How right he was. How does it end, according to Marx? 'The nation feels like a mad Englishman in Bedlam', he says, and I know that feeling too. It seems we're all back to the defunct epoch of Stars in the East . . . for as everyone knows, 'Bedlam' is a shortened form of Bethlehem Hospital.

Of course (as everyone knows), it never really ends. Giving herself an accelerated power of motion, Kylie breaks the shackles of SAWdom, takes on a new identity, reinvents her own body for post-teen SEXdom, and starts all over again. She's got it, she flaunts it, the glossies can't quite believe it (even as they do endless cover features of it), and Kylie Minogue enters the post-Marxist 1990s as a continuing challenge to the critics of a defunct epoch. The tradition of all the dead generations weighs like a nightmare on the brain of this living revolutionary, whose 'borrowed costumes' present 'a new scene in world history', and again we're all back where we started (see chapter 2, p. 21).

II GETTING THE PICTURE?*

The visual arts in the electronic media

I don't think I could have tackled a more difficult task than to review the image of the visual arts in the electronic media, for although TV is a visual art itself it doesn't pay much heed to the fact. Still, here goes. What did 1990 *look like*, and how did it sound at the time?

As I write, there's some art on the more talkative of the electronic media, the radio. It's Dame Joan Sutherland singing her last encore at the Sydney Opera House. It's also the very moment when the two Germanies are becoming one; 3 October 1990. As a matter of fact I have been wandering disconsolately around the house, switching on radios, flicking across TV channels, trying to participate in the one art where the electronic media are undisputed champions: time.

It's 7 a.m. in Western Australia, midnight in Europe. On ABC Television we have an Abbott and Costello cartoon, on SBS a nice black screen, on Channel 7 a commercial, and on Channels 9 and 10 we have the delayed telecast of the morning current affairs shows, both smilingly promising that they'll cross to Berlin throughout the morning. That is, I am watching what Sydney said two hours ago was going to be on in the next two hours in the two Germanies. I don't want to know that; I want to see the moment of fusion. Now. Only TV can do this, but it didn't.

I can almost hear the strains of 'Deutschland über alles' belting out from the Brandenburg Gate. I rush for one of my radios . . . Radio National is playing some music. All my preset stations . . . 6PM, The Eagle, 6UVS, 96FM – are playing some music. But not that music. At last, ABC 6WF in Perth tells me what I want to hear. They have a 7 a.m. news bulletin, and on the line from Berlin I can hear the bells ringing out in the two Germanies . . . in the one Germany.

It's done. But I'm suspicious. Is this report actually live, or is it a pre-recorded package? Have I become so used to edited grabs and delayed broadcasts that I can't tell what's live any more? Or maybe reality is a fake. Have the electronic media gone out of sync. with real time, their most essential attribute, preferring to create the impression of liveness with ambient sound, informed commentary, eyewitness accounts, and fade up music *über alles*, so we can spend our real time profitably listening to what it really means, never mind wasting time on the accidental discontinuities of real actuality, which is always a bit off-mike in any case?

Apparently so, for I subside back into my computer seat, switch on another radio, and find myself grinning at the stupendous rendition of a song I had not expected to hear as the two Germanies become one. Two

* Originally published as John Hartley (1990) 'Getting the picture? The visual arts in Australia in the electronic media', *Artlink*, 10(4), 33–5.

careers, each spanning over forty years, come to a simultaneous ceremonial end, filling the house with sound in an electronic link between my private and the world's public affairs, waking the children and marking the occasion. As East Germany comes in from the cold, La Stupenda sings her last encore, art coterminates with politics, and verily, 'There's No Place Like Home'.

Of course, it's all happened before. It happens all the time. I was at home on Bastille Day too, 14 July 1990, bustling about the house in the weak sunshine of a pleasant winter morning, doing family things and the washing up, listening to the radio. Bastille Day; the day when The People irrupted decisively into History, inaugurating the age of the Popular, and doing it with an act of criminal appropriation.

On this day, on the radio arts show *In Tempo*, we in Perth heard the newly appointed supremo of the Western Australian Art Gallery, whose name I've forgotten, talking to our local TV news presenter and gardening buff Peter Holland. It seems, from their conversation, that art should be popularized, but what this means is to add international artists to the 'gene pool' of local talent. The garden of Australian art is to be hybridized with cultivars of imported tall poppies. On the same day *Arts National* reported on the relationship between art-theft and drug-money; and on the British Museum's latest and most successful art exhibition: *Fakes*.

Fakery, international crime, the laundering of ill-gotten gains through the most prestigious marketplace on the planet, the use of that marketplace to purchase genes for home consumption. Here at home I'm left wondering what it all amounts to. Am I getting the right picture?

The reporting of the arts on radio and TV must itself be dedicated to popularization; why else broadcast it? But if popularization is larceny, Bastille-style, or merely the triumph of market forces, where capitalism and democracy are united like two Germanies and packaged for export, then the image of the visual arts in Australia in the electronic media is this: the authentic icon of art is the fake, imported with dirty money for dissemination to domestic consumers to enjoy in the privacy of their homes.

The authentic icon of 1990 was, therefore, Madonna, belting it out live to millions of adoring fans on TV, wearing the authentic icon of post-feminist art, the external bra, designed by Jean Paul Gaultier, but originated by Vivienne Westwood, Mancunian couture-punk and former co-conspirator, with master-faker Malcolm Maclaren, of clothes-as-politics and popular art as swindle. Jean Paul is clearly an artist too, for as Australian *Elle* enthuses:

> The type of subversion he practices is not only visual but also political. He believes clothes have always been a cipher for the broader currents of society. Admirers of his work credit him with extending to ugly people the right to have impact, and making clothes more of a challenge

to the spirit than the purse. Critics dismiss him as a special-effects man, couture's answer to Fritz the Cat.[1]

So Jean Paul's eight seamstresses work for four months to make Madonna a special effect, clad in '175 kilograms of satin, sequins, leather and steel', for her *Blonde Ambition* tour, her corsetted body an exhibition hall for the shock of the neo, her performances dedicated to kinetic art, and her voice, well, dubbed.

Is she actually singing in front of those adoring fans? Or is live music, like reality, merely an over-produced fake? Are those lips, never off-mike because the thing is strapped to her face, really uttering these sounds? Don't ask: it's the TV audience's democratic right to hear what's already known on CD, and anyway the live performance is merely a marketing strategy, selling the fans the image of their own liveness.

Meanwhile the body politic, Madonna with bra *über alles*, is in any case already a statement of opposition to the ideology of authenticity and originality upon which the entire concept of liveness rests. Postfeminist body in postmodernist performance; the material girl is *iconoplastic*.

They do say that Australia is an egalitarian sort of place, apt to cut down tall poppies even while nurturing them with imported biotechnology, prone to iconoclasm in art as in life. Perhaps this explains why the sublime, the beautiful, the true, the stupendous, appear in the electronic media, as in life, not as art but as news.

The public, iconoclastic or iconoplastic, it doesn't matter which, loves fakes for their democratic potential; everyone can have one, share the joke, get in the picture.

So what was the most newsworthy art sale of the year? Was it the resale of Van Gogh's *Irises*, as local tycoon Alan Bond strove to convert debt into equity? Here the doubts about authenticity attached not to the work of art but to its owner, whose own newspaper (the *West Australian*) and TV station (Channel 9) had so recently shown him at the peak of corporate credibility, emblematically pictured standing in front of the then most expensive piece of canvas and pigment on earth, unselfconsciously throwing his considerable shadow, sharpened by the glare of his own TV lights, right over the painting.

Or was this sale overshadowed by news of the release on to the art market of thousands of original Disney animations, a plenitude of scarcity, given that each cell is hand-painted original artwork, but there are thousands upon thousands of cells, at 1,440 frames a minute and so many cells per frame, adding up to a marketing coup, sell by cell, creating a new class of artistic connoisseurs out of people who're glad to shell out for a respectable representation of their own childhood's not so innocent pleasures; Fritz the Cat's answer to high culture.

And what was the newsworthy art anniversary of the year? Van Gogh's

100th? Or Bugs Bunny's 50th? Maybe both, for the definitive art of the new decade is an amalgam of painterly imagination and cartoon characterization; the art of special effects, computer animation and graphics, images created and manipulated on machinery whose name – Harry – is better known than those of the artists. But their day has come, along with high-definition TV screens, which are also home computer monitors, integrating public art and private consumption, crossing the line between doing and seeing. Who knows, the pre-teens of today, who muck about with Amigas and thrill to the antics of Michaelangelo, Donatello, Raphael and Leonardo, may already know more about contemporary art than we do.

One thing is for sure: the popularization of visual arts is going on everywhere, except in those very places especially designed for the job. The promotion of contemporary art is undertaken not by the WA Art Gallery, for example, where Jimmy Pike's Aboriginal paintings hang, but by Desert Designs, who sell us Jimmy Pikes and Doris Gingingarras for our backs and bottoms. Other visual artists, like Ken Done, have abandoned galleries altogether, preferring to hang their art on our persons, making public galleries out of the people's private spaces.

As for specialist arts programmes on TV itself, it seems they're not designed for the popularization of art, for they serve a different purpose. The best of them look good precisely because they don't pose as arts television at all, they just do good television, like Annette Shun Wah's *Eat Carpet* slot on SBS, which often springs a surprise, getting away with art because it's not an art slot at all.

But the ABC's *Arts Australia* is something else again: a specialist arts programme that must come somewhere near the bottom of the league by any artistic criterion you could name. Its ten minutes of drear embarrassment take the place of what Sunday evenings used to be for; it's the God-slot. Art on the ABC is the secularization of the category of God. Like its radio equivalent, the so-called sacred reading at 7.10 a.m. on Radio National, *Arts Australia* reeks of low-budget dutiful production values, dedicated to accessing special pleaders who are not chosen for their ability to be interesting, but for their authenticity as representatives of something called art, which comes across to the viewer as a coercive and tedious sermon about what we ought to believe, squashed in between what we may have wanted to watch. *Arts Australia* may be the worst programme on Australian TV.

Bugger it, let's switch to Channel 10, where they're screening one of the glories of Australian art of the 1980s, a movie of such eye-catching quality that it might stand as a foundation myth for Australia itself, a *photopoem* that clinically analyses the culture of Saturday night, of men and motor cars and the conquest of a landscape, a metaphor for the colonization of a continent by people who are no better than they should be. And what's more this movie is made by just about the most important production house of our times, and stars Australia's best-known actor since Errol

Flynn. I refer of course, in reverse order, to Mel Gibson, to Kennedy Miller, and to *Mad Max II*.

But hold on a minute. The voice-over intro doesn't even mention that this is an Australian film, nor that Mel Gibson's international career began here; he's billed as the star of *Lethal Weapon*. And Channel 10 is loyal enough to Kennedy Miller, its long-time supplier of major mini-series, to mangle this movie so badly, in an effort to 'modify' it for Channel 10's idea of acceptable television, that the plot frequently doesn't make sense, the action is jump-cut at absolutely crucial moments, and all the good bits – you know, the villain's fingers being sliced off by the feral child's steel boomerang – are missing. In short, real Australian visual art is popularized on television by those who think the proper way to package it for the public is to pretend it's American and chop its fingers off.

No-one cares. In fact the treatment of art in the electronic media teaches the viewing public precisely not to care, by bowdlerizing the art of our age and sacralizing the art of any other, while specialist arts programmes preserve a reverential image of an outmoded aesthetic consensus in which no-one believes, least of all artists.

The aesthetic consensus is not only the traditional evaluation of *this* work over *that* one (my taste is better than yours), but the more fundamental and insidious consensus, shared right across the media from those who espouse the sublime to those who export the cor-blimey, an unholy alliance of those who agree that the coverage of art in the media means one thing: the life story of the artist.

That isn't exactly an advanced theory of textuality, nor does it teach the public anything at all about visual arts. It reduces one domain to another; turning art into story, artists into fictional characters who represent neither themselves nor their work, but the ideology of originality, living proof in biotechnological colour that the explanation of art is the personality, genius, life-experience or character of the author.

Enter Jane Rutter, alias the 'naughty flautist', according to the *Weekend Australian* colour-supplement's cover story of 14 July 1990, Bastille Day. Rutter's life story, written up as the triumph of a name-dropping 'Hooray Harriet' over the people ('it was a real pop pub audience and they went wild for me'), reduces art to personality, personality to body, and body to this:

> If this 30-year-old renaissance woman has the face of a Botticelli cherub, she has the body of a Manet odalisque . . . she was dubbed 'the Samantha Fox of classical music.' . . . Pert, pretty and petite, with the personality of a soubrette and a coloratura laugh, Rutter exudes the kind of sexuality that has male audiences drooling down their shirt collars.[2]

I looked up both soubrette (maid, flirt, coquette) and odalisque (female slave in a harem); Rutter's aural art is explained in terms of her visual resemblance to a prostitute. This may not sound like a very good lesson in how to appreciate flute music, but if that's what you think then you haven't been listening. Let's try again:

> Even before Madonna made fifties underwear fashionable outer-wear, Rutter ripped off her blouse and played a Bach sonata in a Hestia bra during a concert at the Sydney Opera House.[3]

Now do you get the picture? Says Rutter: 'If it makes the music more accessible, then why not?' Exactly what I'm supposed to access from her Hestia bra I'm not at all sure, but I can't help wondering what La Stupenda was hiding as she brought the Opera House down last October.

What Jane Rutter's body hides, however, is that you don't have to hear a bar of the music. All you need is a visual icon of artistic authenticity. Then the great enterprise of public education can begin. You just rip off the blouse of high culture to reveal the bra of high fashion and under that the Samantha Fox of low sex.

I thought that a review of the image of the visual arts in Australia would be difficult. Obviously I was wrong, at least if the world of quality colour supplements is to be believed. For them the appreciation of Australian art is as easy as drooling down your shirt collar.

But for me a difficulty does remain. It's hard to find self-confident experiments in the visual arts, and serious coverage of the arts, in the electronic media, but the blame does not rest entirely with them. There's no climate of criticism which takes the media themselves seriously *as* art, so it's hardly surprising if the media return that compliment *to* art.

In fact the climate of criticism in cultural journalism takes nothing seriously except the aesthetic prejudices of people educated in the authoritarian certainties of the cultural cold war. But the cultural cold war is not what it used to be. Just as the line between Lübeck and Karl Marx Stadt fades from the map, so the former effortless superiority of high art is crumbling. Having lost the courage of its own convictions, it poses art as religion and classical music as Madonna.

But there's still a difference. Madonna's postmodern body is a serious undertaking; Rutter's image is pornography (Gk 'prostitute-writing'). Under Madonna's conical bra is *muscle*; something the *Weekend Australian* might find less than reassuring.

As for me, here at home, I think it's time to go out in the garden. I've just finished watching Don Burke, an electronic visual artist if ever there was one, at the bottom of whose garden there are theories, and whose weekly home-and-garden show *Burke's Backyard* may well be the most popular arts programme on Australian TV, taking both visual pleasure and ordinary people seriously, and not squeamish about cutting down tall poppies when they get in the way of a clear view.

Now where are those secateurs?

Notes

2 TELEVISION AND THE POWER OF DIRT

1 Karl Marx (1968) *Karl Marx and Frederick Engels: Selected Works in one volume*, London: Lawrence & Wishart, 96.
2 Mary Douglas (1966) *Purity and Danger: An Analysis of the Concepts of Pollution and Taboo*, London: Routledge & Kegan Paul.
3 Hans Magnus Enzensberger (1972) 'Constituents of a theory of the media', in Denis McQuail (ed.) *Sociology of Mass Communication*, Harmondsworth: Penguin.
4 Edmund Leach (1976) *Culture and Communication*, Cambridge: Cambridge University Press, 62.
5 Jonathan Culler (1979) 'Jacques Derrida', in John Sturrock (ed.) *Structuralism and Since*, Oxford: Opus (Oxford University Press), 167.
6 Spens Committee (1938) *Report of the Consultative Committee on Secondary Education, with special reference to Grammar Schools and Technical High Schools*, London: HMSO.
7 Ferdinand de Saussure (1974) *Course in General Linguistics*, London: Fontana.
8 Stuart Hall (1982) 'The rediscovery of "ideology": return of the repressed in media studies', in Michael Gurevitch, Tony Bennett, James Curran and Janet Woollacott (eds) *Culture, Society and the Media*, London: Methuen, 56–90, 79.
9 Enzensberger, op. cit., 108–9.
10 Roland Barthes (1981) 'Theory of the text', in R. Young (ed.) *Untying the Text: A Post-Structuralist Reader*. London: Routledge & Kegan Paul, 32.
11 Hall, op. cit., 81.
12 Valentin Volosinov (1973) *Marxism and the Philosophy of Language*, New York: Seminar Press.
13 Hall, op. cit., 80.
14 John Hartley (1982) *Understanding News*, London: Methuen; and Tim O'Sullivan, John Hartley, Danny Saunders and John Fiske (1983) *Key Concepts in Communication*, London: Methuen.
15 Roland Barthes (1973) *Mythologies*, London: Paladin. See also John Fiske and John Hartley (1978) *Reading Television*, London and New York: Methuen, 176.

3 REGIMES OF TRUTH AND THE POLITICS OF READING

1 Kurt Vonnegut (1981), *Palm Sunday: An Autobiographical Collage*, London: Jonathan Cape, 14.
2 ibid., 223.

3 ibid., 13.
4 West Australian Newspapers (1973) *Style Book*, Perth: West Australian Newspapers, 36.
5 BBC Television Service (1972), *Principles and Practice in Documentary Programmes*, London: BBC; 'drawn up' by Richard Cawston (head of documentary programmes), Stephen Hearst (head of arts features), Robert Reid (head of science features), Anthony de Lotbiniere (producer, documentary programmes), Antony Jay (writer, former head of talks features and former editor of *Tonight*), Roger Cary (secretariat), at the request of Huw Wheldon (managing director, BBC Television), 14, 6, 15, 20–2.
6 ibid., 20–1.
7 ibid., 7.
8 Vonnegut, op. cit., 165.
9 Silvester Jourdan (1613) *A Plaine Description of the Barmudas, now called Sommer Islands*. Quoted in Robert Foster Jones (1953) *The Triumph of the English Language*, Stanford, Cal.: Stanford University Press, 32–4n (spelling updated).
10 Walter Haddon (1581) *Against Ierome Osorious*. Quoted in Jones, op. cit., 32–4n (spelling updated).
11 Peter Ramus (1543) *Training in Dialectic*. Quoted in Walter J. Ong (1958) *Ramus: Method, and the Decay of Dialogue: From the Art of Discourse to the Art of Reason*, Cambridge, Mass.: Harvard University Press, 175-80 (trans. from the Latin by Walter J. Ong).
12 (1574) *The Book of Homilies: Certain Sermons Appointed by the Queen's Majesty to be declared and read by all Parsons, Vicars and Curates, every Sunday and Holiday in their Churches; and by Her Grace's advice perused and overseen for the better understanding of the simple people*, repr. 1850, Cambridge: Cambridge University Press, 218–19.
13 ibid., title and 369.
14 ibid., 177, 265 and title.
15 Vonnegut, op. cit., 85, 157.
16 Stanley Harrison (1974) *Poor Men's Guardians*, London: Lawrence & Wishart, 10.
17 Vonnegut, op. cit., 167.
18 Frances Taylor Patterson (1920) *Cinema Craftsmanship: A Book for Photoplaywrights*, New York: Harcourt, Brace & Howe, 8.
19 Quoted in Harrison, op. cit., 98.
20 Royal Commission on the Press (1948) *Minutes of Evidence: Twenty-Sixth Day*, Cmnd 7416, London: HMSO, para. 8660. Quoted in Graham Murdock and Peter Golding (1978) 'The structure, ownership and control of the press 1914–76', in George Boyce, James Curran and Pauline Wingate (eds) *Newspaper History: From the Seventeenth Century to the Present Day*, London: Constable/ Beverly Hills: Sage, 142.
21 James Curran and Jean Seaton (1985) *Power without Responsibility: The Press and Broadcasting in Britain* 2nd edn, London: Methuen, chapter 5.
22 Vonnegut, op. cit., 214–15.
23 Ken Loach (31 October 1985) 'Broadcasters who uphold the established order through the charade of impartiality', London: *Guardian*.
24 ibid.
25 ibid.
26 Quoted in Michael Tracey (1982), 'Censored: the *War Game* story', in Crispin Aubrey (ed.) *Nukespeak: The Media and the Bomb*, London: Comedia, 38–54.

27 *The Listener* (15 August 1985), 'National Top Tens', London: BBC Publications.
28 Hugo Young (1 August 1982), 'Time to be unbalanced', London: *Sunday Times*.
29 ibid.
30 Vonnegut, op. cit. 166.

4 CONSCIOUSNESS RAZING

1 Annan Committee (1977) *Report of the Committee on the Future of Broadcasting*, London: HMSO, 30.
2 ibid., 235.
3 Glasgow University Media Group (1976) *Bad News*; and (1980) *More Bad News*, London: Routledge & Kegan Paul.
4 More information about Diverse, Broadside and Gambles–Milne, as well as ITN, can be found in Simon Blanchard and David Morley (eds) (1982) *What's this Channel Four? An Alternative Report*, London: Comedia, especially chapters 6 (by Barry Flynn) and 7 (by Lesley Hilton).
5 Annan Committee, op. cit., 281.
6 *IBA Handbook* (1982) London: Independent Broadcasting Authority, 57.

5 HOME HELP FOR POPULIST POLITICS

1 Cited in Graham Murdock (1973) 'Political deviance: the press presentation of a militant mass demonstration', in S. Cohen and J. Young (eds) *The Manufacture of News: Deviance, Social Problems and the Mass Media*, London: Constable, 157
2 See also Stuart Hall (1983) 'The great moving right show', in Stuart Hall and M. Jaques (eds) *The Politics of Thatcherism*, London: Lawrence & Wishart, 19–40.
3 Both Eco and Laclau have drawn attention to the way in which popular discourses may revolve around fundamental oppositions. Montgomery and I saw both press and TV news operating 'Manichaean' distinctions in the original version of this chapter, of which 'we/they' is only one. See Umberto Eco (1981) *The Role of the Reader*, London: Hutchinson; and Ernesto Laclau (1980) 'Populist rupture and discourse', *Screen Education*, 34, 87–93.
4 Other aspects of the same news story are analysed in John Hartley (1982) *Understanding News*, London: Methuen, chapter 7.
5 See, for example, Roland Barthes (1975) *S/Z*, London: Jonathan Cape.

6 INVISIBLE FICTIONS

1 E. Ann Kaplan (ed.) (1983) *Regarding Television: Critical Approaches – An Anthology*, New York: American Film Institute/University Publications of America, xi.
2 John Ellis (1982) *Visible Fictions: Cinema, Television, Video*, London: Routledge & Kegan Paul, 5.
3 See, for instance, Raymond Williams (1974) *Television: Technology and Cultural Form*, London: Fontana; James Carey (1977) 'Mass communication research and cultural studies: an American view' in James Curran, Michael Gurevitch and Janet Woollacott (eds) *Mass Communication and Society*, London: Open University/Edward Arnold, chapter 16; Stuart Hall (1982) 'The

rediscovery of "ideology": return of the repressed in media studies', in Michael Gurevitch, Tony Bennett, James Curran and Janet Woollacott (eds) *Culture, Society and the Media*, London: Methuen; Special issue: 'Ferment in the field' (1983) *Journal of Communication*, 33(3).

4 Willard D. Rowland and Bruce Watkins (eds) (1984) *Interpreting Television: Current Research Perspectives*, Beverly Hills: Sage, 33, 25.
5 Ellis, op. cit., 5.
6 Benedict Anderson (1983) *Imagined Communities*, London: Verso, 16.
7 ibid., 31.
8 ibid., 39.
9 Edward Said (1978) *Orientalism*, London: Routledge & Kegan Paul.
10 Edward Said (1985) 'Orientalism reconsidered', *Race and Class,* 27(7).
11 Ellis, op. cit., 169.
12 David Morley (1980) *The 'Nationwide' Audience*, London: British Film Institute, 40, 42, 46, 68.
13 ibid., 27.
14 David Morley (1986) *Family Television: Cultural Power and Domestic Leisure*, London: Comedia.
15 Todd Gitlin (1983) *Inside Prime Time*, New York: Pantheon, 324.
16 Quoted in ibid., 188.
17 ibid.
18 ibid., 136, 137.
19 Quoted in ibid., 138.
20 ibid., 139.
21 Quoted in ibid., 22.
22 Valentin Volosinov (1973) *Marxism and the Philosophy of Language*, New York: Seminar Press, 95.
23 Annan Committee (1977) *Report of the Committee on the Future of Broadcasting*, London: HMSO, 25.
24 ibid., 246.
25 ibid.
26 Australian Broadcasting Tribunal (1984) *Manual*, Canberra: Australian Government Publishing Service, 11.
27 ibid., 15.
28 ibid., 27.
29 Nicholas Garnham (1987) 'Concepts of culture: public policy and the cultural industries', *Cultural Studies*, (1)1, 31. The phrase 'expansion of difference', which I find to be a suggestive and satisfying definition of culture, does not in fact appear in the more accessible published version of Garnham's paper referenced above. It is corrected to the much less interesting phrase 'expression of difference'. But 'expansion of difference' is so apt that even if Garnham wants to discard it I don't, so I have decided to retain it from the first published version, which was issued as a house-printed pamphlet (giving no author or date) by the Greater London Council in 1983.
30 Gitlin, op. cit., 26.
31 ibid., 21.
32 Cf. Ien Ang (1986) 'The battle between television and its audiences: the politics of watching television', in Philip Drummond and Richard Paterson (eds) *Television in Transition*, London: British Film Institute.
33 Gitlin, op. cit., 300.

7 THE REAL WORLD OF AUDIENCES

1 Martin Allor (1988) 'Relocating the site of the audience: reconstructive theory and the social subject', *Critical Studies in Mass Communication*, 5(3), 217–33.
2 ibid., 228.
3 Karl Popper (1983) 'Knowledge: subjective versus objective' [1967], in David Miller (ed.) *A Pocket Popper*, London: Fontana, 58.
4 Valentin Volosinov (1973) *Marxism and the Philosophy of Language*, New York: Seminar Press, 95.
5 Popper, op. cit., 69, 72, 60.
6 E. Ann Kaplan (1986) 'History, the historical spectator and gender address in music television', *Communication Inquiry*, 10(1), 3–14, quoted in Allor, op. cit., 222.
7 Allor, op. cit., 228.
8 ibid., 219.
9 Umberto Eco (1987) *Travels in Hyperreality* (originally *Faith in Fakes*), trans. William Weaver, London: Picador, 81–2.
10 ibid., 143
11 ibid., 148, 150
12 ibid., xi–xii.
13 Allor, op. cit., 228.
14 Todd Gitlin (1983) *Inside Prime Time*, New York: Pantheon. See also my review of Gitlin's Americanism; John Hartley (1987) 'Been there – done that: on academic tourism', *Communication Research*, 14(2), 251–61.
15 Frances Taylor Patterson (1920) *Cinema Craftsmanship: A Book for Photoplaywrights*, New York: Harcourt, Brace & Howe, 150–1. One of the fascinating things about this book, apart from its contents, is that my copy was a gift from the British Board of Film Censors to the British Film Institute, who withdrew it from their library in 1977 after fifty years, and sold it off at a bargain price (to me) at the International Television Studies Conference, which the BFI co-sponsors, in 1986. In such satisfyingly complex ways does the colloquy of Popper's third world continue; reminding me at least that official film censorship, *Screen* theory, and the latest thinking on television, have historical connections that are objective and which 'we' would be wise not to ignore.
16 ibid., 149–50.
17 ibid., 149.
18 ibid., 150.
19 ibid.
20 Allor, op. cit., 229.

8 OUT OF BOUNDS

1 *BBC Annual Report and Handbook 1984* (1983) London: BBC Publications, 130.

10 THE POLITICS OF PHOTOPOETRY

1 Humphrey Jennings (1987) *Pandaemonium: The Coming of the Machine as seen by Contemporary Observers*, ed. Mary-Lou Jennings and Charles Madge from materials compiled by Jennings *circa* 1937–50, London: Picador.
2 ibid., xxxviii.
3 T.S. Eliot (1932) *Selected Essays*, London: Faber & Faber, 458–9.

4 ibid., 459.
5 Cited in Jennings, op. cit., 343–4.
6 ibid., 344.
7 ibid., xi.
8 Cited in ibid., xi.
9 See also John Tulloch (1990) *Television Drama: Agency, Audience and Myth*. London and New York: Routledge.
10 See Tony Bennett, Susan Boyd-Bowman, Colin Mercer and Janet Woollacott (eds) (1981) *Popular Television and Film*, London: British Film Institute/Open University, part 4 *passim*, for a critical debate on *Days of Hope*.
11 See, for instance, Tania Modleski (ed.) (1986) *Studies in Entertainment: Critical Approaches to Mass Culture*, Bloomington and Indianapolis: Indianapolis University Press; Cary Nelson and Lawrence Grossberg (eds) (1988) *Marxism and the Interpretation of Culture*, Urbana and Chicago: University of Illinois Press; Ian Angus and Sut Jhally (eds) (1989) *Cultural Politics in Contemporary America*, New York and London: Routledge.
12 See Frances Borzello (1987) *Civilising Caliban: The Misuse of Art 1880–1985*, London: Routledge.
13 See John Fiske and John Hartley (1978) *Reading Television*, London and New York: Methuen; and John Hartley (1982) *Understanding News*, London: Methuen, 102–6.
14 See Geoffrey Hurd's essay in Bennett *et al.* (eds), op. cit., 53–70.
15 Todd Gitlin (1983) *Inside Prime Time*, New York: Pantheon, 335.
16 ibid., 334.

11 CONTINUOUS PLEASURES IN MARGINAL PLACES

1 Sorry about that. Perhaps a better way of putting it would be as in Dana Polan (1988) 'Film theory re-assessed', *Continuum: An Australian Journal of the Media*, 1(2), 15–30.
2 H. Marshall McLuhan (1964) *Understanding Media,* London: Routledge & Kegan Paul.
3 The information on the first television shows is taken from a BBC radio programme made to mark television's fiftieth anniversary: *TV Began Here*, broadcast on the BBC World Service 27 October 1986.
4 An especially clear example of this would be John Ellis (1982) *Visible Fictions: Cinema, Television, Video*, London: Routledge & Kegan Paul.
5 I'm told these savoury snacks are unknown in Australia, which is fine for Australia, if not for my attempted calembour. Come to think of it, Twiglets are unknown to cultural theory too, so that's OK.
6 Umberto Eco (1987) *Travels in Hyperreality* (originally *Faith in Fakes*), trans. William Weaver, London: Picador, 150.
7 The term enslavement is Don McLeod's, who uses it explicitly to gloss the preferred colonial euphemism 'protection': Don McLeod (n.d.) *How the West was Lost*, Port Hedland: D.W. McLeod.
8 Benedict Anderson (1983) *Imagined Communities*, London: Verso.
9 Nicholas Garnham (1987) 'Concepts of culture: public policy and the cultural industries', *Cultural Studies*, 1(1), 23–37.
10 This information, like so much really useful knowledge, comes from television – a British series called *The Politics of Food*, broadcast in Australia on SBS-TV in June 1988. The ABC science series *Quantum* has also investigated agribusiness along the same lines.

11 Christopher Hill (1969) *Reformation to Industrial Revolution,* Harmondsworth: Penguin, 89.
12 On the complexities and contradictions provoked by reading Shakespeare the popular dramatist as a capitalist landlord see Terence Hawkes's *tour de force* 'Playhouse–workhouse', in Terence Hawkes (1986) *That Shakespeherian Rag*, London and New York: Methuen, 1–26.
13 This useful concept comes from S.L. Bethell (1944) *Shakespeare and the Popular Dramatic Tradition*, St Albans, Herts.: Staples.
14 Jane Feuer (1987) 'The two weather channels', *Cultural Studies*, 1(3), 383–5.
15 Horace Newcomb and Paul M. Hirsch (1983) 'Television as a cultural forum', repr. in Horace Newcomb (ed.) (1987) *Television: the critical view* 4th edn, New York and Oxford: Oxford University Press, 455–470.
16 Todd Gitlin (1983) *Inside Prime Time*, New York: Pantheon.
17 Camilla Mowbray (March 1988) 'Bright new identities', *Broadcast (Australia)*, 28–31.
18 Maria Del Sapio (1988) ' "The question is whether you can make words mean so many different things": notes on art and metropolitan languages', *Cultural Studies*, 2(2), 196–216.
19 This and the ensuing comments of TV executives are all quoted in Mowbray, op. cit.
20 At the time of writing the fifth national network, SBS, had not released its new logo ID (which turned out to be worth waiting for).
21 Perth *Sunday Times TV Extra Magazine* (24 July 1988), 38.
22 Janet Wolff (1978) 'Bill Brand, Trevor Griffiths, and the debate about political theatre', *Red Letters*, 8, 57.
23 John Fiske and John Hartley (1978) *Reading Television*, London and New York: Methuen, 178–88.
24 And this is it:

Eighty-five will come alive
When 9's stars step out strutting;
When daytime turns to night-time,
Hey! Here's the place to be.
Downhill hitting top gear,
Stealing hearts and falling clear,
Sail into a brand new year with 9.

From today until next Sunday,
And the Minutes in the middle,
When will you see a team you trust like ours?
When raquet, bat and boot hit ball,
When Keke Rosberg hits the wall,
Where Eagles dare we'll take you there;
The super sports on 9.

We're the people for the movies
When a movie's really moving,
When a special's super-special,
We're just the place to be.

We're flying high – The Aussie Flag!
We're climbing high – And we're proud!
We're still the one – To shout out loud!
There's never been a year like this before.

12 A STATE OF EXCITEMENT

1 Exemplified most spectacularly, soon after the Cup, by the opening of what should prove to be the world's largest iron ore mine, aptly named McCamey's Monster, developed by local millionaire Lang Hancock in a unique barter deal with Romania's President Ceaucescu.
2 See Martyn Webb (1987) 'Regionalization and the making of Western Australia', paper presented at the *Imaging Western Australia* symposium, April 1987, and deposited in the J.S. Battye Library of Western Australian History, Perth.
3 The reference is now not confined to Joseph Conrad's nineteenth-century invocation of white terror, but extends, interestingly, to Francis Ford Coppola's contemporary version of it, *Apocalypse Now*.
4 Thomas Hardy (1930) 'The convergence of the twain (lines on the loss of the *Titanic*)', in *The Collected Poems of Thomas Hardy*, 4th edn, London: Macmillan, 288–9.
5 Paolo Prato and Gianluca Trivero (1985) 'The spectacle of travel', *Australian Journal of Cultural Studies*, 3(2), 25–43.
6 The photogenia of the event is perhaps gauged by the estimated consumption in the America's Cup Media Centre of 36,500 sheets of monochrome print paper per month and 20,000 rolls of film per month during the five months of the Cup (Source: *Western Mail Magazine*, 27 September 1986).
7 ibid.
8 Several months later, the euphoria having been killed off, a competition in the local papers revealed some popular images of WA – 14,420 suggestions for a new slogan for the state's vehicle licence plates. Leading candidates were *The Friendly State* (which received most nominations), *The Great State*, *The State For All Seasons*, *The Wildflower State*. Unlikely, but revealing, were *Smoking – No WA* and *WA – Beer Bull and Brawl*. So there was in fact an overwhelming majority *against* the officially chosen 'winner': *WA – The Golden State*. However, this regression to the hole in the ground – and flattery by imitation of Dennis Conner's home state of California – was appropriately rewarded: the competition winner received a half 'Nugget', the new, ideologically sound Australian version of the Krugerrand made from gold extracted, naturally, from Western Australia (Source: *Sunday Times*, Perth, 7 June 1987).

13 LOCAL TELEVISION

1 Source: Todd Gitlin (1983) *Inside Prime Time*, New York: Pantheon, 51.
2 Shown on midweek prime-time television, the locally produced episodes of *Australian Mosaic* got a rating of 1 per cent in Perth (Source: McNair Anderson).
3 Source: *Marketing*, September 1988, 10.

14 QUOTING NOT SCIENCE BUT SIDEBOARDS

1 Quoted in Barbara Radice (1985) *Memphis: Research, Experiences, Results, Failures and Successes of New Design*, London: Thames & Hudson, 142.
2 Quoted in ibid., 142.
3 E.M. Bianchi (1961) 'History of Television in Western Australia', Graylands Teachers College, manuscript deposited in the J.S. Battye Library of Western Australian History, Perth, 3.

4 Personal interview.
5 Radice, op. cit., 140.
6 Personal interview.
7 Bianchi, op. cit., 26.
8 Radice, op. cit., 140.

15 TWO CHEERS FOR PAEDOCRACY

1 William Langley, Australian *Elle*, October 1990, 56–8.
2 Linda Van Nunen, *The Australian Magazine*, 14–15 July 1990, 17–22.
3 ibid.

Bibliography

Allor, Martin, 'Relocating the site of the audience: reconstructive theory and the social subject', *Critical Studies in Mass Communication*, 5(3) (1988), 217–33.

Anderson, Benedict, *Imagined Communities*, London: Verso, 1988.

Ang, Ien, 'The battle between television and its audiences: the politics of watching television', in Philip Drummond and Richard Paterson (eds) *Television in Transition*, London: British Film Institute, 1986.

Angus, Ian and Sut Jhally (eds), *Cultural Politics in Contemporary America*, New York and London: Routledge, 1989.

Annan Committee, *Report of the Committee on the Future of Broadcasting*, London: HMSO, 1977.

Aubrey, Crispin (ed.), *Nukespeak: The Media and the Bomb*, London: Comedia, 1982.

Australian Broadcasting Tribunal, *Manual*, Canberra: Australian Government Publishing Service, 1984.

BBC Television Service, *Principles and Practice in Documentary Programmes*, London: BBC, 1972.

Barthes, Roland, *Mythologies*, London: Paladin, 1973.

Barthes, Roland, *S/Z*, London: Jonathan Cape, 1975.

Barthes, Roland, 'Theory of the text', in R. Young (ed.) *Untying the Text: A Post-Structuralist Reader*, London: Routledge & Kegan Paul, 1981.

Bennett, Tony, Boyd-Bowman, Susan, Mercer, Colin, and Woollacott, Janet (eds), *Popular Television and Film*, London: British Film Institute/Open University, 1981.

Bethell, S.L., *Shakespeare and the Popular Dramatic Tradition*, St Albans, Herts.: Staples, 1944.

Beynon, John, Doyle, Brian, Goulden, Holly, and Hartley, John, 'The politics of discrimination: media studies in English teaching', *English in Education*, 17(3) (Autumn 1983), 3–14.

Bianchi, E.M., 'History of Television in Western Australia', Graylands Teachers College, manuscript deposited in the J.S. Battye Library of Western Australian History, 1961.

Blanchard, Simon and Morley, David (eds), *What's this Channel Four? An Alternative Report*, London: Comedia, 1982.

Borzello, Frances, *Civilising Caliban: The Misuse of Art 1880–1985*, London: Routledge, 1987.

Boyce, George, Curran, James and Wingate, Pauline (eds), *Newspaper History: From the Seventeenth Century to the Present Day*, London: Constable; Beverly

Hills: Sage, 1978.
Carey, James, 'Mass communication research and cultural studies: an American view', in James Curran, Michael Gurevitch and Janet Woollacott (eds) *Mass Communication and Society*, London: Open University/Edward Arnold, 1977.
Cohen, S. and Young, J. (eds), *The Manufacture of News: Deviance, Social Problems and the Mass Media*, London: Constable, 1981.
Culler, Jonathan, 'Jacques Derrida', in John Sturrock (ed.) *Structuralism and Since*, Oxford: Oxford University Press, 1979.
Curran, James, Gurevitch, Michael and Woollacott, Janet (eds), *Mass Communication and Society*, London: Open University/Edward Arnold, 1977.
Curran, James and Seaton, Jean, *Power without Responsibility: The Press and Broadcasting in Britain*, 2nd edn, London: Methuen, 1985.
Del Sapio, Maria, '"The question is whether you can make words mean so many different things": notes on art and metropolitan languages', *Cultural Studies*, 2(2) (1988), 196–216.
Douglas, Mary, *Purity and Danger: An Analysis of the Concepts of Pollution and Taboo*, London: Routledge & Kegan Paul, 1966.
Drummond, Philip and Paterson, Richard (eds), *Television in Transition*, London: British Film Institute, 1986.
Eco, Umberto, *The Role of the Reader*, London: Hutchinson, 1981.
Eco, Umberto, *Travels in Hyperreality* (originally *Faith in Fakes*), trans. William Weaver, London: Picador, 1987.
Eliot, T.S., *Selected Essays*, London: Faber & Faber, 1932.
Ellis, John, *Visible Fictions: Cinema, Television, Video*, London: Routledge & Kegan Paul, 1982.
Enzensberger, Hans Magnus, 'Constituents of a theory of the media', in Denis McQuail (ed.) *Sociology of Mass Communication*, Harmondsworth: Penguin, 1972.
Feuer, Jane, 'The two weather channels', *Cultural Studies*, 1(3) (1987), 383–5.
Fiske, John and Hartley, John, *Reading Television*, London and New York: Methuen, 1978.
Garnham, Nicholas, 'Concepts of culture: public policy and the cultural industries', *Cultural Studies*, 1(1) (January 1987), 23–37.
Gitlin, Todd, *Inside Prime Time*, New York: Pantheon, 1983.
Glasgow University Media Group, *Bad News*, London: Routledge & Kegan Paul, 1976.
Glasgow University Media Group, *More Bad News*, London: Routledge & Kegan Paul, 1980.
Gurevitch, Michael, Bennett, Tony, Curran, James and Woollacott, Janet (eds), *Culture, Society and the Media*, London: Methuen, 1982.
Gurevitch, Michael and Levy, Mark R. (eds), *Mass Communication Review Yearbook*, vol. 6, Newbury Park: Sage, 1987.
Haddon, Walter, *Against Ierome Osorious*, 1581.
Hall, Stuart, 'The rediscovery of "ideology": return of the repressed in media studies', in Michael Gurevitch, Tony Bennett, James Curran and Janet Woollacott (eds) *Culture, Society and the Media*, London: Methuen, 1982.
Hall, Stuart, 'The great moving right show', in Stuart Hall and M. Jaques (eds) *The Politics of Thatcherism*, London: Lawrence & Wishart, 1983.
Hall, Stuart and Jaques, M. (eds), *The Politics of Thatcherism*, London: Lawrence & Wishart, 1983.
Hardy, Thomas, *The Collected Poems of Thomas Hardy*, 4th edn, London: Macmillan, 1930.

Harrison, Stanley, *Poor Men's Guardians*, London: Lawrence & Wishart, 1974.

Hartley, John, *Understanding News*, London: Methuen, 1982.

Hartley, John, 'Encouraging signs: television and the power of dirt; speech and scandalous categories', *Australian Journal of Cultural Studies*, 1(2) (1983), 62–82. Published in the USA in Willard D. Rowland and Bruce Watkins (eds) *Interpreting Television: Current Research Perspectives*, Beverly Hills: Sage, 1984.

Hartley, John, 'Regimes of pleasure', *One-Eye* (Magazine of Chapter Film Workshop, Cardiff), 2 (1984), 6–17.

Hartley, John, 'Out of bounds: the myth of marginality', in Len Masterman (ed.) *Television Mythologies: Stars, Shows, Signs*, London: Comedia, 1984.

Hartley, John, 'Regimes of truth and the politics of reading: a *blivit*', *Cultural Studies*, 1(1) (1987), 39–58.

Hartley, John, 'Invisible fictions: television audiences, paedocracy, pleasure', *Textual Practice*, 1(2) (1987), 121–38. Published in the USA in Robert J. Thompson, and Gary Burns (eds) *Television Studies: Textual Analysis*, New York: Praeger, 1989.

Hartley, John, 'Been there – done that: on academic tourism', *Communication Research*, 14(2) (1987), 251–61.

Hartley, John, 'A state of excitement: Western Australia and the America's Cup', *Cultural Studies*, 2(1) (1988), 117–26.

Hartley, John, 'The real world of audiences', *Critical Studies in Mass Communication*, 5(3) (1988), 234–8.

Hartley, John, 'The Eighteenth Brumaire of Kylie Minogue', *Australian Left Review*, 107 (1988), 7.

Hartley, John, 'Local television – from space to time' (Two-part article), *In the Picture*, 3(4) and 3(5) (October/November 1988 and December 1988/January 1989).

Hartley, John, 'Continuous pleasures in marginal places: television, continuity and the construction of communities', in John Tulloch and Graeme Turner (eds) *Australian Television: Programs, Pleasures and Politics*, Sydney: Allen & Unwin, 1989.

Hartley, John, 'Culture and popular culture: the politics of photopoetry', in Martin Coyle, Peter Gardside, Malcolm Kelsall and John Peck (eds) *Encyclopedia of Literature and Criticism*, London and New York: Routledge, 1990.

Hartley, John, 'Getting the picture? The visual arts in Australia in the electronic media', *Artlink*, 10(4) (December 1990), 33–5.

Hartley, John, Goulden, Holly and Wright, Trevor, 'Consciousness razing: Channel 4 news and current affairs', in Simon Blanchard and David Morley (eds) *What's this Channel Four? An Alternative Report*, London: Comedia, 1982.

Hartley, John and Montgomery, Martin, 'Representations and relations: ideology and power in press and Television news', in Teun van Dijk (ed.) *Discourse and Communication: New Approaches to the Analysis of Mass Media Discourse and Communication*, Berlin and New York: Walter de Gruyter, 1985.

Hartley, John and O'Regan, Tom, 'Quoting not science but sideboards: television in a new way of life', in Tom O'Regan and Brian Shoesmith (eds) *The Moving Image: Film and Television in Western Australia 1896–1985*, Perth: History and Film Association of Australia, 1985. Published in the USA in Michael Gurevitch and Mark R. Levy (eds) *Mass Communication Review Yearbook*, vol. 6, Newbury Park: Sage, 1987.

Hawkes, Terence, *That Shakespeherian Rag*, London and New York: Methuen, 1986.

Hill, Christopher, *Reformation to Industrial Revolution*, Harmondsworth: Penguin, 1969.

Homilies, The Book of; Certain Sermons Appointed by the Queen's Majesty to be declared and read by all Parsons, Vicars and Curates, every Sunday and Holiday in their Churches; and by Her Grace's advice perused and overseen for the better understanding of the simple people, repr. 1850, Cambridge: Cambridge University Press, 1574.

Jennings, Humphrey, *Pandaemonium: The Coming of the Machine as seen by Contemporary Observers*, ed. Mary-Lou Jennings and Charles Madge from materials compiled by Jennings *circa* 1937–50, London: Picador, 1987.

Jones, Robert Foster, *The Triumph of the English Language*, Stanford, Cal.: Stanford University Press, 1953.

Jourdan, Silvester, *A Plaine Description of the Barmudas, now called Sommer Islands*, 1613.

Journal of Communication, Special issue: (1983) 'Ferment in the field', 33(3).

Kaplan, E. Ann, 'History, the historical spectator and gender address in music television', *Communication Inquiry*, 10(1) (1986), 3–14.

Kaplan, E. Ann (ed.), *Regarding Television: Critical Approaches – An Anthology*, New York: American Film Institute/University Publications of America, 1983.

Kelsall, Malcolm, Coyle, Martin, Gardside, Peter and Peck, John (eds), *Literature and Criticism: A New Century Guide*, London and New York: Routledge, 1990.

Laclau, Ernesto, 'Populist rupture and discourse', *Screen Education*, 34 (1980), 87–93.

Leach, Edmund, *Culture and Communication*, Cambridge: Cambridge University Press, 1976.

McLeod, Don, *How the West was Lost*, Port Hedland: D.W. McLeod, n.d.

McLuhan, H. Marshall, *Understanding Media*, London: Routledge & Kegan Paul, 1964.

McQuail, Denis (ed.), *Sociology of Mass Communication*, Harmondsworth: Penguin, 1972.

Marx, Karl, *Karl Marx and Frederick Engels: Selected Works in One Volume*, London: Lawrence & Wishart, 1968.

Masterman, Len (ed.), *Television Mythologies: Stars, Shows, Signs*, London: Comedia, 1984.

Modleski, Tania (ed.), *Studies in Entertainment: Critical Approaches to Mass Culture*, Bloomington and Indianapolis: Indianapolis University Press, 1986.

Morley, David, *The 'Nationwide' Audience*, London: British Film Institute, 1980.

Morley, David, *Family Television: Cultural Power and Domestic Leisure*, London: Comedia, 1986.

Mowbray, Camilla, 'Bright new identities', *Broadcast (Australia)*, (March 1988) 28–31.

Murdock, Graham, 'Political deviance: the press presentation of a militant mass demonstration', in S. Cohen and J. Young (eds) *The Manufacture of News: Deviance, Social Problems and the Mass Media*, London: Constable, 1973.

Murdock, Graham and Golding, Peter, 'The structure, ownership and control of the press 1914–76', in George Boyce, James Curran and Pauline Wingate (eds) *Newspaper History: From the Seventeenth Century to the Present Day*, London, Constable; Beverly Hills: Sage, 1978.

Nelson, Cary and Grossberg, Lawrence (eds), *Marxism and the Interpretation of Culture*, Urbana and Chicago: University of Illinois Press, 1988.

Newcomb, Horace (ed.), *Television: The Critical View*, 4th edn, New York and Oxford: Oxford University Press, 1987.

Newcomb, Horace and Hirsch, Paul M., 'Television as a cultural forum', in Horace Newcomb (ed.), *Television: The Critical View*, 4th edn, New York and Oxford: Oxford University Press, 1987.

Ong, Walter J., *Ramus: Method, and the Decay of Dialogue: From the Art of Discourse to the Art of Reason*, Cambridge, Mass.: Harvard University Press, 1958.

O'Regan, Tom and Shoesmith, Brian (eds), *The Moving Image: Film and Television in Western Australia 1896–1985*, Perth: History and Film Association of Australia, 1985.

O'Sullivan, Tim, Hartley, John, Saunders, Danny and Fiske, John, *Key Concepts in Communication*, London: Methuen, 1983.

Patterson, Frances Taylor, *Cinema Craftsmanship: A Book for Photoplaywrights*, New York: Harcourt, Brace & Howe, 1920.

Polan, Dana, 'Film theory re-assessed', *Continuum: An Australian Journal of the Media*, 1(2) (1988), 15–30.

Popper, Karl, 'Knowledge: subjective versus objective' [1967], in David Miller (ed.) *A Pocket Popper*, London: Fontana, 1983.

Prato, Paolo and Trivero, Gianluca, 'The spectacle of travel', *Australian Journal of Cultural Studies*, 3(2) (1985), 25–43.

Radice, Barbara, *Memphis: Research, Experience, Results, Failures and Successes of New Design*, London: Thames & Hudson, 1985.

Ramus, Peter, *Training in Dialectic*, 1543.

Rowland, Willard D. and Watkins, Bruce (eds), *Interpreting Television: Current Research Perspectives*, Beverly Hills: Sage, 1984.

Said, Edward, *Orientalism*, London: Routledge & Kegan Paul, 1978.

Said, Edward, 'Orientalism reconsidered', *Race and Class*, 27(7) (1985).

Saussure, Ferdinand de, *Course in General Linguistics*, London: Fontana, 1974.

Spens Report, *Report of the Consultative Committee on Secondary Education, with special reference to Grammar Schools and Technical High Schools*, London: HMSO, 1938.

Thompson, Robert J. and Burns, Gary (eds), *Television Studies: Textual Analysis*, New York: Praeger, 1989.

Tracey, Michael, 'Censored: the *War Game* story', in Crispin Aubrey (ed.) *Nukespeak: The Media and the Bomb*, London: Comedia, 1982.

Tulloch, John, *Television Drama: Agency, Audience and Myth*, London and New York: Routledge, 1990.

Tulloch, John and Turner, Graeme (eds), *Australian Television: Programs, Pleasures and Politics*, Sydney: Allen & Unwin, 1989.

Volosinov, Valentin, *Marxism and the Philosophy of Language*, New York: Seminar Press, 1973.

Vonnegut, Kurt, *Palm Sunday: An Autobiographical Collage*, London: Jonathan Cape, 1981.

Webb, Martyn, 'Regionalization and the making of Western Australia', paper presented at the *Imaging Western Australia* symposium, April 1987, and deposited in the J.S. Battye Library of Western Australian History, Perth, 1987.

West Australian Newspapers, *Style Book*, Perth: West Australian Newspapers, 1973.

Williams, Raymond, *Television: Technology and Cultural Form*, London: Fontana (republished by Routledge), 1974.

Wolff, Janet, 'Bill Brand, Trevor Griffiths, and the debate about political theatre', *Red Letters*, 8, 57 (1978).

Young, R. (ed.), *Untying the Text: A Post-Structuralist Reader*, London: Routledge & Kegan Paul, 1981.

Index